Marine,
Public Servant,
Kansan

Marine, Public Servant, Kansan

The Life of Ernest Garcia

Dennis Raphael Garcia

With a Foreword by Bob Dole

University Press of Kansas

Published by the University Press of Kansas (Lawrence, Kansas 66045), which was organized by the Kansas Board of Regents and is operated and funded by Emporia State University, Fort Hays State University, Kansas State University, Pittsburg State University, the University of Kansas, and Wichita State University.

Library of Congress Cataloging-in-Publication Data
Names: Garcia, Dennis Raphael, author. | Dole, Robert J., 1923– , writer of foreword.
Title: Marine, public servant, Kansan : the life of Ernest Garcia / Dennis Raphael Garcia ; with a foreword by Bob Dole.
Description: Lawrence, Kansas : University Press of Kansas, [2018] | Includes index.
Identifiers: LCCN 2018016378 | ISBN 9780700626670 (cloth : alk. paper) | ISBN 9780700626687 (ebook) | ISBN 9780700643707 (paperback)
Subjects: LCSH: Garcia, Ernest, 1946- | Mexican Americans–Kansas–Biography. | United States. Marine Corps–Officers–Biography. | Mexican American soldiers–Biography. | Dole, Robert J., 1923-–Friends and associates. | Iraq War, 2003-2011–Biography. | Kansas Highway Patrol–Biography. | Garcia family. | Mexican Americans–Genealogy. | Garden City (Kan.)–Biography.
Classification: LCC F690.M5 G37 2018 | DDC 978.1/44033092 [B]–dc23.
LC record available at https://lccn.loc.gov/2018016378.

British Library Cataloguing-in-Publication Data is available.

EU Authorised Representative Details:
Easy Access System Europe
Mustamäe tee 50, 10621 Tallinn, Estonia
gpsr.requests@easproject.com

To Jose Garcia and Rosa Campos Garcia,
for all they gave

Contents

Photographs

Foreword

Following Ernie Garcia's studies at the University of Kansas in the late 1970s, he pursued a career in Washington, DC, where he would become a member of my Senate staff. It was then that his childhood friend and college roommate, Randy Bowling, encouraged him to write about his developing career. Thirty years later, Ernie's cousin, Dennis Garcia, approached Ernie with the idea of organizing those notes and memorializing his life's experiences. Ernie agreed, and the process of writing this book began soon thereafter.

This book is the story of Ernie's family's migration to the United States to escape the hardships of Mexico, including possible capture by national military forces during the Mexican Revolution of 1910. The family's story also includes the trials and tribulations incurred upon their arrival in the United States. Though no longer pursued as enemies of the Mexican government, Ernie's family still endured poverty, poor living conditions, and limited educational opportunities. The family members eventually made their way to Kansas, where they struggled to support themselves through difficult and demanding field labor.

The book also details the events and experiences of Ernie's immediate family in Kansas, including the untimely death of his father as well as the challenges and consequences of ethnic discrimination. Despite the obstacles facing him, Ernie became a young man whose character and personality would pave the way for success beyond his wildest dreams.

Many of Ernie's aspirations were tied to the University of Kansas. As a young boy, he listened to radio broadcasts of Jayhawk basketball with his father. Ernie ultimately played basketball in high school and went on to attend KU. Later, when Ernie came to work with me in the US Capitol, he took advantage of the opportunities afforded him there—and developed into a capable and knowledgeable Senate staff professional. His successes continued in Washington long after he left my office.

In the mid-1980s, Ernie achieved another of his many goals by becoming an officer in the United States Marine Corps. Even after retirement from the corps, Ernie remained a protector and public servant when he went on to serve as superintendent of the Kansas Highway Patrol.

Ernie's story is a compelling tale of a talented and highly motivated member of an immigrant family here in the United States—a family that came to Kansas with a determination to become self-sufficient and, ultimately, one whose children and grandchildren would proudly serve the people of Kansas and our nation.

Senator Robert Dole
October 2016

Preface

The life of Ernest E. Garcia validates the continuing viability of the American dream. The road that Ernie, as he is affectionately nicknamed, and his family traveled is a compelling tale that needs to be told. An examination of the family history reveals that the origin of Ernie's story lies in family experiences before his birth. The first two chapters of this book detail the migration of Ernie's great-grandfather Pedro and grandfather Jose from Mexico to Kansas. His grandparents Jose and Rosa Garcia entered the United States in 1917 at El Paso, Texas. They and their six sons, two of whom were born in Mexico, eventually settled in Garden City, Kansas. By 1951 their sons had fathered more than half of their forty-four grandchildren who reached adulthood.

The remaining chapters detail Ernie's life over the course of six decades. It is a story filled with an extraordinary array of rich and unique experiences and successes in his government and military careers. But along the way there were many difficult challenges. He overcame those hardships and took advantage of the opportunities created by the hard work of his parents and immigrant grandparents.

This book relies on the oral histories provided by Ernie and many family members who recounted precious stories told to them by parents and grandparents and generously shared their family photographs. Additionally, many of Ernie's friends recalled with delight their school days together. Many places and events in Garden City were observed firsthand. When possible, information was gleaned from official documents such as military, census, immigration, and property records, as well as birth, marriage, and death certificates. An abbreviated family tree is included just before the prologue for reference. Historical events were researched to provide context for the path the family traveled.

Ernie's story and family history over the last 150 years are a part of American history—as are the histories of every family in America. Each family's experience includes fascinating and compelling events that beg for discovery and should be shared with others. The more everyone knows the experiences of others, the more we can understand and appreciate one another. In that way, Americans will have a kinship that is a hallmark of a strong society and nation.

My thanks go to Ernie and to family and friends who shared their experiences. My thanks also go to the University Press of Kansas and its staff for their support and guidance. Thanks also go to Amy Sherman for her assistance in the development of the manuscript. Last but not least, thanks to the many who supported this project, especially Celeste and Elizabeth.

Marine, Public Servant, Kansan

Ernest Garcia Abbreviated Family Tree

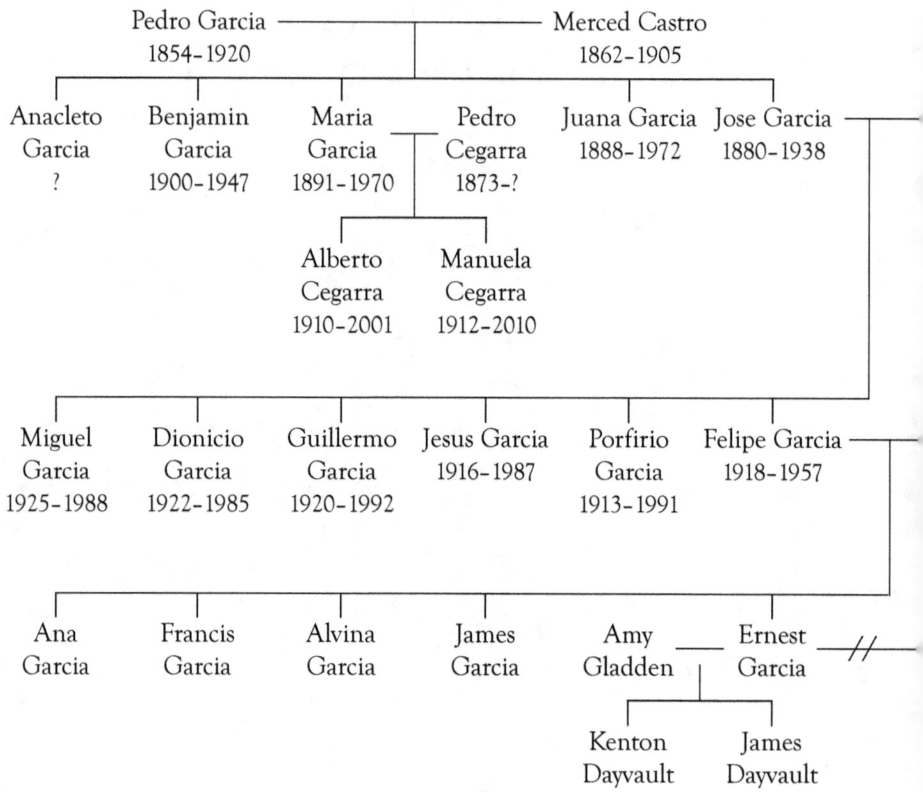

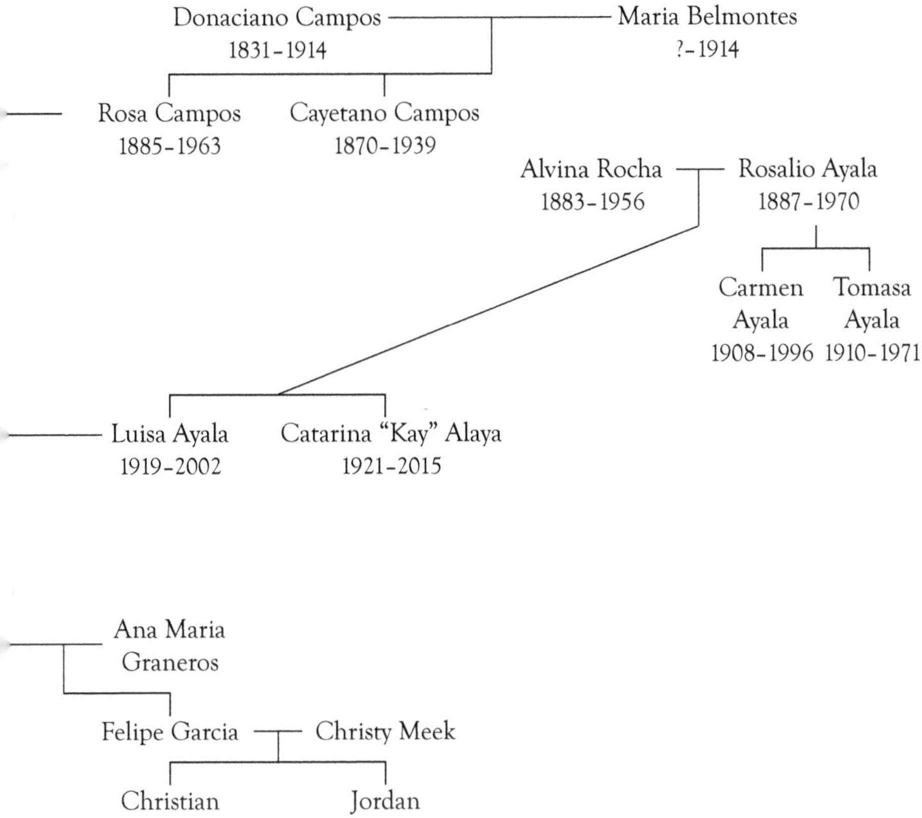
Donaciano Campos
1831–1914
Maria Belmontes
?–1914
Rosa Campos
1885–1963
Cayetano Campos
1870–1939
Alvina Rocha
1883–1956
Rosalio Ayala
1887–1970
Carmen Ayala
1908–1996
Tomasa Ayala
1910–1971
Luisa Ayala
1919–2002
Catarina "Kay" Alaya
1921–2015
Ana Maria Graneros
Felipe Garcia
Christy Meek
Christian
Jordan

Prologue

Francisco Vasquez de Coronado, a Spanish nobleman, set out from Mexico in 1540 to find the fabled cities of gold. Thirty horsemen, foot soldiers, guides and a Franciscan Friar, Juan de Padilla, who wrote a diary, accompanied Coronado.

On June 29, 1541, after much hardship, the group crossed the Arkansas River (called the St. Peter & St. Paul River) near present day Fort Dodge, Kansas. Father Juan de Padilla held a mass of thanksgiving on the nearby hills, the first Christian service held in the interior of the continent, predating the landing of the Pilgrims almost 100 years.

–Coronado Cross Monument, Ford County Historical Society, Dodge City, Kansas

On March 23, 1957, the third night of spring, a howling blizzard swept across the southwestern plains of Kansas. Travelers were stranded on the highways and taken to shelters after their rescue. Residents were told to remain indoors. Sixty-mile-per-hour winds roared into Garden City, shaking and rattling the doors and windows of the wood-framed homes in the Mexican barrio on Santa Fe Street. The families within could measure the storm's intensity only by the density of the snowflakes as they flew horizontally through the illumination of a single porch light and by the rising snow drifts outside their doors.

In their home on Santa Fe Street, Felipe Garcia assured his sons, Ernie and Jim, that they were safe from the wind and snow. He tried to keep their attention on the radio broadcast of the national basketball championship final between the University of Kansas and the University of North Carolina. With ten-year-old Ernie on his lap and Jim, two years older, sitting next to him, Felipe was ready to lead them into a night of cheering for the Jayhawks. However, any exuberant physical outbursts of cheers had to be avoided, as Felipe suffered from heart disease and was in a weakened state.

Though Felipe was born in El Paso, Texas, in 1918, he was raised in Kansas from the age of two. He was a sports fan and had developed a passion for KU basketball. Anticipating a repeat of KU's 1952 national championship season, he and the boys had closely followed the 1957 Jayhawk season. Their hopes were spiked by the addition of Wilt Chamberlain to the varsity team. In his debut, Chamberlain scored fifty-two points and grabbed thirty-one rebounds, and he went on to dominate play during the regular season. To reach the championship final, KU had survived the regional games in Dallas the week before. The Jayhawks not only prevailed on the scoreboard but also overcame the racial slurs and coins hurled at them by the fans supporting Southern Methodist University and Oklahoma City University. With their contentious wins in Dallas, the Jayhawks advanced to the final round in Kansas City, Missouri.

The final game against North Carolina was hard fought, intense, and stressful. In the Garcia home, hope and despair rose and fell with each shot made or missed. Each team had opportunities to win the game with a basket at the end of regulation play and overtime. By the time the game went into a third overtime, the snowy tempest in Garden City had left nearly two feet of snow and drifts reaching five to six feet high. The electricity in homes flickered during the storm, resulting in moments of darkness and garbled radio broadcasts. Some homes completely lost power.

Back in Kansas City, KU missed its last shot, and North Carolina won the championship 52–51. The Garcias were deeply disappointed, having come so close to winning. With a father's wisdom, Felipe assured his boys that the Jayhawks would have a chance the following year. As the lights in the house continued to flicker, he suggested to his sons in a tone of calm determination that the team needed to work harder to win another championship.

As with most people, only a select few moments of Ernie's childhood, those with extreme and intense emotions, were secured in his mind and available for recall during his lifetime. Among Ernie's precious few memories of Felipe were the events on the night of the blizzard of 1957. It was a night unlike any other in his young life, bursting with apprehension, tension, and excitement.

* * *

Nearly thirty years after that snowy night in southwestern Kansas, a shiny black presidential state car, adorned with diplomatic flags, slowed to a stop at the steps of the Senate entrance to the US Capitol building. A member of the Secret Service dutifully opened the door for President Ronald Reagan. With a cheerful "Hello, Ernie," the president greeted the waiting Senate sergeant at arms, who responded, "Welcome, Mr. President."

Ernie Garcia led the president and his entourage through the Capitol building to the House chamber, where the president was to deliver the 1986 State of the Union address. Moments after the House doorkeeper, James Malloy, announced the arrival of the president, Ernie slowly led President Reagan down to the House speaker's podium. Legislators and government officials, men with gray hair in dark suits and a few women in red dresses, rushed to the end of their rows to see—or be seen with—the president. As they walked down the aisle, Ernie's focus on the business of moving the president along was frequently broken with a smile as he noted the president's enthusiastic admirers. When the president handed copies of his speech to the vice president and the speaker of the House, Ernie took a seat to the president's right.

As Ernie listened he could not avoid stepping back and thinking about his presence in the House chamber at that moment. He was thrilled to be in the presence of the Congress, the president, and the justices of the Supreme Court of the United States—the heart of the most powerful government on earth. He was appreciative of the good fortune that enabled him to lead the president to the podium. He wished that his father, Felipe, was alive to see his role in the evening's events.

At the conclusion of the address, in the midst of seemingly endless applause, Ernie led the president and a procession of legislative leaders out of the House chamber and back to the Senate entrance. With his duties completed, Ernie was amazed that a young man from Garden City had accompanied the president, albeit for just a short walk. In the years to come, his amazement would continue to grow as he began learning the road that his family had taken and that had led him to the House chamber. It was an improbable journey filled with hardships, forged by perseverance and the events of Mexican and American history.

1

Escape
1854–1920

Pedro Garcia, Ernie's paternal great-grandfather, was raised in poverty on the same *hacienda* where he was born in 1854 in the state of Zacatecas in central Mexico. Most haciendas at that time consisted of a large tract of land, sometimes twenty thousand acres or more, give or take a few thousand. They were usually owned by a single wealthy owner and serviced by a number of laborers—the *campesinos*. For many campesinos, living and dying occurred on the hacienda. Their work days were long and difficult, beginning at sunrise and ending at sunset. They used many tools made of heavy iron and steel, and the misuse of those tools easily resulted in serious injury. The animals were frequently bad tempered and dangerous. Summer working conditions were hot, dry, and dusty. Winter days and nights were cold and just as miserable.

The *hacendados*, the landowners, paid Pedro and the other campesinos little for their labor and ranching skills. The minimal compensation trapped and tied them to the hacienda. For the campesinos, accumulating financial savings or any other wealth was virtually impossible. They were forced to choose low pay and survival on the hacienda or a slow death in the gold and silver mines of Mexico. All the while, their labor enriched the enormous ranching and mining estates of the wealthy hacendados.

In 1877 when Pedro was twenty-two years old, he married Merced Castro. She was fourteen years old. Pedro, Merced, and their children who survived birth—four sons and four daughters—were in the 90 percent of Mexico's 15 million people who did not own land or wealth and were poorly educated. The remaining 10 percent, the elite class, including the hacendados, held all the wealth of Mexico. Pedro's family and his determination to escape the near-slave existence on the hacienda were his only resources. Such an escape from this subsistence living in Mexico was rare. It required an opportunity, good fortune, or an act of divine providence.

Pedro came to believe that his pathway out of poverty was the railroad in Torreón. In the 1800s railways had become, literally, vehicles for accumulating wealth in both the United States and Mexico. A railroad was built connecting El Paso–Juárez and the city of Torreón in the state of Coahuila by the 1880s. Torreón was roughly the halfway point between Juárez and Mexico City. To the north of Torreón were the states of Durango and Chihuahua. To the south was the state of Zacatecas. From its inception, the railroad in Torreón was the essential means for transporting people and goods from Mexico's interior to its northern border. The construction and maintenance required enormous amounts of brute physical labor. The railroad barons and the hacendados were not above raiding each other's workforces and taking each other's labor with the allure of higher pay. By 1905 Pedro and his oldest son, Jose, were determined to take advantage of this competition for cheap labor.

Now twenty-five years old, Jose had married Rosa Campos. Rosa's older brother, Cayetano Campos, confirmed Pedro's belief when he reported from Torreón that he had found work on the railroad. In February 1905, before the family could depart the hacienda, Merced passed away from kidney failure. Nonetheless, sometime later in the year, Pedro risked the meager security of the hacienda and traveled with his children to Torreón. Once there both Pedro and Jose found work with the railroad. The Garcia family appeared to be on its way to a level of stability. But that stability quickly unraveled.

In Torreón the calls for revolution against the Mexican government were becoming louder and louder. If revolution were to erupt, Torreón, then a hub of commerce, would emerge as a strategic prize for any army able to seize and hold the city. Francisco Madero, who led the call for revolution, had been born into one of Mexico's wealthiest families. Though he was a mild-mannered intellectual and stood only five foot two, he was a giant in his advocacy for land reform and social justice for Mexico's poor.

After decades of failure to improve the conditions of the campesinos, the revolt against the Mexican government did indeed arise across the country in November 1910. Madero's best-known supporter in northern Mexico was a campesino with the nom de guerre of Pancho Villa. Even before the outbreak of revolution, Villa and his militia of irregulars had begun seizing property from wealthy hacendados by force. Separate and independent counterrevolutions, local resistance movements, and military coups soon followed the outbreak of the revolution. The people of Mexico were among the first of millions worldwide to experience the killing engines of the twentieth century—poverty and warfare. As in many countries at war, Mexico's railroads were transformed into essential weapons of warfare, and Torreón's was no exception. It became vital to the transport of men and artillery.

During the course of the Mexican Revolution, politicians, generals, and outlaw militias engaged in a mad scramble for power. They aligned themselves, betrayed one another, and then executed their former allies and their rivals in their attempts to take the reins of power. Within three years Villa himself had twice taken each of the cities of Juárez, Chihuahua, and Torreón, had been taken prisoner and condemned to death, had escaped to El Paso, and then later returned to the state of Chihuahua, where he was appointed its governor.

With no end to the fighting and killing in sight by 1914, the revolution's promise of land and liberty remained unfulfilled. Both the rebel and government forces remained threats to the members of Pedro's family still living in Torreón and to those who had fled to Juárez. Both armies continued to conscript boys and young men for battle. They also took without compensation the few livestock and grain stores held by the campesinos. The only safety was to continue to move north to Juárez and into El Paso.

In 1905 when Pedro's youngest son, Benjamin, was five years old, he was sent to El Paso to be raised by his oldest sister Juana and her husband. In 1913 at age fifty-nine, already having lived twice the average lifespan of his countrymen, Pedro fled the chaos of his native land. He joined Juana and Benjamin in El Paso.

Juana lived in a small apartment in an adobe tenement on Leon Street in the Mexican barrio of Chihuahuita on the city's southwest side, adjacent to the Rio Grande. The barrio was El Paso's poorest and included the red light district on Overland Street. The first stop for many poor Mexican immigrants fleeing the poverty and warfare of Mexico was the Chihuahuita barrio. The City of El Paso directed few, if any, resources to the barrio. It was essentially without law enforcement and other government services. An infamous bordello operated there, and an apartment a few blocks down the street once served as a hideout for Villa's brother, Hipólito. Despite the proximity to the border and an occasional bullet straying into the El Paso side during the battles over Juárez, the barrio served as a safe haven for Pedro and his children.

At the time, El Paso residents, newspaper reporters, and photographers took positions on the international bridge or the Rio Grande's bank to observe the fighting on the other side in Juárez. After one particular skirmish, a white man approached Pedro, who was seated in front of the screen door to his apartment. The man carried a small, handheld, box-like device with a circular lens attached to the end of bellows that expanded and contracted like an accordion. The man said his name was Alexander, and in Spanish he asked Pedro if he would allow his photograph to be taken. The reporter then pointed the lens at Pedro and extended an open hand toward Pedro, then swept it toward Juárez. The reporter explained that Pedro was part of the historical events occurring on the border. Pedro nodded in agreement.

When the photographer stepped back and peered through his lens, he saw a man in a long-sleeve, collarless white shirt buttoned to the top and what can best be described as khaki-colored pants. His shoes were worn and dusty. His clothing did not obscure his sturdy build and thick torso. Pedro's facial features—for example, the heavy white stubble covering his cheeks and chin—and light coloring were clearly European without any noticeable native Central American traits. His plain, dark wide-brimmed hat hid any hair he might have had on his head. Pedro's brow was slightly furrowed, and his face was worn but without wrinkles. His expression was one of firmness and determination with a gaze that was clear and focused.

Just as the photographer was ready, Pedro called to his dog. Othello, a pooch of medium size and unrecognizable breed with a large head and a curly, thick white coat, responded and sat next to him. Apparently, Alexander thought better of asking Pedro to keep the dog out of the photograph. Or perhaps Alexander thought the dog was part of the history as well. With his large hand Pedro steadied Othello by holding the scruff of his neck. Maria, another of Pedro's daughters who had fled to El Paso, was inside the apartment. With her new infant daughter, Manuela, in her arms, Maria went to the screen door to see who was speaking with her father. Alexander pressed the plunger on the hand grip and captured the moment.

* * *

In the spring of 1915, Pancho Villa suffered a major defeat at the Battle of Celaya. With the heavy losses there, he rapidly lost his ability to command a fighting force of any significance. There were no assurances that the forces rushing to replace Villa would conscript fewer citizens or provide better security for the people and territories, including Torreón.

When Pedro fled to El Paso, Jose remained behind in Torreón with Rosa. With the revolution's continuing danger and uncertainty, thirty-five-year-old Jose understood that he should flee before the opportunity closed. But he would have to wait until Rosa delivered the child she was carrying. Infant mortality was common at that time in Mexico. Five of Rosa's pregnancies resulted in stillbirth or the death of the child within a year. Her first child to survive was Porfirio, a son born in Torreón in 1913 when she was twenty-nine. Rosa delivered her second son, Jesus, in January 1916. Soon after Jesus was born, Jose gathered the family and the belongings they were able to carry. They boarded a train and set out to join Pedro and the others in El Paso.

Jose had heard from other railroad laborers, including Rosa's brother Cayetano, stories of available work in El Paso. The accounts proved accurate—soon after his arrival, Jose found work at the Galveston Harrisburg and San Antonio Railroad roundhouse. He was hired as a wiper, the lowest-paid laborer. A wiper kept the internal parts of the locomotive engine greased. It was difficult and dirty work done in twelve-hour shifts.

Border crossers like Jose frequently came and went as they pleased via trolley car, on foot, or by wading across the Rio Bravo (as it is known in Mexico) itself. The border crossing was essentially guarded by one or two US inspectors, except when the US cavalry from Fort Bliss in El Paso patrolled the Rio Grande to prevent the revolution from spilling over the border. The revolution did in fact spill into the United States when Villa's militia raided Columbus, New Mexico, in 1916. General John J. "Black Jack" Pershing, the commander at Fort Bliss, and a force of five thousand troops unsuccessfully pursued Villa into northern Mexico.

For Jose the challenge was not crossing the border. It was, instead, acquiring the lawful paperwork to remain and work in the United States. The US Congress at the time was experiencing one of its recurring spells of anxiety over admission of immigrants believed to be "defective." The Immigration Act of 1917 expanded the list of defective immigrants to include those over the age of sixteen who were illiterate. Unable to read or write English fluently, Jose faced yet another obstacle in acquiring the paperwork for lawful admission. After a lengthy battle between Congress and President Woodrow Wilson, the law passed in early February, to be effective May 1, 1917. The railroad companies moved swiftly to avoid the restrictions by convincing the Department of Labor Immigration Service to approve as many railroad work permits as possible before May 1. In the interim, the railroad barons, along with growers and the sugar beet industry in the American Southwest, continued their lobbying efforts to persuade Congress to eliminate the literacy requirement and preserve their source of cheap labor.

Back in El Paso, on March 29, 1917, a clerk at the Department of Labor gave Jose an information card to complete. The card included the following prestamped information: "Race MEXICAN," "TRACK LABORER," "Dest. EL PASO," and "Admitted at EL PASO." Jose provided the information requested, and with that he and his family lawfully entered the United States.

Eight days later, on April 6, the United States entered World War I, placing General Pershing in command of US forces in Europe. The government's demand for soldiers created the need for workers, not only to replace those marched off to war, but also to support the manufacture of materials and supplies necessary for the war effort. By the end of May, the low-cost labor lobbying effort paid dividends. Exceptions were made to the literacy requirements for railroad workers and temporary agricultural workers. Within months, with relative ease, tens of thousands of Mexicans acquired their paperwork and lawfully entered, or remained, in the United States.

By this time another of Pedro's daughters, Guadalupe, was living with her family in San Antonio, Texas. Pedro, Juana and her husband, and Benjamin had joined Guadalupe in San Antonio as Juana's husband looked for better-paying work. But after Jose's arrival in El Paso, they returned, leaving Benjamin, now age sixteen, with Guadalupe in San Antonio. Ultimately, all of Pedro's children entered the United States with the exception of his son, Anacleto, who had stayed behind to join the invincible Villa. Without any detail of the circumstances, Pedro and the family received word that Anacleto had been lost in the revolution.

Pedro's efforts to keep his family safe were nearly a complete success. He had moved them off the hacienda and kept them moving, navigating the events of history and staying a step beyond the clutches of Mexico's revolution and poverty. His effort was an extraordinary accomplishment given his times and circumstances. However, 1918 brought the arrival of an evil more deadly than the revolution itself, an evil that would threaten the security Pedro had forged for the future success of his family.

Experts in medicine and history have debated the origin of the 1918–1919 flu pandemic, but many would agree that the first wave of the flu in the United States was observed in January 1918 in Haskell County, Kansas, in the southwest corner of the state. The county seat, Sublette, was just thirty-three miles south of the Atchison, Topeka and Santa Fe railroad main line that connected El Paso, Kansas City, and Chicago. Within two months of the Haskell County reports, more than five hundred soldiers at Fort Riley, Kansas, in the center of the state, were hospitalized. Some of the men had reported from Haskell County. There was speculation that the flu suffered by the soldiers originated in Europe and that the afflicted soldiers brought it with them when they returned from the Great War. Regardless, in August 1918 a more virulent strain appeared across the globe, including the United States. Estimates are that in the first twenty-four weeks the flu killed 25 million people. Some historians believe perhaps 50 to 100 million people died in the worldwide pandemic.

The flu arrived in El Paso in September 1918. With its fluid international border, the railway center, and nearby Fort Bliss, the city became fertile ground for the flu—the number of people traveling though the city enabled the virus to spread easily and quickly. The flu struck the Chihuahuita barrio with a fury. No medical facilities or personnel served the barrio, and quickly dozens of people died. The number of illnesses and deaths in El Paso began to decline by the end of the year, but by then more than six hundred people had perished, a majority from El Paso's south side, including the barrio. Jose, Rosa, their two boys, and a newborn, Felipe, were living in the barrio during this time. Unlike most flu pandemics, this strain did not strike hard at the very young or old. By a random biological stroke, the boys were left untouched.

In response to the loss of manpower due to war casualties and the flu pandemic, the local draft board in El Paso began to register legal immigrants—Jose had fled the revolution only to again be within reach of an army in need of soldiers. He did not want to jeopardize his place in his new country, so he duly registered for military service in World War I in September 1918. It was unlikely that Jose would be summoned to serve, as thirty-eight-year-olds were not prized candidates for army recruits. But in any case, within a month of Jose's registration, the war began to draw to a close. Germany's allies collapsed, and the Allied forces were approaching the German homeland. For the good of Europe, the United States, and Jose, the armistice of November 11, 1918, ended any chance of Jose's service.

On February 3, 1920, Edward Stearn, a census taker, bravely made his way through the Chihuahuita barrio, completing his duties. At 915 Chihuahua Street he recorded Jose, Rosa, and their three sons. The next day, at 912 Leon Street, Stearn duly recorded Pedro and his new wife, Julia, as residents of the United States. But by this time Pedro was in declining health. The flu pandemic began to subside in early 1919, but Pedro and many others were left weakened to respiratory illnesses. As the year progressed, it became apparent that Pedro was gravely ill. Tuberculosis was the culprit. On February 9, 1920, Jose was able to convince Dr. Ira J. Bush to attend to Pedro at his home on Leon Street. Bush, then in his mid-fifties, had moved to El Paso from Louisiana for his health. He had tended to the wounded of the battles that raged in Juárez and Chihuahua. He sympathized with the rebels and is said to have assisted in the theft of a cannon for use by the revolutionaries. Bush advised Jose that Pedro was on his deathbed and that nothing could be done to save him.

The next day Rosa delivered her fourth surviving son, Guillermo. Jose's great joy in cradling his new son was tempered by the great sadness of his final embrace of his father. Pedro's determined journey of survival ended two days later on the evening of February 12. He was laid to rest in the dry, rocky desert ground of Concordia Catholic Cemetery on El Paso's east side.

At the time of Pedro's death, Jose had ceased working with the Galveston, Harrisburg and San Antonio Railway. The pressure of a growing family sent him looking for better wages, so he took his labor to the Atchison, Topeka and Santa Fe Railway, commonly referred to as the Santa Fe, which also operated in El Paso. The Santa Fe was one of the railways built to reach the west coast. It generally followed the old Santa Fe Trail, extending from Topeka in northeast Kansas to the southwestern corner of the state and into Colorado. Construction began in 1860. In 1862, in pursuit of a transcontinental railway system, the US Congress passed the Pacific Railroad Act, which granted nearly 4 million acres in public lands to the State of Kansas for handouts to railways. The state and railroads divided the lands between themselves. Both were free to sell the lands for homesteading or for profit.

The incentive for railroad construction was the increase in value of their lands once the railways were completed. The Santa Fe reached Colorado in the early 1870s and eventually reached the Pacific Coast to the west and El Paso to the south in 1881.

At the Santa Fe, Jose worked for better wages, servicing the locomotives in the Santa Fe roundhouse. However, the need for his labor fluctuated, and on some days he did not work. This recurring shortfall in pay was soon dramatically remedied. From time to time the Santa Fe gathered its men in the railyard of the roundhouse. Crew leaders then announced that men were needed to work at different locations on the railway that stretched from California to Chicago. On one such occasion, crew leaders called for men to work in California and Kansas. A friend of Jose's whispered to him that Kansas was the place to go: the work in Kansas was steady, while crews that had gone to California soon found themselves without work. Jose was interested, and with Pedro's passing, he had considered the possibility of leaving El Paso to work in other Santa Fe locations. Rosa did not entirely oppose the move—Cayetano and his daughter's family had gone to Kansas with the Santa Fe to a place called Garden City. On the suggestion of his friend and Cayetano's experience, Jose raised his hand for a Kansas crew.

In the spring of 1920, Jose, Rosa, and their four sons boarded a Santa Fe train bound for Kansas. They, along with other Santa Fe workers and their families, began the trek that would take them north to New Mexico and Colorado before turning east into Kansas. Jose paid no fare for his family to ride in their assigned boxcar, but the Santa Fe would collect its toll for as long as this forty-year-old man could deliver low-cost labor.

The family's journey through New Mexico and Colorado was slow as the train stopped along the way to allow Jose's section crew to perform maintenance on the track. At some locations the duration of the stop was a few days; at others, a few weeks. Along the way, the crew and their families were housed in one-room structures. If no structures were provided, they were housed in tents or boxcars. The women provided the men with meals and cared for the children.

Within a month of Jose's departure from El Paso, he learned the intricacies of building and maintaining a "section"—approximately ten miles of mainline track. His section crew, with pick and shovel, began by building a bed of gravel or crushed stone to support the steel rails and wood ties. The wood ties were ten feet long and weighed two hundred pounds. The steel rails were approximately ten yards long and weighed one thousand pounds. Two men with tie tongs laid the wood ties in place, and a number of men with heavy rail tongs laid the steel rails on the ties. Crew members—called section hands—then used specially designed sledgehammers to drive spikes into the wood ties to anchor the rails in place. Jose became adept at using a sledgehammer with a curved head. If his swing missed the spike head, the hammer head would strike instead the wood tie, the rail, or the thin metal plate connecting the two. The more accurate Jose's swing, the less energy he wasted. He learned to swing the hammer with accuracy, striking the spike head with maximum force.

The work of section hands was not for physically or mentally weak men. The locomotive was a powerful and imposing beast, standing fifteen feet tall. Its protruding iron teeth narrowed to a point that would kill any man or animal that had the misfortune to be in its path. It ate fire and blew black puffs from its smokestack nostril. Even when standing in place, the beast snorted hot steam from its underbelly. It let out an incredibly loud scream to demand the way be cleared as it prepared to move.

Jose's section crew—most of whom were of Mexican heritage—warned him that hands suffered catastrophic injuries, even death, if they were careless or did not work in unison. Despite their warnings, Jose took comfort in the support his crew provided by speaking in Spanish and offering teasing encouragement if a man tired or faltered.

After nearly three months of moving slowly northward, the train transporting Jose and Rosa turned east. As it rumbled through southeast Colorado and into the plains of southwest Kansas, the Rocky Mountains slowly slipped from sight. From his vantage point, Jose began to see fields thick with rows of short green plants. He saw men, women, and children working with teams of horses in the fields in small groups and in groups as large as thirty. A few of the laborers held long-handled hoes. Many others, including the children, were on their hands and knees. Jose asked his fellow crewmen about the workers and the crop in the fields. They told him the workers were Mexicans, the crop was sugar beets, and the fields and horses were owned by a farmer or a sugar beet company. They added in a tone of empathy that the work was hard, and the pay was poor. Jose felt some gratitude for the small good fortune that at least he and his family were not in the fields.

The Santa Fe train soon arrived at Jose's assigned location: Holcomb, Kansas, a small village in the southwest corner of the state, fifty miles east of Colorado and seventy miles north of Oklahoma. At Holcomb the Santa Fe Railway ran parallel to the Arkansas River. Between 1803 and 1845, the river had marked the US border with Mexico. The land south of the river was Mexico; north of it was the United States. The town was only five miles west of Garden City, where Rosa's brother Cayetano and his daughter were living. Holcomb's landscape included a small wooden depot and loading dock, a few farmhouses, and miles and miles of mostly flat prairie, and wind—an ever-present wind.

When Jose and his family stepped off the train, they were escorted to a labor camp where new arrivals were sheltered until they were able to find suitable residences. Men with families were under pressure to quickly find housing to keep their children out of the elements. Spring temperatures in Kansas can drop into the forties at night and become even more biting with the constant wind. Some workers and their families resorted to abandoned train cars for shelter. Jose went farmhouse to farmhouse in search of cover from the wind and cold. Within a few days he found a farmer who allowed Jose and his family to stay in the barn. In return Jose agreed to tend to the horses and other livestock also occupying the barn.

After a couple of weeks, the farmer's one-room wood-frame shed with a small window, dirt floor, and a wood stove for cooking and heating became available. The shed, previously occupied by migrant field workers, stood behind the farmer's residence. The Santa Fe's main line was nearby, so every train whistle awoke anyone sleeping within a quarter-mile. The trains that rumbled past caused the shed to vibrate and tremble. Like the work camps on the journey to Kansas, the shed was far less comfortable than the apartment the family had occupied in El Paso, but Jose and Rosa believed that over time they would save for a more comfortable home. Their sacrifice did not diminish their hope that their children would avoid hard labor at a tender age, and that they might attend school, learn English, and know success.

2

Jose's Foothold

1921–1940

Over the next four years Rosa and Jose worked according to plan. Rosa maintained the household in the shed, while each day Jose went out to battle both the black iron beast and the elements on the prairie. Springs were harsh; northern cold fronts rushed in, creating intense thunderstorms and tornadoes. Winds were constant and blustery. Ninety-degree temperatures were common in the summer months and occasionally climbed into the hundreds. July, August, and September were sticky with higher humidity. And, of course, the winds were constant. Autumn temperatures were mild, but nighttime temperatures fell quickly into the twenties and thirties by mid-November. Winters were brutal with temperatures in the forties during the day and teens at night, even falling below zero from time to time. Snow storms and blizzards, with their winds intensifying the bite of the winter's cold, laid white blankets of snow across the fields.

In April 1922 Rosa gave birth to a fifth son, Dionicio, adding to the already crowded shed. She delivered him in the shed with the help of Mexican midwives. In these times, giving birth was even more of a miracle if both mother and baby survived. Rosa's efforts in the care of the family equaled if not exceeded those of Jose. Mile after mile, hardship after hardship, she kept pace despite eventually bearing six sons who reached adulthood and enduring five pregnancies that resulted in miscarriage, still birth, or infant death. No matter the city or village on their path—Torreón, Juárez, El Paso, Holcomb—Rosa provided the cooking, the sewing, the nurturing, and the comforting for the family. She insisted that Roman Catholic prayer and practices be followed by the household to help strengthen the family's faith and hope for a better future. She kept the males in her household in line, including Jose, scolding him when he drank too much. Although she could wear the hard shell of determination, she could also unveil a sense of warmth and kindness.

Rosa understood, as did women in other Mexican households, that keeping the breadwinner in good working order was the family's first priority. Each work day Rosa readied a suit of armor for Jose to shield him from the elements during the workday—a hat for warmth or protection from the sun and gloves to warm and protect his hands—as well as a full lunch bucket to fuel him through the course of the day. Despite awakening in the night to provide care and comfort for the boys, Rosa began her day before sunlight to prepare a breakfast with the staples: beans, eggs, potatoes, bacon or sausage, and corn tortillas. All tortillas were homemade, as there were no other kind in 1920. Rosa soaked kernels of maize in water and lime (technically calcium hydroxide), then removed the kernel skins after they had softened. Using a *metate*, a rectangular stone with a smooth, shallow depression, and a *mano*, a handheld grinding stone, she ground the kernels into masa. She then formed the dough into a small ball from which the tortillas were pressed.

Each day she filled Jose's sturdy gray tin lunch bucket with large servings of the morning staples with beef, pork, or chicken replacing the breakfast eggs, bacon, and sausage. She included a small stack of tortillas wrapped in wax paper. Jose spooned the staples from a mason jar onto the tortillas, then ate them with small bites of a chili pepper. A cup of coffee completed his meal. His lunch bucket always included a tin cup along with his jar of coffee, in the event he encountered a hot stove or grill on which to heat the coffee. When Jose returned to the shed at the end of the work day, Rosa prepared a family meal of yet more staples. In the harsh winters, with temperatures below freezing and howling winds, she frequently prepared the ultimate comfort food, *caldo de pollo*, chicken and vegetable soup.

In Holcomb Jose and Rosa became part of the community of Mexican section hands and their families. The families typically lived near one another close to the main line. Members of both Jose's and Rosa's families were part of that community as well. Jose's younger sister Maria, who had been captured in Pedro's photo with baby Manuela, and her family also lived in Holcomb, while Cayetano and his family still resided in Garden City, five miles east. The two dozen or so families, bound by their labors, living conditions, and language, knew each other well. When a family or an individual was in need of food, shelter, or care when ill, the others would respond and provide if possible. Many families planted gardens of corn, squash, tomatoes, chilies, cilantro, *yerba buena* (mint), and many other vegetables and herbs common in Mexico. Their food, music, and religion, along with their work ethic and aspirations, steadied them through the hardships of their lives in this new country.

In 1924 Rosa gave birth to another son, Miguel. He too was born in the shed. With a sixth son, the pressure for more living space for the family was extreme.

In 1926 Jose's section crew was sent to Garden City to lay track for a new spur that paralleled the main line. Access to the new spur was especially valuable to lumberyards and grain elevator operators in Garden City. With few trees on the prairie, wood was brought in by rail and warehoused, and wheat harvests were stored in grain elevators until they were shipped to mills. To facilitate access, the spur was set five feet from the property line of businesses and residences. Family homes so close to the new spur did not have the same increase in value as did the commercial property. Residential property near the main line was already considered undesirable because of the noise and commercial activity. Despite the fact that the spur was not used on a daily basis, the risk the iron beast posed to residents and their children at play left the homes with even lower value. However, a man with a wife and six children living in a one-room, dirt-floor shed might think otherwise.

While Jose's crew constructed the new spur on the north edge of the Santa Fe's property line, Jose learned that the owner of the small house where Fourth Street, running north and south, intersected the new spur had decided to sell. The front of the wood-frame house was set back a few feet from the east edge of Fourth Street, facing west. The house was on a lot much deeper than it was wide, with a backyard extending forty feet from the house, creating a relatively sizable space for play and storage. The front door opened into a small living room with a north-facing wall and a bedroom with a south-facing wall. The kitchen extended straight back from the living room with sufficient space for a table, stove, sink, and cabinets. The bedroom also extended straight back into two smaller bedrooms. And in a welcome contrast to the dirt floor of the shed, the floors were tiled.

The owner, Hubert Callahan, was eager to sell to Jose. They agreed that he would take possession and make installment payments totaling $800. Upon full payment Callahan would convey legal title of the house and lot to Jose.

Jose and Rosa gathered their boys and belongings and moved into the house at 102 North Fourth Street. With their new home, the older boys were able to attend public school regularly. Jose knew they would struggle in the classroom because they spoke primarily Spanish, but he believed that, as all children seem to do, they would learn to speak the new language along the way. Jose and Rosa were diligent in their house payments, and in August 1928 the last payment was made and the property deeded to Jose. For the first time, at age forty-eight, Jose lived in a home on land he owned.

Jose and Rosa's family was part of the beginning of the Mexican barrios that emerged on either side of the Santa Fe's main line in Garden City. The city, with 3,500 residents, had developed in the late 1800s with the arrival of irrigation farming and the railway. Many European immigrants and their descendants in Garden City viewed the barrio as the proverbial wrong side of the tracks. But to the Garcias and the other families, homes in the barrio were the foothold for a better future at long last.

With the final house payment made, Jose immediately set his sights on a new prize—an automobile, and with it, mobility. He purchased a used Willys-Overland Whippet. It had a small engine and cost less than most other automobiles at the time. It was small and sturdy, yet had room for a family of two adults and six boys. Although not a luxury auto, Jose nonetheless took great pride in this possession that also served the needs of his family. Clearly, the family was approaching a level of comfort unknown to them in the past.

Despite the influence of the robber barons, urban America saw a remarkable era of economic expansion as the 1920s progressed. The Great Gatsby types as described by F. Scott Fitzgerald saw an explosion in wealth. The very rich became a great deal richer during these times. Big cities experienced, even if only for a short time period, the rise of a middle class. Black Tuesday, October 29, 1929, signaled the beginning of the end of this rising prosperity. The roar of the 1920s ultimately ended with the Wall Street crash and its aftermath. At the time of the crash, few Americans actually owned any stock. So while it was almost entirely the very rich who lost their fortunes on the stock market itself, the new middle class lost its paychecks and standard of living when the upper class lost its businesses.

For most people in the United States, the Great Depression began after the crash. For Jose and Rosa, however, the turn for the worse began a few months earlier. Jose had won the race to establish a foothold for the future when he purchased his home before suffering any serious injury laboring for the railroad. But the black iron beast did not relent. One day, Jose's body gave way while he and a fellow section hand lifted a wood tie. He felt a sharp pain in his abdomen. For a short time he tried to work despite the pain. When possible, he avoided the heaviest labor with the cooperation of his fellow section hands. When his absence would not be detected, he lay in a field, high weeds, or some other out-of-view location to try to relieve the pain. He massaged the bubble on his abdomen in an attempt to put his intestine back in a comfortable position within the abdominal wall. Jose was reluctant to see a doctor but finally did so at Rosa's urging. The doctor confirmed what Jose dreaded most: he had suffered a hernia. With that diagnosis, he understood that at age forty-nine, his days of heavy lifting on the railroad had passed.

Jose had no insurance nor access to any social programs to compensate him for his injury and loss of pay. The Santa Fe did not grant severance pay. He was out on his own again. He and Rosa had sacrificed so much and labored so hard to attain a foothold. Now they would have to be resourceful to keep and maintain it. Jose immediately began to search for work. He went farmhouse to farmhouse, door to door, offering his labor and carpentry skills as might be needed. From time to time, he worked temporarily on small projects or supplied farm labor that did not involve heavy lifting. He searched in Garden City as well, but home construction and remodeling work was limited. He did find carpentry work on structures at the Garden City Airport, but that project soon ended. He began to accept that he could not support his family with his carpentry skills alone.

Mexican immigrants in Garden City worked either for the Santa Fe or in *el betabel*, the sugar beet fields. They spoke little English and had little education, and few had skills for other types of employment. Jose had first seen the Mexican families in el betabel eight years earlier, when the Santa Fe brought him into Kansas. His work with the Santa Fe had spared Rosa and the boys from the hardship of field labor. But after his injury, he suspected that he would have no other choice. He felt some disappointment at his inability to keep them out of the fields.

In the barrio tavern, over beer and a game of dominoes with Antonio Rodriguez and Andres Mora, Jose learned that labor in el betabel did not require a prolonged blast of energy for moving heavy objects as did the railroad. Instead, the work required small bursts of energy for each slash of the hoe. But the slashing was unending and, after ten to twelve hours, exhausting. Rodriguez and Mora, who worked with their families in el betabel, told Jose that sugar beets were not a crop that required simply planting and harvesting after a few months. If left unattended, the crop failed. The men explained with a bit of pride that field laborers were responsible for the crucial step of sugar beet thinning, twice in a growing season. They added that the thinning must be completed at the right time—if it was completed too soon, a farmer would have to pay for a third thinning. If completed too late, the plant would produce less sugar. Both results reduced the farmer's profits.

When Jose asked how their pay was determined, the men looked at each other and chuckled. They answered that the farmer paid whatever he wanted to pay. The going rate was $20 to $25 per acre. The amount of pay varied depending on the price the farmer received from the sugar companies for his crop, the number of families available for thinning, and the condition of the fields. The experience of the two men was that laborers rarely negotiated for higher pay. They agreed that a farmer might pay more than the going rate only when he had delayed and needed a field thinned immediately or when he tried to prevent a family of laborers from going to a farmer willing to pay more. The men reminded Jose that farm laborers had families to feed and had no other place to go for work, so they accepted the price the farmers offered.

Jose admitted to them that he had never thinned sugar beets. Rodriguez responded that he and his family would be in the fields in two weeks. He told Jose that he was welcome to work alongside him and his family. He promised to show Jose how the thinning was completed and pay him for his work as well. Jose accepted the offer. Rodriguez told him to bring a hat, a pair of gloves, and a big lunch.

A couple of weeks later, Jose drove to the Rodriguez home at daybreak. He carried with him a lunch that Rosa had prepared just as she had done for years. As directed, he brought along his hat and work gloves. When he arrived, he found Rodriguez and his younger brother, Eduardo, and their families sitting alongside the dirt road. The owner of the field had agreed to pick up the men and their families and transport them to his fields. Rodriguez and his wife had two daughters, ages 12 and 14, and two sons, ages

8 and 11. Eduardo was accompanied by his wife and their two sons, ages 6 and 9.

At dawn the families climbed aboard the farmer's flatbed truck. Rodriguez and Jose loaded the tools, the jugs of water, and the lunches that would fuel them through the day. Rodriguez rode with Jose in the Whippet following the flatbed as it made its way to the fields three miles away. "Antonio, how long have you been going into el betabel?" Jose asked.

"Pues, most of my life. I'm thirty-five and I can't remember a time when we were not in the fields. Mi papa told me that when I was little, we lived in Alamo, in the Rio Grande Valley in Texas. When I was about five years old, un Americano came to Alamo looking for families to work in the sugar beet fields in Colorado. He wanted families with a lot of kids. I was one of eight kids."

"De veras?!"

"Si. My parents considered us kids gifts from God. We were just a bunch of poor kids fighting over food and clothes."

At that Jose laughed.

"Anyway, this Americano told mi papa that the sugar company he worked for guaranteed work and housing for families willing to work in el betabel. They wanted families so they only had to pay one adult. If you have twelve adults working one acre, nobody is going to make any money. So papa signed a contract, and they gave him money for the train tickets. Then he dragged us off to Colorado."

"All of you?"

"Yes. I don't remember the train ride. But I remember that when we were in Colorado it was cold. There were no houses. There were tents, boxcars and a few people got 'beet shacks.' They were just wood frames with dirt floors."

"That's what we lived in when we first came to Kansas," Jose said.

"The sugar companies and farmers had no work for us after the season. Their guarantees for other work weren't worth a damn. So when the beets were done, mi papa took us to wherever we could find work, California, Washington, Nebraska, and back to Texas. I've been doing this ever since." Jose nodded in understanding. Antonio looked at Jose and said, "You know what the hardest part of this work is?" Jose waited for the answer.

"It's getting after your kids. You have to be on their asses all the time. You know they're tired, and they wish they were out playing. And you wish that too. But you can't let up on them. They do a very important part of the work. If they mess it up, it will cost you time and money." Antonio paused. "Maybe someday they'll get lucky and find work in some town and get out of these fields."

Jose empathized, "Si, si Dios les da licensia. If God permits it."

When the flatbed pulled to a stop, the Rodriguez crew unloaded the tools and supplies. Antonio met briefly with the farmer, who sternly gave final instructions, then drove away. Antonio told Jose to grab a hoe and follow him. As they walked to the corner of the field, Eduardo and the rest of the crew readied themselves, taking final drinks of water, adjusting their clothing, and sharpening the blades of their hoes with a metal file.

Antonio squatted at the plants in the first row. He reached down and held between his fingers the narrow green stems of three plants. They were two to three inches high and opened into full leaves. "This is the sugar beet plant. See how there are two or three growing together? That's a problem, because el patron wants only one plant to grow. The farmers plant a ball of seeds, it might have one seed, or two, or three, or four. They can't control how many plants will come up. The more that come up, the more work for us. You have to cut out the rest of the plants, and all the weeds. You can get most of them with a hoe."

Antonio demonstrated with a swift slash of his hoe wiping away all but two plants. "I had to be careful and not take out both plants. I don't want the patron yelling at me. When he gets mad, he wants to pay you less, and he won't hire you again. This is where your kids come in. They have to get one of those plants, either with a hoe or their fingers. And they have to get any weeds you miss, root and all. When we are done, in every row, the plants will grow about six inches apart without anything growing in between them. Entiendes?"

"Entiendo."

Antonio took the first row, Eduardo the second, and Jose a third. The women and children lined up behind the men, each with a handheld hoe. Antonio looked at them and yelled, "Listos cabrones?! Are you bastards ready?! Vamonos!"

With that command the workday began. Immediately the air was filled with the sound of the blades of the hoes slashing through the earth. The children crawled down the rows. Their hands constantly reached for and pulled out plants and weeds as they followed the men. Occasionally they slashed with the handheld hoe. The sun was up and began to warm the day. The crew worked this way until the noon break, except for short breaks for water.

Jose could not keep up with Antonio and Eduardo. They moved down the rows seemingly without breaking stride. On reaching the end, they immediately started back up new rows. They assured Jose as they met that he was doing well. They told him to stretch his neck and shoulder muscles at the end of each row. Jose tried not to look up and see the end of the row. He quickly realized that the more he looked, the longer it seemed before he got there. As the morning progressed, Jose tracked the time with each train that passed the field. He remembered the times they were scheduled to pass through Garden City.

After two days, Jose had slashed his way through more than an acre of sugar beet plants (one acre is slightly smaller than an American football field). He was exhausted after each day. His shoulders and neck stiffened after the first day. Despite working only two ten-hour betabel work days, it was enough for Jose to know what his family was about to endure.

Without any hesitation, he became the driving force of his family's labor in el betabel. Within a few days of his time with Antonio, Jose met with a farmer needing a family of laborers. Jose made no attempt to negotiate the farmer's offer of $22 per acre for a field similar to Antonio's. It was the first of hundreds of acres to be thinned by the family during the decade to come.

Sugar beets were usually planted in late March. Four to five weeks later, the first thinning began. For Jose's family, the process was essentially nonstop labor during those weeks. A month after the first thinning, the family returned to the fields and began the second thinning. These were the moneymaking months for the family, until the early fall. During the harvest in September and October, Jose and the older boys returned to the rows in el betabel to pull out the fully grown plants by hand. They tossed them into a pile to have their leafy tops slashed away with a sharp knife. The topped beets were then transported by truck to the factory for processing.

During the thinning season, a day in el betabel for the Garcia boys began with a rude awakening. Jose did not awaken the boys with soft words and gentle strokes of affection. Instead, he loudly whistled at them, and commanded them to get out of bed. He barked that a day of labor lay ahead of them. By daybreak the family was moving about in the house trying to ready themselves for the day. Rosa had awakened before everyone and prepared breakfast and lunch baskets. She checked that everyone wore the appropriate clothing. They piled into the Whippet with their provisions and tools and drove out of Garden City to the fields. Most were within a few miles of the city, but some were as far as thirty miles away.

On arrival at the field, Jose slipped on a pair of gloves to sharpen the hoes with a metal file. He, and usually one of the older boys, Porfirio, Jesus, or Felipe, started down a row. With long-handled hoes, they slashed, and slashed some more, clearing plants and weeds, hour after hour, row after row. After completing a row, the slashers sometimes walked backward down the next row to use the other shoulder to absorb the blows. If any of the older boys using long-handled hoes forgot gloves, they had blistered hands by the end of the day. The younger boys, Guillermo and Dionicio, pulled out the weeds and plants barehanded.

To compete with other families for the available acres in need of thinning, they worked as quickly and precisely as possible, then moved on to the next field. The formula was direct. The more acres thinned, the more the family was paid. Jose frequently halted his slashing to follow behind the younger boys and examine their work. Any seedlings or plants left intact would result in a sharp and thunderous condemnation and an occasional strike across the back with the handle of the hoe. Jose scolded the boys if they worked too slowly or began to fall asleep from fatigue. He did not tolerate complaints from the boys about the work. He pushed them to move quickly and to get it right the first time. During the drive home at the end of the work day, they could sleep.

Intentionally or unintentionally, Jose's methods hardened the boys. They learned there was no point in trying to avoid or delay the hard labor. They learned to follow Jose's approach to the challenges of hard labor: do it right the first time, save the complaining, complete the job, and move on.

The labor in el betabel produced a majority of the family's income for the year. In the interim, Jose and the older boys took on any work requiring manual labor, regardless of whether the labor was needed only for a day, a week, or a month. They became skillful handymen out of necessity. Farm labor, yardwork, construction, painting, roofing, plumbing, ditch digging—the type of work did not matter. If Jose or the boys had no experience with work that became available, they taught themselves on the job.

Apart from their place in the local farm labor pool, Jose and his family became part of the Mexican immigrant community in Garden City, just as they had in Holcomb. Their common experiences and hardships brought them together. They supported one another in the care of their families and neighbors. Community members gathered together to share their Catholic faith and celebrate birthdays, baptisms, and weddings. Musicians in their community almost always provided music at these celebrations.

By 1932 the oldest boys, Porfirio and Jesus, at ages nineteen and sixteen respectively, were approaching adulthood. Felipe and Guillermo were in their early teens, and Dionicio and Miguel were not far behind. The family seemed to be approaching stability despite its reliance on seasonal and sporadic work. Jose, Rosa, and their sons began to enter the flow of American culture. The Garcia boys, as they were then known in the barrio, had become fluent in English. They had attended Garden City's public schools through the eighth grade when not in el betabel. The boys played baseball and followed the exploits of Babe Ruth and the Yankees. They were fans of football and were saddened at the death of Knute Rockne, the famed Notre Dame coach who died in a plane crash in Bazaar, Kansas, 275 miles from Garden City. The boys followed boxing and the heavyweight champions. Each of them was anxious to learn how to drive the Whippet. They listened to the popular music of the day. The family began to celebrate Thanksgivings with a turkey dinner.

The winter of 1932–1933 was unusually dry on the southwestern prairie, with many large dust storms. In January one of the largest storms that winter struck Amarillo, Texas. That dust cloud was estimated at ten thousand feet high. The following spring, the wheat crop showed the effects of the poor winter weather. The wheat stalks in the fields did not stand as high as in previous years. The sugar beet crop suffered less damage from the spring storms, as the fields were often irrigated. When Jose and the family returned to el betabel for the first thinning, they found themselves in the middle of blowing dust on many occasions. Jose and the boys stayed in the fields until the dirt and sands made seeing and breathing difficult. Then they took refuge in the Whippet until the storms passed.

One afternoon Jose and the boys were driving home when the winds stirred remnants of a dust storm. Jose was unable to clearly see the farm road ahead and drove off the side into a deep ditch. He checked to see that all were safe and uninjured, then ventured out of the car into the dust to check on his Whippet, his beloved metal horse. The Whippet had come to rest at a steep angle with its nose at the bottom of the ditch. The driver's side rear wheel was left slightly off the ground.

Jose got down on one knee, rested his opposite elbow on the other knee, and examined the front end of his Whippet. The damage was not severe, and the car appeared to be operable if put back on the dirt road. But Jose did not immediately rise to his feet. Instead, he was motionless and continued to look at the Whippet. The boys saw his eyes water and redden. He then reached for the top of a nearby weed and firmly snapped the tip off the stem. He rolled the tip in his fingers for a few seconds, then tossed it aside. After a few more moments, Jose stood up and wiped under his eye with his index finger, then swiped it on his pant leg.

Jose was not a man to pity himself. Perhaps the emotion of that moment escaped him out of fatigue. He had faced a life of challenge after challenge, hardship after hardship. Yet he met them head on and kept pushing forward. He had left the Santa Fe as an injured man and with his family went into el betabel and farm labor. The loss of the Whippet would be an added burden, and a wholly unnecessary challenge. It was the only time Jose's sons saw that emotion in him.

He turned to the immediate issue—getting the Whippet back on the road. Any attempt to push the Whippet out of the ditch by its nose was dangerous. It could roll back on them if their combined strength was insufficient. Jose concluded they would have to wait on the farm road for help from a passerby or send one of the boys to ask for help from the nearest farm house. They did not wait long. Soon a tractor headed toward them was visible. The farmer driving the tractor kindly attached a cable to the frame of the Whippet and pulled it back on to the road. The farmer's quick appearance was a minor but welcome blessing and sent Jose and the boys on their way.

In the end, the 1933 wheat crop choked for lack of water and excessive winds. The wheat farmers and investors suffered double blows: the price of wheat had fallen even more during the year, and the farmers did not have a crop to harvest. Most farmers and investors kept a stiff upper lip and belief in the next year. They planted again in the fall season and prayed for rain. But their prayers were unanswered. The next three years were even worse. The rains failed to arrive, and the number of dust storms increased year after year.

By this time millions of Americans across the country were unemployed. The value of farms dropped well below the money owed on the land. Farmers began shutting down their operations. At the same time, hundreds of thousands of acres of topsoil turned to dust and were blown across the country. People living in what became known as the Dust Bowl, particularly the very young and the very old, began to suffer lung and breathing illnesses. The need for field labor to thin sugar beets diminished, leaving Jose to drive to Colorado, Nebraska, and California to find fields to thin, fruit to pick, or other crops to harvest. From 1936 to 1938, the drought and dust storms continued. Each year the number of storms approached or reached one hundred. Nearly one in four residents of the Dust Bowl began to leave the region, joining many victims of the Great Depression who left their homes for California. They too were seeking a better life.

Jose began to take the family to California for weeks at a time in the winter months when there was no work in Garden City. Jose's nephew, Alberto Cegarra, had found his way from El Paso to Los Angeles. Alberto was the older brother of Manuela Cegarra-Rodriguez, the infant held by her mother, Maria, when Pedro Garcia was photographed in El Paso two decades prior. Alberto and his family graciously opened their modest home to his aunt and uncle and his six cousins, and made Los Angeles home base in Jose's search for farm work. Together the families picked fruit and vegetables in nearby orchards and farms. When the harvest seasons came to a close, Jose and his family often extended their stays for a few days and visited with the cousins. They had no desire for a quick return to the windy, cold, barren plains of southwestern Kansas.

On Sunday evening, January 16, 1938, Jose, Rosa, and the family enjoyed a supper with plenty of food and drink at the home of one of the cousins. The following morning as Rosa prepared breakfast in the kitchen, she noticed that Jose had not yet joined her. She went to check on him and found him still in bed. "Aren't you getting up?" she asked Jose in a mildly surprised tone.

"Rosa, I can't get up. I don't feel well."

"What's the matter?" she asked with concern.

"I just can't get up. I don't understand," Jose responded.

"Does your stomach hurt? Are you hungry?"

"It hurts. I don't know if I can eat."

"I will get you some crackers and see if that helps."

"That's fine," Jose said in agreement.

When Rosa returned with a few saltines, she sat him up and held a saltine to his mouth for him to eat. Jose bit down and began to chew the cracker. But it spilled out of the sides of his mouth as he chewed. "I will get you some water and see if that is better," she said. On her return, she held up Jose's head and slowly raised a cup of water, tilting it to his lips. But again, he could not swallow, and the water spilled out of his mouth. Rosa now grew concerned. "Jose! What is happening to you?" He did not reply. As she laid his head back on the pillow, a tear fell from his eye. "Jose! What is wrong?"

Rosa began to fear Jose was gravely ill, possibly dying. She went into the kitchen and anxiously told Dionicio to run and get the priest who resided some six blocks away. Dionicio left immediately and ran to the parish rectory. Upon arriving, and out of breath, he relayed what Rosa had told him about Jose, and asked him to come quickly. The priest gathered his prayer book and a black pouch containing ashes, holy water and oils, and the Eucharistic hosts. The two of them hurried down the street back to the house. On entry, Rosa approached the priest and asked him to administer the last rites. Rosa rushed the priest to the bedroom, but Jose had already passed away. He was fifty-eight years old.

In a somber ritual, the priest honored Rosa's request. The priest dabbed his thumb into a small vial of holy oil, made the sign of the cross with the oil on Jose's forehead, and said, "May the Lord in his love and mercy, help you with the grace of the Holy Spirit." He then made crosses with the oil on Jose's worn hands, saying, "May the Lord free you from sin, save you, and raise you up."

Rosa and her sons were in shock. For some time, Jose had complained of abdominal pains. In the three days before the Sunday night family supper Jose had been feeling pain on the right side of his abdomen. He was not alarmed, as he had dealt with abdominal pain since he had suffered the hernia. Eventually those pains usually subsided with massaging and avoiding strenuous activity. None of his recent complaints suggested that he was gravely ill. When a member of the Los Angeles Coroner's Office later examined Jose, he concluded that Jose had likely suffered from appendicitis, and, left untreated, it had led to a deadly infection.

People without means often try to fight their way through illnesses without medical care. They unreasonably conclude that an illness is minor and that the body will heal itself in time. Perhaps if Jose had seen a doctor, he may have been properly treated, and he might have survived.

Rosa and her sons had earned enough money in California to sustain them until the next thinning in el betabel. However, the cost of transporting Jose to Kansas for burial would cut deeply into their earnings. Rosa did what she thought necessary to benefit the family, just as she and Jose had always done. She made the difficult choice of burying him in east Los Angeles. He was buried on a slight rise in Calvary Cemetery where the morning sun falls on his gravestone. He rests in a place where the days are cool and breezy, far, far away from the hard labor that was his life.

Though Jose left his family in shock, he did not leave them defenseless. Rosa and the boys had a home. His sons were young men prepared for their adult lives. They did not avoid hard work. Instead, they embraced it as an opportunity to provide for their family. The family was resourceful when faced with a challenge and did not hesitate to take care of one another and their neighbors. They had learned to persevere in pursuit of a better life.

Rosa returned to Garden City with five of her sons. Porfirio, the oldest, had decided to stay in California. Jesus and Felipe, now the oldest in the home, took the lead in support of the household.

3

Ernie's Promise

1941–1957

The Mexican barrio in Garden City stretched over seven blocks on Santa Fe and Maple Streets on the city's southeast side. Santa Fe Street was the first street south of the Santa Fe's main line; Maple Street was the second and like Santa Fe Street, it ran east and west parallel to the main line. The two streets extended to the city's southeast edge. Garden City had provided the Mexican barrio few city amenities, such as lighting and sewer lines. But one amenity the city could not withhold was the city park.

In 1919 George Finnup, a successful businessman and generous community supporter, donated 111 acres to the city for a public park. The donated land's northern boundary was Maple Street, and one-half mile to the south was the southern boundary, the Arkansas River. Garden City could not turn its back to a donation of that size. It accepted that the city park would be adjacent to the barrio. By 1941, with Work Projects Administration programs, donations, and city funds, the city had improved the park with lanes, trees, playground equipment, a small zoo, a baseball field, and an incredibly large pool.

The pool was lined with concrete, measured 110 yards long and 70 yards across, and had a deep end of eight feet. The city installed the water lines and pumps to bring the 2.5 million gallons of water required to fill it, and city promoters advertised it as the "World's Largest Free Concrete Municipal Pool." The pool and park improvements were symbols aimed at potential residents to illustrate the quality of living in Garden City. While it is difficult to measure the effectiveness of the city's promotion, it was clear that barrio residents had the easiest access to and use of the park. Residents on Maple needed only to cross the street, and those on Santa Fe needed only to walk a block.

Many barrio children spent hours and hours playing in the park every day. Teenagers from the barrio used the park as a place to congregate with friends and family. Young couples strolled in the park on its winding shady lanes. On December 7, 1941, after Sunday Mass at Saint Mary's in Garden City, Jose and Rosa's third-oldest son, Felipe, and his new wife walked to the city park to be with friends. That particular Sunday was pleasant and mild for early December in Kansas. Felipe, then twenty-three years old, had married Luisa Ayala eighteen months earlier. She was a year younger than he. They began their married life living in the small garage to the side of the Garcia home on Fourth Street.

Shortly after one o'clock, a friend of Felipe's drove up to the picnic table near the empty pool where Felipe and Luisa sat with other couples and friends. The driver quickly got out of the car and excitedly asked if they had heard the news. No one in Felipe's group was aware of any news, as they had no radio. The driver announced that the Japanese had attacked the United States at a place called Pearl Harbor. No one had heard of Pearl Harbor. The driver explained that it was in the Hawaiian Islands. Felipe asked the driver if the radio said there was going to be a war. The driver nodded his head and answered probably so.

Earlier that December in Japan, the military had approached Emperor Hirohito for his final approval of the naval attack on Pearl Harbor. Whether from a callous indifference to total war, the arrogance of an all-powerful emperor, or a desire to avoid a violent revolt by his own military, Hirohito gave his approval. The attack on Pearl Harbor began at 7:55 A.M., local time. More than 2,400 Americans were killed, and the American naval fleet was crippled. The attack jolted the entire United States, impacting even small towns like Garden City, 3,500 miles to the east.

After hearing of the attack, Felipe and Luisa immediately began walking home. They had been aware of the talk of a possible war with Germany. But there had been less talk of war with Japan. When they arrived, they immediately told Rosa the news. She was shaken. She had lost Jose three years before, and all of her sons except Miguel, who was now sixteen, were of age to be called to war.

For the Garcia home on Fourth Street and in homes all across the United States, the night of December 7, 1941, was a night of great apprehension and prayer. In all the uncertainty of that moment, they could not have foreseen that the burden of fighting and winning the impending war would significantly alter the American social and cultural landscape. America rose to become an economic powerhouse. During and after the war, laborers continued their departure from the farms for the stability of city industrial jobs. Millions of veterans utilized higher education benefits, and the civil rights movement began its ascent with its call for an end to discrimination and racial segregation.

The next day, Felipe and his brothers gathered around a radio at a nearby grocery store. They heard President Roosevelt declare December 7 as a "day of infamy." They listened intently as Roosevelt avowed that the "American people in their righteous might will win through to absolute victory." The commander in chief concluded his speech by asking Congress to declare war on Japan. It did so immediately. Four days later, Germany and Italy declared war against the United States, and Congress responded in kind.

President Roosevelt knew the military was not in a state of full readiness for wars on both the Atlantic and Pacific fronts. The year before, in anticipation of the United States entering the war, he took steps to increase the size of the military. He established the first peacetime draft in US history despite strong opposition in Congress. The involuntary draft was especially unpopular with those who opposed US involvement in the war in Europe. Even Charles Lindbergh, one of America's most famous and popular aviators, spoke out against America's going to war. But virtually all that opposition vanished after December 7.

The massive buildup of men, war materials, and supplies began in earnest. As were all men between the ages of eighteen and sixty-five, Felipe and his brothers were required to register for the draft. And just as Pedro and his sons had, the grandsons would have to navigate the chaos of war. Within weeks of his registration, Felipe received a standard form order from the president directing him to report for induction into the armed forces. He was inducted in the first week of April, three months after Pearl Harbor. When he left for the army, Luisa remained with Rosa in the house on Fourth Street.

After completing basic training, Felipe was assigned to the medical department of the army. Despite his seventh-grade education, the army had confidence in his abilities. The army sent him to Fort Shafter on the island of Oahu in Hawaii, where he was assigned for training as a medic at

Tripler Army Hospital. Tripler was the hospital where most of the casualties of the Pearl Harbor attack received medical care for their wounds. Felipe saw the remnants of the suffering and devastation left in the wake of the attack.

With the US entry into World War II, the populations of American military installations experienced a dramatic increase. Many soon became overcrowded, and the close contact of so many men made the spread of bacterial and viral diseases much easier—it was not uncommon for installations across the country to experience occasional outbreaks of colds and other respiratory illnesses. The military was slow to add the personnel and resources necessary to provide proper medical and health care for the men. Shortly after his arrival at Tripler Hospital, Felipe became ill with a throat infection. The medical staff made no attempt to determine whether his illness was viral or bacterial in its origin. Instead, he was treated for a common cold. After two weeks, Felipe developed a fever, became very weak and lethargic, and experienced severe pain in his joints.

The army medical staff later diagnosed Felipe with rheumatic fever, a disease that develops when strep throat is left untreated with antibiotics. At its worst, rheumatic fever can infect the heart valves, leaving permanent damage. In the end, the army concluded that Felipe's heart had, indeed, been damaged. Felipe was one of the many men who in the early years of the war suffered the worst consequences of this preventable disease. He and the others were not casualties on the battlefield; nonetheless, they were casualties of war. It was not until later in the war that the army began to test men for strep infections in order to treat them properly.

After his diagnosis, Felipe transferred back to the mainland for months of medical treatment. In July 1943 he finally received a medical discharge and returned to Garden City. On his arrival Luisa and Rosa felt great relief that he was home and seemingly away from danger. But none of them knew the severity of the illness lurking in his heart.

To support Luisa, Felipe relied on his military disability benefits and any odd jobs his health permitted him to do. At times he was able to complete a day of routine activity, but he was not able to perform any strenuous labor. He could neither lift heavy objects nor stand or walk for long periods of time. Any overexertion resulted in chest pain, shortness of breath, and fatigue. He needed periods of rest during the course of a day, and each day required caution and vigilance.

Despite his weakened health, Felipe was determined to have a family life. He purchased a lot on Santa Fe Street for the family home. His two older brothers—Porfirio, who had returned from California, and Jesus—had not been drafted. A bad knee caused Guillermo to fail his physical, and Dionicio, who was inducted, had been medically discharged from the army because of the asthma he developed during the Dust Bowl. Their youngest brother, Miguel, was eighteen and had not yet been called to serve. In their spare time, the brothers provided the labor and, whenever possible, the materials, to build a small two-bedroom home for Felipe and Luisa.

The call to active military service of so many from Garden City, including men from the barrio, created steady work for the Garcia brothers. They left el betabel to work for Garden City businesses and the war effort. Women, too, began working outside the home in support of the troops. Kay Ayala, Luisa's sister, worked a 4:00 P.M. to 4:00 A.M. shift mixing concrete for the air base ten miles east of downtown Garden City. Despite being pregnant with her first child, Irene, Dionicio's wife, lay across the wings of military aircraft to complete the wing assembly. For Felipe, his brothers, and their families, days relegated to el betabel and farm labor ended.

Apart from relief from the backbreaking labor and seasonal paychecks, the prize for the brothers was the financial stability to keep their children in the classroom and out of the fields. They vowed that at the very least their children would become better educated and thereby live better lives.

In March 1945, two months before the war ended in Europe, Luisa gave birth to James, her first child, in the living room of the house on Santa Fe Street. After the war, and with barrio men regularly employed, women from the barrio had access to Saint Catherine's Catholic Hospital for childbirth—and so, the following year in July, Luisa and Felipe's second son, Ernest Eugene, was born at Saint Catherine's. Access to Saint Catherine's delivery room and nursery was quite timely for the barrio, which now extended to Garden City's west side. During America's baby boom that followed the end of the war, the barrio did its share of the booming. Eventually, the Garcia brothers and their wives would raise forty-four children to adulthood. Dozens of barrio veterans who experienced combat on both the European and Pacific fronts returned and pursued their dreams of raising families.

Like many other barrio parents, the Garcia families were quick to show their willingness to be Americans by choosing English versions of their children's names. Some parents believed use of English names lessened any potential bias or negative impressions toward their children by classmates and teachers. Felipe and Luisa's oldest, James, was later nicknamed Jim, and Ernest would be nicknamed Ernie. Their concern was not unfounded. By the 1940s a few individuals with Mexican or Spanish heritage had reached national recognition. Perhaps in an effort to avoid the risk of their celebrity losing any value, their heritage received little notice. Among them were Hollywood starlet Rita Hayworth, who was of Spanish, British, and Irish extraction; Academy Award–winner Anthony Quinn, who was born in Mexico to Mexican and Irish parents; and perhaps the best hitter in baseball history and wingman to John Glenn in the Korean War, Ted Williams, who was of Mexican, Welsh, and Irish descent.

Three years after the end of the war, when Ernie was two years old, Felipe was still unable to find work within the limits of his physical strength. If he was discouraged, he set it aside and remained determined to support his family. Using his GI Bill benefits, he enrolled in a watchmaker and jeweler school in May 1948. Like his assignment as a medical corpsman, it was a field in which he had no experience. But what he did have was Jose's attitude: when a work opportunity presents itself, take it, and learn as you go. So he gathered Luisa and their two sons and moved his family 375 miles away to attend the Kansas City School of Watchmaking.

After two years of study Felipe emerged as a certified watchmaker and jeweler. In August 1950, Felipe and Luisa returned to the house on Santa Fe Street. They returned not only with Felipe's new certification but also with a new daughter, Alvina, born earlier that year. Felipe immediately began applying for a position with Garden City's downtown jewelers. The jewelers accepted Felipe's applications, but they had no position for him. He could only wait for an opening. In the meantime, he was still determined to work. He found work as a driver for a lumber company. His duties were not strenuous for a man in good health, but for Felipe they were difficult and tiring.

Finally, in 1953 Dickinson's Jewelry Store on Main Street offered Felipe a position. He accepted. At thirty-five years of age he had made the transition from farm laborer to white-collar worker. He wore a suit and white shirt to work every day at Dickinson's. He was one of the first men of Mexican heritage to work in downtown Garden City in a white-collar position. More importantly, he could support his family with work that was within his physical limits.

Felipe's work at Dickinson's moved his family into a position to thrive, from a day-to-day existence to one of paycheck to paycheck. Even if more difficult times should arise, the family had the support of grandparents, uncles and aunts, cousins, and neighbors in the barrio. Most barrio families were willing to help each other with the tasks of maintaining their households. No school buses operated within the city, so a family able to drive its children to school willingly offered to drive others. Every morning, with books in arms and holding paper lunch bags, children waited at the street (paving and curbs were not yet in place) for their chauffeurs. After school many of the children walked home together and packed the living rooms of homes with television sets to watch the Mickey Mouse Club.

Residents shared the bounty of their gardens and fruit trees and sent children to deliver paper bags of corn, tomatoes, squash, chilies, peaches, pears, and more. On Saturdays one woman would purchase two low-priced cases of eggs from a Mennonite farmer. After keeping three dozen for herself, she distributed the remaining twenty-seven dozen to neighbors at cost.

When additions were added to the houses with growing families, the men offered their labor and skills. One man was a carpenter who made custom cabinets for the often irregularly sized kitchens and bathrooms. Others helped with the framing, the painting, and the roofing. In the winter, when snow fell, men and boys shoveled not only the sidewalks of their own homes but also those of their elderly neighbors.

Everyone knew which homes on their block had a storm cellar or the luxury of a basement. During the spring tornado season, warning sirens sent families running under darkened, rolling, low-lying clouds to the shelters. The residents immediately opened the angled doors of the cellars to facilitate the quick entry of neighbors. Teenagers, usually boys, were sent to the homes of the elderly to bring them to safety. If the cellar filled, women and children occupied the spaces furthest from the entry, while the teenage boys and men gathered at the steps nearest the entrance. More than once, Luisa and her children sat in the next-door neighbor's cramped and poorly lit cellar, sometimes by candlelight, and waited for the storms to pass.

Ernie's earliest memories began during this time period. He had a big brother, a little sister, and a new baby brother, Francis—nicknamed Frank—who was born in December 1951. By then Ernie was a playful child with a mischievous streak and a sparkle in his hazel green eyes. He was mostly mindful of Luisa, but at times he tested her limits for his behavior. When the limits were reached, Luisa called him back from the edge with an exasperated, "Ernesto!" Almost always he responded appropriately to her call to order. In 1951 he started kindergarten at Alta Brown Elementary, a public school. A photo of Ernie and his kindergarten classmates, including a cousin, Gloria (Guillermo's daughter), and a lion cub from the zoo appeared in the *Garden City Telegram*. Ernie had a medium build and was average in height as kindergartners go. In the photo, he looked directly into the camera's lens with a bright gaze. It is clear that he was a boy comfortable and confident in his surroundings.

Ernie's world, especially with the addition of school, was a place full of new and fun places with things to discover and explore. Ms. Adamson, his teacher, was kind and made him feel welcome. He easily made friends with children from outside the barrio, some of whom became lifelong friends. At school, his senses compared his new surroundings to those at home—the soap smelled different, the odor of glue was strong, erasers felt strange and rubbed away letters and drawings. The school provided daily snacks of milk in cartons and sugar cookies. He had his own rug to nap on. There was a shelf full of books and a playground right outside the door. Like many children, he saw this new world as a magical wonderland.

Ernie's admission into public school in Garden City was without issue. The schools at that time were not segregated. In fact, Felipe and his younger brothers had attended Garden City's public schools even in the 1920s. Nonetheless, after World War II, independently or through organized regional advocacy, Mexican Americans across the American Southwest and Midwest placed greater emphasis on education. The motto of one veteran organization from Corpus Christi in south Texas, the American GI Forum, was "Education is our freedom and freedom should be everybody's business." By 1955 the reach of the GI Forum included Garden City and Dodge City war veterans. The group considered military service as passage to the opportunities of first-class citizenship and was determined to take advantage of that passage to improve veterans' and their children's educations. The group's efforts were aimed at Ernie's generation and they advocated not just for high school diplomas but for college degrees as well.

* * *

When Ernie was six years old, Felipe was actively involved in organizing that year's Mexican Fiesta in Garden City. Beginning in 1926, the Garden City Mexican community publicly commemorated Mexico's 1810 revolution for independence from Spanish rule with an annual Fiesta. Felipe's father, Jose, had served on the Fiesta committee in 1929. In a photograph of that committee, Jose took his place among twelve other men. The men did not smile for the photo—instead, they wore serious expressions. Apparently, even when leading a celebration, these men were all business. The majority of the men were of medium or dark complexion with thick black hair. As had his father, Pedro, Jose looked European. His hairline had receded more than those of the other men in the photo, and he wore a mustache. With his light complexion, he stood out from the others.

The Fiesta was a distraction, if only for a day, from the sacrifices made in this new country in pursuit of a secure life free from poverty. Fiestas were held on September 16, or within a few days of that date, and included the selection of a Fiesta queen, traditional dances and music, and the sale of Mexican food. To this day, the Mexican Fiesta celebrating Mexico's independence remains an annual event in Garden City.

When Felipe asked Ernie if he would be willing to dance in the Fiesta, he agreed right away. Ernie had accompanied Felipe and Luisa to many Saturday night Mexican dances and watched them dance together. These Saturday night dances were an important social event for the barrio community—a welcome relief from a week of work and childrearing and an opportunity to enjoy the music, to meet with friends and family, to share a beer or two, and to enjoy a little romance and passion with a sweetheart. Ernie saw dancing as a fun time and eagerly stepped onto the floor and tried to follow in his parents' footsteps, literally. He had already received compliments and praise for his dancing, so he was not shy or apprehensive about dancing for a public audience.

For many years an elderly man from Mexico, Don Cipriano Garcia (not related to Jose's family), taught the Mexican children of Garden City the popular and traditional dances of their families' home country, including the Doble Paso and Jarabe Tapatio, the latter popularly known as the Mexican Hat Dance. Under Don Cipriano's direction, Ernie and the others danced on an elevated stage, dressed in their traditional *charro* outfits and *folklorico* dresses. In his black, white-stitched charro outfit and sombrero, Ernie was a handsome boy. In his performance of the Jarabe Tapatio, Ernie pursued the attention of his female dancing partner. Having won her attention, the dance concluded with Ernie on one knee, the other knee propped up for his partner to rest her foot upon while she lifted his sombrero to her head. As the small crowd applauded Ernie took a bow while his partner curtsied. They left the stage with the sense of having performed well.

Ernie began attending Saint Mary's Catholic School in first grade. Felipe and Luisa believed a Saint Mary's education strengthened their children's Catholic faith. They were confident their children benefited not only from the religious teachings but also from the high educational standards in the school. Nuns from the Dominican order taught at Saint Mary's. They wore traditional long black robes covering all but their hands and faces, with a white coif and black veil atop their heads. They had earned a reputation for strict teaching methods and classroom management.

Saint Mary's was Ernie's first encounter with raw discipline from someone other than his parents. But the threat of knuckle-rapping, ear-pulling, or other corporal discipline did not always deter his classroom socializing, tardiness, and violations of classroom management rules. Occasionally, he tested the limits and suffered the consequences, but he was not willing to endure swats and other physical punishments for defiance's sake.

Still, despite the influence of the nuns, Ernie kept a playful and mischievous manner and looked for fun and adventure, especially in the worries of adults. On one particular spring afternoon when Ernie was in the fourth grade, the students were enjoying recess after lunch. Without warning a Dust Bowl–era storm descended on the school. The nuns rounded up the children as quickly as possible and rushed them into the two-story red brick school house.

The nuns scurried about the school wetting paper towels and directing the students to use them to cover their faces. A few students helped the nuns line the windowsills with wet paper towels as well. The nuns checked every student's breathing. Though it was early afternoon, the schoolhouse was covered in darkness. Most of the children were anxious or fearful as they sat at their desks waiting for the dust to clear. Not Ernie. To him this was exciting. Darkness at midday, wet towels on faces, and putting aside the afternoon lessons made the day an adventure until the dust finally cleared at the end of the school day.

Ernie's exception to the "drill sergeant" nun experience was his fifth-grade teacher, Sister Mary Jeanette. She was young, pleasant, and patient and had been a nun and teacher for only a short time. Ernie felt comfortable in her classroom and was inspired to do well in her classes. He was at ease asking for help with the schoolwork and talking about his family, including Felipe's illness. However, Ernie did lose some favor with Sister Jeanette as a result of a show-and-tell performance he and a neighborhood classmate, Terry Billinger, presented to the class. They performed their rendition of Elvis Presley's "Hound Dog," complete with air guitars and the gyrations of the King himself. Their classmates—especially the girls—loved the performance, but it was the gyrating that crossed the line for Sister Jeanette. She was appalled and was left with no choice but to refer the boys to the parish pastor for the appropriate scolding. When the matter was closed, Ernie did feel bad that he had disappointed his favorite teacher.

Although Ernie improved his effort in Sister Jeanette's classroom, he was never a driven academic whiz kid. He always advanced to the next grade level at Saint Mary's, but he did not strive to be at the top of his class. His best efforts were saved for sports. Sports were the most common topic of discussion for Ernie, Jim, and the boy cousins when they were together. The *primos* spent much of their play time in sand lots or the city park playing the big three: baseball, football, and basketball. Ernie enjoyed baseball, but his passion was basketball. A rim and net were fastened to the family garage that stood in the backyard, where he spent hours shooting hoops.

When school days ended, Ernie hurried home to play basketball. He and most other students walked the mile home, crossing Main Street and Santa Fe's main line to reach the barrio. Some days on the way home he walked down the alley behind Dickinson's Jewelry Store. If the back door was open, he could see Felipe at his work table in a white shirt. Ernie sensed the white shirt was important from watching Luisa as she carefully and precisely ironed Felipe's shirts. If there was time, Felipe and Ernie would talk for a few moments before Ernie continued on home.

In the summer, if Jim and Ernie were not playing baseball, they were listening to game broadcasts. In 1955 the Philadelphia Athletics major league baseball team moved to Kansas City, Missouri. Immediately, radio stations across Kansas picked up the broadcasts of the A's games. Ernie and Jim joined Felipe in listening to as many games as possible. As teenagers and young men before the war, Felipe and his brothers played organized baseball. The six brothers passed on their love of sports to their sons—and after raising the six of them, it was inevitable that Rosa would develop some interest in sports, too. Surprisingly, she became a big fan of Garden City's junior college football team. On Saturdays in the fall, Rosa accompanied Porfirio, Felipe, Jim, and Ernie to the small stadium to watch their games. On one particular November Saturday, a heavy snow began to fall during the game. Rosa was undeterred and insisted they watch the game until it was over!

During this time Felipe's heart continued to weaken. The defective valve over time continued to damage the heart muscle. Medicine had no effective cures or treatments at the time. Felipe began to miss work at Dickinson's more frequently. He was able to get a hospital bed that allowed him to sit up as he rested at home. However, the size of the bed left no room to maneuver in the bedroom, so Luisa moved it to the living room. With the change, the doctor, Luisa, and family tended to his care without obstruction. Some days, Felipe had enough strength to move about the house or even drive the kids to Saint Mary's. But after each chore, he tired and had to rest.

For just a couple of years, Felipe, Luisa, and their children had lived the 1950s middle-class, Ward-and-June-Cleaver life. But now the reality of the hardship of Felipe's health settled in. Jim and Ernie needed to work to help support the family. The family never thought otherwise. This was not the Cleaver family experience—it is hard to imagine Wally and Theodore forced to go to work.

Luisa did not drive, and Felipe knew Jim and Ernie needed to be more mobile in order to help her maintain the family. So Felipe told Luisa to buy a bicycle for each of the boys. She bought each of them a new Schwinn. Jim used his for a newspaper route, while Ernie, at nine years of age, used his to get to and from his first job: shining shoes at Lefty's Barbershop downtown.

Garden City's downtown was classic small-town America in the 1950s. Main Street extended northward for five blocks from the Santa Fe's main line. The businesses on either side of Main Street included banks, gas stations, drug stores, hotels, a theater, clothing stores, a Woolworths, a Montgomery Ward, a Sears, Roebuck, and family-owned jewelry stores. Downtown shoppers angle-parked in front of the stores and shops. At the north end of Garden City's downtown, on the west side of Main Street, stood a long, gray one-story building at the corner of Main and Pine Streets. The rear of the building extended to the alley behind it, with a clothing store at the front of the building facing Main. Toward the rear of the building, two small businesses faced Pine Street. Lefty's was in the far rear space with a Pine Street entrance and a service door to the alley.

The owner of the barbershop was Earl "Lefty" Brickell. Lefty was middle aged, with straight blonde hair and blue eyes, and he wore eyeglasses. He was a down-to-earth, commonsense midwesterner who tried to do the right thing. Lefty's served Mexican men and their boys, including Felipe and Ernie. Lefty cut the hair of African American men as well, but only after dark, and they had to enter and exit through the back door. Remarkably, some barbershops in Garden City would serve men of color under no conditions. Lefty and his wife, Ruth, knew Felipe and Luisa. When they learned Felipe was ill and could no longer work, they offered Ernie a job at the shop.

Felipe asked Ernie to describe his duties at Lefty's. Ernie said he washed the glass in the front door and swept the floor when necessary. Felipe told Ernie to wash the windows as well and to sweep the floor after each haircut. Ernie explained that Lefty had not asked for that. Felipe instructed Ernie, "Always do more than is asked."

Ernie also had access to Lefty's shoe shine stand, where he could earn whatever the shop traffic brought in. Ernie already knew how to shine shoes when he started working at Lefty's. Nonetheless, he improved his technique. He learned to brush in beat and pop that cloth and shine that shoe. He took pride in the brilliance of the shine and charged his customers only twenty-five cents. A shine of that quality might cost fifty cents at any other stand. Downtown businessmen and employees learned that Lefty's was the place for a good shine, and soon men began to come into Lefty's just for a shine. Ernie often rode his bike from home to Lefty's with a cloth bag. Along the way he picked up as many as six pairs of shoes from businessmen. He took them to Lefty's and returned bright, shiny shoes to the men at the end of the day.

Ernie loved his job. After most school days, instead of shooting hoops at home, he now rode his bike to Lefty's and reported for work. He often worked late on Friday and Saturday nights. His best tips came from roughnecks who made their way into Garden City on weekend nights to enjoy a night on the town. Some of the local citizens described them as the riffraff. These men worked long days out on the farms digging and servicing irrigation and oil wells; Lefty's stayed open late on Fridays and Saturdays to accommodate them. Many had already been drinking by the time they arrived for their haircut and shoe shine. In their merriment, they often tipped Ernie two or three dollars for a twenty-five-cent shine. When the men left the shop, they walked across the alley to a small diner, the Midway Café. After supper the roughnecks headed back across the alley to the Windsor Hotel.

When the Windsor was built in 1886, it stood alone in the open prairie. It was out of place in western Kansas given its size and structure. But over time Garden City had grown up around it, and now it was in the heart of downtown. Standing alongside Lefty's building, the red brick, four-story Windsor extended to the alley as well, with its back door opening to the alley. It was a widely held belief in Garden City that working girls practiced their trade at the Windsor. Ernie's experience was that when he emptied Lefty's trash into bins in the alley, he sometimes encountered women smoking just outside the hotel's back door. Some of the women said hello, asked for his name, and asked what he was doing. Ernie politely answered that he worked at the barbershop. The women usually responded with an approving comment.

Ernie took satisfaction in working and supporting his family. When he arrived home after especially good days, he would pour a bag full of quarters and bills into Felipe's lap. Felipe praised him and assured Ernie that he and Luisa appreciated all the help he provided.

Hiring Ernie to work at the shop was not the only help Lefty gave Felipe's family. He and Ruth visited Felipe and Luisa at the house on Santa Fe, and sometimes after their visits they treated Jim and Ernie to a drive-in movie and popcorn. On days when Ernie was unable to ride his bike, Lefty and Ruth drove him home at the end of the day. They also treated Ernie to his first restaurant experience. He ordered a hamburger steak, a salad with French dressing, and a Pepsi, a dinner that was so much more appetizing to him than the staples of beans, rice, and tortillas. For Ernie the meal was as though he had died and gone to heaven. But it was only the Midway Café across the alley from Lefty's in Garden City, Kansas.

By the time Ernie started shining shoes, he had completed the first three Catholic rites after baptism as an infant—confession, Holy Communion, and confirmation, a rite performed by the bishop of the diocese. At Saint Mary's, the nuns were instilling in him a strong Roman Catholic faith. Along with the three traditional Rs of education—readin', 'ritin', and 'rithmetic—a fourth R was taught: religion. Every school day began with a Latin mass. Classes began with a prayer, the Our Father, followed by reciting the Pledge of Allegiance. Lunch in the cafeteria started with a prayer, and the school day ended with a prayer. Every student was taught the basic Catholic principles set out in the Baltimore Catechism, which had been assembled by Catholic bishops in the 1880s. On certain Friday afternoons, the entire student body prayed a rosary in the church.

By the time Ernie was ten, he had a belief in God, knew that there was good and sinfulness in the world, and understood that good would be rewarded and sinfulness punished. He learned that in times of need, prayers would be answered.

On many summer mornings before eight o'clock, in the early coolness before the heat took hold of the day, Ernie rode his Schwinn through the city park. He used clothespins to attach baseball cards to the spokes of the rear wheel. The snapping of the cards announced his presence as he cruised on the winding, paved, and shaded lanes. Not only were the lanes lined with trees, but so many other trees stood within the park that the shade in large sections of the park was virtually unbroken. It was such a contrast to the dry, treeless, flat plains that surrounded Garden City.

Early weekday traffic in the city park was almost nonexistent, except for the zoo keepers who moved from pen to pen to tend to the animals. By the time Ernie was riding his bike through the park, the zoo featured a variety of exhibits, including a lion, an elephant, polar bears, brown bears, sea lions, buffalo, zebras, peacocks, alligators, and a fish pond. Ernie watched as the keepers fed, watered, and hosed down the animals. Some mornings he saw Penny the elephant out on her morning walk with a keeper. Young people Ernie's age knew about these animals from books and may have seen them in person only on rare occasion. But Ernie saw them often and from a close distance.

On summer nights he could see from his porch the glow of the light towers at the baseball field three blocks away. At the opposite side of the park at the softball fields, fans drove up to the fence to watch the games from the comfort of their cars. Exciting plays on the field led to cheers and blasts of car horns easily heard by those living on Maple and Santa Fe Streets. Ernie and Jim were drawn to the ball parks, where they enjoyed the competition of the games, five-cent bags of popcorn, and five-cent bottles of soda. One of their favorite fast-pitch softball teams was the Latin Club, a highly competitive team consisting mainly of men of Mexican heritage.

* * *

In the spring of 1957, after the University of Kansas's loss in the national basketball championship game, Felipe's condition worsened. His heart was not pumping enough blood with oxygen throughout his body, and he was using an oxygen mask to try to improve his condition. Luisa needed more and more help in caring for Felipe and the children. She was also expecting a new baby. Luisa's sister—Aunt Kay, as she was called by the family—spent an increasing amount of time at the house. Felipe's brothers, the uncles, also helped as needed. The exception was Jesus, who had moved to Wichita five years earlier.

Felipe's doctors sent him to the University of Kansas Medical Center in Kansas City for surgery, in an attempt to repair the damaged heart valves. A few days after the surgery, Felipe was released from the hospital. But he did not immediately go to the train station for the trip home to Garden City. Instead, he took a cab to Kansas City Municipal Stadium to watch an Athletics major league baseball game. Luisa was quite upset with Felipe's diversion. She knew for some time that his heart condition was very precarious, and she could not understand why Felipe had recklessly put himself at risk for a ball game. Perhaps Felipe realized his chances to see a game were diminishing, so he attended while he was able. Or perhaps he had a mischievous streak, like his son.

When the new baby, Ana, arrived in July 1957, it was clear that surgery had not improved Felipe's condition. As his father had experienced twenty years earlier, the routine, highly successful surgical treatment he needed was two decades away. He still required the oxygen mask and was very fatigued. By this time Ernie had an understanding of death. His grandmother Alvina, Luisa and Aunt Kay's mother, had died the year before. And Aunt Sophia, Guillermo's wife, had died unexpectedly in 1955. Ernie feared Felipe's death, but he was taught at Saint Mary's that with faith and prayer, righteousness would prevail. So Ernie planned on Felipe's survival.

That summer in his nightly prayers Ernie asked God to allow his father to live. Some nights he lay awake unable to escape his thoughts and the uncomfortable heat. He kept his bedroom window open to catch any stray cool breeze. He waited for an answer from God, but all he heard were the angry roars of a lion and the wild calls of a peacock.

When the new school year began for Ernie and his siblings, Felipe's heart was extremely weak. He was essentially bedridden and always used an oxygen mask. Ernie offered a new prayer to God—a bargain. If He would allow his father to live, Ernie promised he would become a priest. He knew becoming a priest was a real possibility—recruiters had spoken to Saint Mary's students to explain how such a vocation could be pursued, and the nuns and parish priests did not hesitate to encourage students, including Ernie, to consider a religious vocation. With this new proposal, Ernie turned his focus to attending the seminary.

But Ernie's proposal to God went unanswered. In mid-November Felipe was taken to Saint Catherine's Hospital. Ernie, Jim, Alvina, and Francis were taken out of Saint Mary's and waited at home with Aunt Kay and baby Ana. Later that afternoon Ernie saw a cab pull up in front of his house. The driver walked Luisa to the door. When Ernie saw his mother alone, he knew that his father had died. Luisa, Rosa, and Dionicio were with Felipe when his heart failed on November 14.

The Garcia and Ayala families were devastated. They held each other and prayed. How could it be that Felipe could die at age thirty-nine? Luisa went into mourning and, in Ernie's eyes, never stopped. Rosa buried yet another child. It was a pain and heartache she believed had ended with her childbearing years. In such moments, no one can see an end to the pain and sorrow in their hearts and souls.

The Garcia and Ayala families gathered for Thanksgiving two weeks later. There seemed to be little reason to give thanks. The conversation among the women was tempered as they served the meal and watched over the children. Many of the men drank alcohol, some heavily. A priest joined the family for the dinner. Later the priest pulled Jim and Ernie aside. He told them that they were now the men of the house, that they were now responsible for caring for their mother, brothers, and sisters. Other family members, people who loved Ernie and cared for him, told him the same. At age eleven, Ernie did not fully understand the adult meaning of "man of the house." All he knew was that it was something serious and that he must help Luisa and his brothers and sisters.

4

Sanctuary in Ohio

1958–1961

When the breadwinner of a family dies, a family without wealth finds itself not knowing whether it will eat the next day. With Felipe's passing, Luisa had to set aside for the moment dreams of a future for her children. In her situation, any detailed long-term plans she might consider were too easily derailed by life's events. Her focus instead was meeting the day-to-day needs of her children.

In the aftermath of Felipe's death, Luisa remained dedicated to providing for her children and maintaining their modest house on Santa Fe Street. She relied on Felipe's veteran's benefits and Jim's and Ernie's earnings for income. During the school year she rose early to ensure the kids were off to school on time. She dressed them in clothes that she had set out the night before, including pressed jeans. In addition to breakfast, she prepared their sack lunches, which frequently included egg or bologna sandwiches and a piece of fruit. Saint Mary's cafeteria served hot lunches, but Luisa was one of the parents who could not afford the cost. Many in the sack lunch crew were children of Mexican heritage. On occasion, Ernie did enjoy a hot lunch after negotiating a trade with classmates who found the cafeteria cuisine not to their liking.

It might seem that Ernie, so young at Felipe's passing, would become lost without Felipe's direction. Felipe's time with him allowed only a small amount of fatherly guidance about family, education, and sports. But Ernie was not without direction. His aunts, uncles, friends, and neighbors, inside and outside the barrio, offered their encouragement and assistance. Their efforts assured Ernie that help was available if he or the family was in need.

During one particular evening, Luisa called Uncle Dionicio over to the house when Jim and Ernie would not stop fighting. Dionicio resolved the dispute with a threat that the loser would have to fight him afterward. He scolded the boys, reminding them that Felipe expected them to help their mother.

Luisa's father, Rosalio Ayala, nicknamed Chalio (pronounced cha-LEE-o), was another of those who kept an eye on Ernie. Chalio was born in 1883, in central Mexico near Penjamo in the state of Guanajuato, about 230 miles northwest of Mexico City. As in the state of Zacatecas, the Spaniards settled Guanajuato in pursuit of mining, agricultural, and cattle interests. Like other campesinos of numerous generations, Chalio was willing to embrace any work available. He understood that his labor meant survival. Many of the men who went to the United States to work, including Chalio, left a wife and children behind in Mexico. Sometime after 1910 Chalio left Penjamo and landed in Kansas City. There, approximately seven years later, he met and married Alvina Rocha. Eventually, like Jose and Rosa, they made their way to Holcomb, Kansas. Their two daughters were born and raised in Holcomb: Luisa in 1919 and Catalina—Aunt Kay—in 1921.

When Luisa and Kay were in grade school, Chalio worked on a farm in Holcomb. On many occasions he took the girls out of school to help with the farm work, including digging irrigation ditches and cutting milo. Like Felipe and his brothers, the Ayala sisters worked alongside their father in el betabel and in the potato fields in Nebraska. Neither of the girls completed their schooling beyond the eighth grade. Eventually, the Ayala family moved to the Garden City barrio on Santa Fe Street.

Initially, Chalio had not approved of Luisa's marriage to Felipe, but he warmed toward the arrangement with the births of his grandsons, Ernie and Jim. Luisa and her children frequently visited her parents and Aunt Kay at the Ayala home, a small house located where Santa Fe Street dead-ended on Garden City's southeast edge. The distance between the two homes was only three blocks. After Felipe's death, Chalio stopped to check on Luisa virtually every day. If she needed help of any sort, he tried to provide it.

Ernie saw his grandfather as a strict, no-nonsense figure. He often accompanied Chalio as he worked odd jobs and performed chores around the home. The two of them had little time for play or fun. If there was a chore to complete, a yard to be cleaned, or a lawn to be mowed, that was their priority. If there was a task Ernie could do, Chalio required him to help complete it.

Born and raised on a ranch, Chalio worked with cattle and other livestock. He became a butcher and was adept at dressing the animals on the ranch. He remained a skilled butcher into his sixties. A meat packing plant in Garden City called him in to work as needed, and people in the community who raised farm animals knew that Chalio butchered and dressed animals, including lambs, goats, and venison. On one occasion, when Ernie was about seven, he helped Chalio butcher and dress a goat. He watched his grandfather sharpen his knives and cleavers in preparation. Ernie saw the blood empty from the hanging carcass and followed Chalio's blood-stained hands as they moved with swift and efficient cuts and slashes. In a matter of minutes the goat was skinned and the viscera removed. Chalio had no concern for the brutality of his work—his concern was to put food on the table. The bloody scene made Ernie squirm, uneasy. It was not a pleasant experience, but even at his young age, Ernie knew that the meal that followed the butchering was good for the family.

Ernie continued to work at Lefty's after Felipe's death. The work was still fun, and the responsibility steadied him at a time when he might have faltered. Lefty generously accommodated Ernie's schedule to allow for his attendance at school and sporting events. At Saint Mary's, Ernie continued to be an average student at best. But he kept his passion for sports, especially basketball. He became a starting player on the seventh grade basketball team, and his passion for the game appeared in his play. Ernie was all-out hustle. He displayed skills and smarts for the game and gave the extra effort, running hard down the court, diving for the basketball, and constantly moving his feet as he defended.

Ernie's basketball coach was Art Wilson, a lay teacher. Initially, Saint Mary's Parish relied exclusively on nuns as teachers, but by the time Ernie reached the seventh grade, Saint Mary's had begun to add men and women to the faculty who were not members of a religious order. The male teachers were expected to coach basketball as part of their duties. Wilson had taken note of Ernie's play on the court and his popularity with teammates and classmates.

Unfortunately, it was Coach Wilson who opened Ernie's eyes to another part of the world at this stage in his childhood. Many people of color experience their first encounter with "the man"—a white person declaring superiority because of another's nationality—at school. Sometimes the declaration is an explosive in-your-face burst. Sometimes it is a slithering slight, undetected until after the bite. For most, including Ernie, those moments are etched in their memories for the rest of their lives.

Ernie admired a pretty classmate of Irish background named Ann Regan. By coincidence, her father owned a jewelry store on Main Street. One afternoon Ernie was talking to Ann outside the classroom just before the class bell. He entered the room seconds late. Wilson directed Ernie to come to the front of the classroom. Ernie complied, not knowing what to expect. The coach began to tell the rest of the class how he was "misguided" by flirting with Ann and insinuated that there was an ethnic issue at play. Ernie stood and suffered the stares of his classmates while Wilson delivered his lecture about him. Ernie did not understand why he was put on display. Finally, he was allowed to sit at his desk. He then felt for the first time that someone viewed him in a way that separated him from everyone else. He realized the separating factor was being Mexican.

The event was vivid in Ernie's memory. He had witnessed racial discrimination—he saw black men enter Lefty's only through the back entrance. But until Wilson's slight, he had not been conscious that his Mexican heritage might result in different treatment. Perhaps his light complexion had shielded him from this type of treatment until Wilson stood him before the class.

Fortunately, Ernie concluded that Wilson's acts were part of a Saint Mary's experience but not a part of the religious beliefs of the people at Saint Mary's. Though the event hurt and disappointed Ernie, he did not become discouraged or cowed. Instead, he now saw with an eye open for any prejudice that might come his way. He also decided to keep flirting with Ann. She thought he was very likable and, like many in her class, quietly appreciated the hard time he and his pals gave the nuns. She and Ernie remained friends through high school and even throughout their lives to this day.

It is safe to say that he also kept the sparkle in his eye and his mischievous streak. He continued to see the magic of his world and to look for adventure.

Most of Ernie's classmates, in their early teens, counted the days to the end of middle school or junior high school. They looked forward to high school with great expectations of fun and excitement, eager to begin their lives as young adults. Most of all, they were pleased that they would no longer be considered children. Ernie's view of high school, however, was much more subdued. He had committed to high school at the seminary.

Before Felipe died, Ernie, in his youthful innocence and faith, believed in his genuine commitment to become a priest if God would mercifully allow Felipe to live. Despite Felipe's death, Ernie's faith in God and prayer was not shaken. Although the bargain failed, he did not want to feel that it had failed because he had not intended to fulfill his obligation. He wanted to demonstrate that he fully intended to uphold his end of the bargain and that he did not consider himself excused from his obligation. He reasoned instead that perhaps Felipe died because it was God's will that he become a priest.

Ernie's opportunity to attend the seminary arose from the generosity of Saint Mary's parish and a Society of the Precious Blood priest Father Fredrick Lang. They agreed to help Luisa pay the cost of Ernie's tuition and room and board at Brunnerdale Seminary near Canton, Ohio. Brunnerdale was a four-year Catholic high school operated by the Precious Blood priests. Ernie knew that priests made a vow of poverty, so he did not understand how Father Lang was able to pay anything. Nonetheless, Luisa, who was very conscientious about paying bills on time, appreciated and accepted the generosity of the parish and Father Lang. She, Aunt Kay, and Chalio were willing to suffer the financial hardship to cover her share of the cost in support of Ernie.

Brunnerdale was 1,160 miles from Garden City. For Ernie, it was a world apart from Garden City's barrio and Lefty's Barber Shop. He knew Brunnerdale was far away, but because of his promise, and a growing sense of adventure, he was determined to go to Ohio. It was unlikely that at age thirteen, Ernie understood the magnitude of the impending changes to his daily life.

The seminary offered a summer orientation program for the students planning to attend in the fall. The goal of the week-long orientation program was to present a realistic preview of the structure and discipline required of seminarians. The students would be guided through a typical seminary school week. They were awakened each morning for 6:30 Mass and taken to the chapel for prayer, the first of four daily trips to the chapel. Mornings were spent in the classroom, followed by afternoon work periods that included house cleaning, tending to farm animals, preparing meals, and cleaning the kitchen and dining facilities. Late afternoons included athletics and free time. Their meals were served in the cafeteria, and they slept in open dormitories.

It was the railways, particularly the Santa Fe, that delivered Ernie to a life-changing destination, just as they had Pedro and Jose before him. In June Ernie and four other boys from Saint Mary's assembled at the train depot in Garden City. The plan was to ride the El Capitan passenger train on Santa Fe's main line to Chicago, then change trains to Canton. For each of the boys, it was their first trip away from home on a train. Any apprehension the boys felt was far outweighed by the anticipation of the adventures and mystery of the journey before them. The boys did not know, nor did their parents, that the adventure and mystery would begin before the boys stepped aboard the El Capitan.

Ernie, Luisa, his classmates, and their parents waited for the El Capitan in the small Garden City Depot. They sat together on long bench pews. Another train passenger, a nicely dressed man, began polite conversations with Ernie and the waiting group. Shortly after their conversation began, the El Capitan announced its arrival with loud blasts of its horn. The boys said their goodbyes over the noise of the train engines and eagerly boarded. The nicely dressed man who had befriended them followed. The conductor seated the boys together toward the rear of their car.

After leaving Garden City, a different man in a suit walked past where the boys were seated. The man stopped at the door of the small corridor that connects the train cars. The man caught Ernie's attention and signaled with his hand to come to him. He also put his index finger over his lips signaling to Ernie that he remain quiet. As the man in the suit waited for Ernie to respond, he quickly glanced forward and backward. Ernie recognized this was a time for caution. He paused for a moment but decided he would not be hurt, so he proceeded, carefully. Ernie left his seat and walked toward the man. The man identified himself as some type of policeman, showing Ernie a badge. The policeman asked Ernie, "Do you remember the man who talked to you at the Garden City train station?"

Ernie answered, "Yeah, I do."

"Good. Do not get off this train with that man. You understand? And that goes for your friends too. They are not to get off the train with him. Make sure you tell them that. You got that?" Ernie nodded that he did. "Good, now go tell your friends."

Ernie returned to his seat and shared his conversation with his classmates. Perhaps disbelieving and not overly concerned, they did not react to Ernie's surprising information.

Two days later as the train approached Chicago, his classmates' disbelief ended. The nicely dressed man from the Garden City station approached them. He invited them to get off the train with him. The boys refused his offer. The man then attempted to entice them with a promise to buy them something to eat and drink in the station. The boys held their ground and responded that they were not interested. The man's friendly face turned to one of spite. He walked away without saying anything more and was quickly out of sight. Immediately after the suspicious man slipped away, the policeman approached the boys from the adjoining car. He asked the boys about their conversation with the man. The boys eagerly told him about their encounter.

When the train arrived in Chicago, the policeman escorted the Garden City boys off the train. There they were met by several other men in suits. They learned that the policeman on the train and the men meeting with them were agents with the Federal Bureau of Investigation. The agents took the boys to an office and questioned them about the suspicious, nicely dressed man. The agents never confirmed the reasons for their interest in the man, but the boys were certain the agents were investigating him for kidnapping or harming children. After they were interviewed, the high drama and suspense ended for the small-town boys. But before they boarded a train for Canton, the agents treated them to a meal fit for boy-kings—a hamburger, French fries, and a soda pop.

When the boys arrived at the Canton station, they were met by a Brunnerdale priest, the director of seminarians. He appeared to be filled with dread as they began to retell their adventure with the FBI agents and the mystery man. As he drove them to Brunnerdale, his apprehension did not subside until the boys assured him they were not harmed in any way. The director silently recited prayers of thanks to God.

It was twilight when the director and the boys neared Brunnerdale. The main building of the seminary, which had been built on five hundred acres of land in 1931, was set back in the woods and not visible from the roadway. Ernie was able to see steep green hills and wooded areas as they drove onto the lane leading to the main building. He was anxious for his first sight of the seminary, his anticipation rising with each winding turn through the woods to the top of a hill. As they rounded the final bend, the woods opened to reveal a broad, four-story brick building. The only visible entrance extended outward from the middle of the building. A bell tower rose up from behind the entrance. The façade of the structure resembled the front of a large stone hotel or luxury estate in the English countryside.

They drove into the paved quarter-mile circle drive in front of the building. The area within the circle was covered with green grass and shrubbery. The grounds surrounding the seminary and the hilltop were a carpet of green. From the entrance, Ernie was able to look back toward the road. To the right of the circle and set back a short distance was a large pond of still blue water. A bench had been placed on the pond's edge. To Ernie this instantly seemed a wonderful and beautiful place.

By the time the boys completed registration, it was nearly time for lights out. The first night of orientation was one of the rare instances when seminarians were permitted to speak in the dormitory, and the boys nervously talked among themselves in preparation for the first of their five days as seminarians.

Ernie's primary purpose in attending Brunnerdale was to fulfill his obligation arising from the bargain for his father's life. But he also welcomed a break from the pressure of earning money to support his family. Apart from those adult aspects of his decision, the prospect of daily access to a pool and a basketball gym was enticing. He was also mindful that he would be in line for three square meals a day, minus, of course, Luisa's tortillas, tacos, enchiladas, beans, and other staples.

For most of the students, the conclusion of orientation was the decisive moment in their decision to return for the fall semester. Some attendees could now make a final rejection of their parents' wishes. They were then able to say that they had tried the seminary life and did not like it. For a few others, orientation was a preview of an unwanted life away from home at the insistence of their parents. For still others, orientation was a confirmation that Brunnerdale was where they wanted to be. By the end of the week, Ernie had no doubt that he wanted to attend the seminary. After just one week as a seminarian, he felt a sense of belonging.

On his return to Garden City—without any incidents along the way—he told Luisa of his final decision to attend in the fall. Luisa took great pride in his decision to pursue becoming a priest. So did barrio residents when they learned one of their own would become a seminarian miles away from home. On one occasion Ernie was with a group of friends when a girl used the word *damn* and drew disapproving looks for use of the cuss word in the presence of a priest-to-be. While Luisa took pride in Ernie's vocation, she was not so enthusiastic about his year-long absence.

At Brunnerdale, Ernie felt all the dramatic changes of freshman life. He lost the daily support of his family and the contact with his friends from the barrio and Saint Mary's. He no longer had spending money from the tips of the entertaining characters at Lefty's. Ernie had always enjoyed dancing in Garden City's Fiesta, and it gave him a strong sense of belonging in the Mexican community. But his seminary commitment ended his Fiesta performances (though not his love for dancing).

The seminary replaced those losses with a great deal of prayer, schooling, and work. This devout living was often conducted in silence and in the flicker of votive candlelight or in otherwise dimly lit chapels and halls. Prayer included meditation and reflection as well as recitations of scripture. Ernie accepted the subdued atmosphere of strict discipline and periods of total silence because of his promise to God.

Brunnerdale followed the Catholic practice of the Great Silence. Seminarians were not allowed to speak at all during the first Sunday of the month. During the remaining Sundays and weekdays, they were barred from speaking during particular periods of the day. The longest period of silence began at the close of night prayers at 9:00 and ended with the breakfast prayer. The seminarians were not allowed to begin speaking or eating breakfast until all were seated and the prayer completed. The church believed that silence led to solemn reflection and holiness. Even if that result did not always occur, the Great Silence made management of the student body of 120 or so a much easier task.

In the first weeks, Ernie's enthusiasm eased the adjustment to the strict daily routine. Seminarians were awakened at ten minutes after 6:00. Ernie did not linger in bed, as he was to be in the chapel for Mass by 6:30. He dutifully dressed and groomed himself in silence. Over a polo shirt and pants, he wore an ankle-length black cassock with a white collar and black shoes. Breakfast was served after Mass at 7:00. The school day began at 8:00, with ten minutes of chapel prayer before lunch, and ended at 3:00 with ten more minutes of chapel.

Every seminarian, regardless of grade level, was enrolled in a Latin class. Brunnerdale's emphasis was not conversational Latin; instead, it focused on the terminology and phrasing used in Catholic rites and rituals and Gregorian chants. After years of daily Mass in Latin and religion classes at Saint Mary's, it was no surprise that Latin and religion were Ernie's better subjects. Most days the classroom was not the highlight of Ernie's day. With minimally passing grades at best, his academic performance still lacked his best efforts.

The best part of Ernie's day was the time spent on a ball field or in the pool or on the gym floor, particularly the basketball court where he excelled. His athletic skills, combined with his penchant for fun times, paved the way to acceptance by his fellow freshmen and a few upperclassmen as well. Most seminarians developed a small circle of two or three close friends. The free time available to them was simply insufficient to make more. Their time was consumed with classes and chapel during the day, more chapel before supper, a daily two-hour evening study hall, and yet more chapel for evening prayers. Close friendships required conversation and the exchange of stories and information. But at Brunnerdale, there was little time for such exchanges given the priorities of prayer and silence.

After a short time, just as Ernie was adjusting to his strict surroundings, he was summoned to the director's office. As he sat nervously waiting, he could not imagine why the director had summoned him. On arrival, the director sat behind his desk and sternly looked across at Ernie. He began to speak with a firm voice. "Seminarians must not be distracted from their studies and religious obligations." He continued, "In order to prevent distractions, all incoming and outgoing mail and parcels are censored here at Brunnerdale. It is my job to intercept any such communications or items."

Ernie asked himself, *Why am I getting this lecture?* In an attempt to put the director at ease, Ernie nodded in agreement and answered, "I understand the reasons the mail has to be censored." The director paused to gather himself. He reached for a white envelope on his desk. "You—" he paused to let the tension build, "received a letter from a young girl from Garden City. I read this letter. It is distracting!"

Ernie sat in shocked silence. For the moment he could not think of anyone who might send him such a letter. The director held up the letter for Ernie to see. "Your girlfriend's letter is distracting because it uses the word 'love' and contains 'puppy-love' sentiments."

It was never openly stated, but everyone knew seminarians and priests alike adhered to a vow of celibacy. Seminarians were expected to refrain from entering into romantic relationships with girls and young women. They were further expected to relinquish all prior romantic relationships. It was the duty of the director of seminarians to protect and shelter the seminarians from any such romances.

Ernie was speechless and embarrassed that the director had become aware of a letter sent to him that contained sweet nothings. After a few moments of silence, he told Ernie that he would not be allowed to read the letter. Instead, he read the letter aloud, adding to Ernie's embarrassment. He concluded without announcing who had sent the letter and tossed the letter into the trash can with disgust.

"There won't be any more letters," Ernie said in an attempt to assure the director.

"Ernest, there better not be. You are excused."

Ernie was quite relieved to leave the director's office.

Throughout the rest of the day Ernie thought about the events in the director's office. He wanted badly to read the letter for himself. The temptation was too great for him to resist. He waited until later in the day when the director was out of his office. When the office was unoccupied and unguarded, Ernie made his way in. He searched for his letter in the trash can, only to find it torn to pieces. But without hesitation he laid out the pieces on the director's desk, quickly assembled them, and discovered the letter was from a friend and classmate named Jana. He bent close to the tattered pieces to read it and as he did so inhaled the scent of perfume.

Ernie wanted to send an answering letter to Jana, but because of the ever-vigilant director, he was never able to do so. It was not surprising that Ernie never received another letter from his "girlfriend," or perhaps he was never advised that another letter from her had arrived. In any event, the director had done his duty—he had squashed a "puppy love." Ernie then realized with disappointment that fun and flirtatious friendships with girls were not possible while he was at Brunnerdale, even through the mail.

Soon autumn began to take its place in the Ohio hills and woods. Temperatures began to fall, and the leaves began to unleash an array of colors. By this time Ernie had been able to settle comfortably into Brunnerdale's routines and discipline. Some freshmen were unable to do so. During some nights, his classmates cried in their sleep. If Ernie was within reach, he gently woke them. If not, he could only lie awake waiting for the crying to stop.

Snows in early December changed Brunnerdale's grounds into a bed of pure white, glistening softness. The limbs of the surrounding evergreen trees and shrubs bent under the snow that piled upon them. From the pond, the golden light in Brunnerdale's windows glowed in the cold air like the warm embers of a fireplace.

The snowfall did not keep the seminarians from their assigned chores. Many were from the upper Midwest and East Coast and were accustomed to the inconveniences of snowfall. Ernie and the others cleared away the snow from the building's walkways and driveways. They tended to the farm animals before the winter daylight slipped away. It was only during Saturday free time that they were able to ride sleds down the hills, throw snowballs, and otherwise enjoy the snow.

Most seminarians returned home for the Christmas holiday, but not everyone returned for a second semester. One of the major concerns of seminarians returning for spring semester was an accounting of those who did not and why. The reasons their religious vocations ended after four months varied: the stress of strict rules and challenging schoolwork, the unending prayer and meditation, the loneliness, or any combination of those reasons. Ernie returned, but the time spent with his family and friends during the holiday remained fresh in his thoughts. Five months would pass before he could see them again. His time at home made it clear, without question, that the more interesting people to know and events to experience were outside the solemn and candlelit halls of the seminary.

The energy and excitement of the fall semester were lacking when the new spring semester began. In January the winter's harsh cold and winds took hold of Brunnerdale. The pond in front of the building turned to solid ice. It became too difficult to enjoy the snowfall when the temperatures began to fall into the teens. During these weeks of gray days and overcast skies, the seminarians avoided the outside whenever possible, with the exception of one group—the ice skaters. These East Coast and Upper Midwest classmates invited Ernie to lace up a pair of skates and give hockey a go. Always open to new ways to have fun, he accepted the challenge. Within a few days, using borrowed skates and a hockey stick, the Santa Fe barrio kid learned to stay upright and maneuver around the frozen pond in a game of ice hockey—a most unlikely circumstance.

In the middle of this January dreariness, Brunnerdale held its annual vocational retreat. For three days, everyone, priests and seminarians alike, prayed and meditated. Their purpose was to reflect on and strengthen their vocations by rededicating their lives to God. From Friday evening through Sunday evening, in solemn silence, they prayed, read scripture, penned their thoughts, and attended Mass. Especially in these moments, Ernie felt he was in the presence of God and His holy people. Nevertheless, it is fair to say that a teenage boy left in silence to pray and meditate will daydream as much as he remains on task in prayer. But to some degree, the retreat introduced him to notions of reflection, self-control, and resolve, traits necessary for a foundation of mental strength in the future.

The winter months dragged on, but eventually gave way to warmer days. With the arrival of spring weather, the campus grass turned green, and the leaves began to return to the trees. The changes of spring inspired Ernie with hope for better and happier days. He began to think that those better days were outside of the solemnness of the seminary. He felt that his time at Brunnerdale had satisfied his end of his bargain with God, and that he could remain devout in his Catholic faith. In many of Ernie's meditations and prayers, he had asked God to reveal His plan for him. But by the end of the school year, he still did not know the plan. As the school year came to a close, many more of his thoughts were about Garden City High School, playing sports, making friends, dating, and dancing.

In late May 1961, Uncle Dionicio drove to Brunnerdale with Luisa, Jim, and Frank. The moment Ernie saw them he knew he would not return to Brunnerdale. Despite his positive experiences at the seminary, he felt he was not a good candidate for the priesthood. His family brought Ernie back to Garden City for his sophomore year of high school. They drove for three days in a packed station wagon without air conditioning. The highlight of the road trip was the constant play by rock and roll stations of the Marcels version of Rodgers and Hart's "Blue Moon." The repeated riff, "bomp-baba-bomp, dang-a-dang dang," drove Luisa and Dionicio crazy. For Ernie, the hit song was a return to rock and roll and dancing, and it was far, so very far, from the solemn Gregorian chants at Brunnerdale.

5

New Heights
1961–1964

On Ernie's return to Garden City, he immediately resumed contributing to the support of Luisa and his brothers and sisters. He found a job as a stock boy at the Woolworths store across the street from the Windsor Hotel on Main Street. At the first opportunity, he took the time to stop in at Lefty's and say hello. Lefty, always supportive, congratulated Ernie and encouraged him to keep working hard.

That summer Ernie played third base on a baseball team sponsored by the Knights of Columbus, a charitable service organization made up of Catholic men. Many of the players on the team had been Ernie's classmates at Saint Mary's. He fit in right away and avoided the awkward moments of an unknown player joining a new team.

Fitting in was not quite as easy when high school began in the fall. At Saint Mary's, Ernie had established a place among his classmates. From first through eighth grade he had shared a classroom with essentially the same thirty classmates. They studied together, ate lunch together, prayed together, and played together. They knew who among the class was smart, who was rich, who was an athlete, who behaved, and who did not. They had a reliable social order with relatively stable expectations of one another.

For all their differences, the Mexican and non-Mexican students at Saint Mary's shared a common experience. They were anchored in a Catholic faith and an immigrant heritage. Many of the non-Mexicans were the grandchildren and great-grandchildren of Volga Deutsch (people of German descent whose ancestors lived in Russia in the area of the Volga River) and Irish immigrants who settled in Kansas during the late 1800s. Typical class rosters at Saint Mary's included the surnames Hahn, Bauer, Rupp, Brungardt, McMillan, Regan, Mesa, Servantes, and Garcia.

But Saint Mary's did not offer classes beyond the eighth grade, so the structure and expectations built at Saint Mary's collapsed on the students' first day at Garden City's public junior high school. When Saint Mary's students arrived at the junior high, which included grades 7–9, they were without Mass, nuns, and an assigned single classroom. Instead, they were separated and scattered in classrooms across the campus and found themselves with new teachers and dozens of unfamiliar classmates. The result was that most Saint Mary's friendships and ties withered quickly or were eventually discarded. For some the process of establishing new friends and alliances was difficult, if not painful. But by the end of the school year, most Saint Mary's students had new friends and had found a new place among the student personalities and cliques. To a lesser degree, all freshmen at the junior high school would experience a similar transition when they began their sophomore year at Garden City High School. At the high school, most sophomores did not venture beyond the security of their fellow sophomores.

When Ernie started his sophomore year, he knew virtually none of the five hundred high school students. Since he had been away in Ohio, he was not part of a new circle of friends or a clique that emerged from the junior high school. His circle of friends at Saint Mary's had dissolved and scattered. Some days he recognized faces from Saint Mary's in the halls, including Ann Regan. But often there was only time for a "Hi" without conversation. He began to feel that he was missing two of the better American high school experiences—new friends and belonging. Ernie was nice-looking with an engaging smile, and he knew how to talk with people. He just needed a key to find his way into a circle of friends.

He accompanied his brother Jim to the first Friday night football game of the year. They arrived early so Jim could dress out, as he was a lineman on the team. He had grown husky and excelled not only in football but in baseball and wrestling as well. In addition to Garcia, Garden City's football roster included such names as Mendoza, Sandoval, Ortiz, and Escalada. The growing list of Mexican American students engaged in the American high school experience reflected the previous decade's promotion of education in the community. Ernie, whose passion was basketball, chose not to play football. So he sat alone for the start of Jim's game in the same stadium where as a boy, he, Jim, Felipe, and Rosa had cheered for the junior college team.

Shortly before the game began, Ernie's key appeared before him in the form of a pretty blue-eyed blonde girl. The pretty blonde boldly approached Ernie and said, "Hi! Who are you?" Ernie was surprised that she would confidently approach him and introduce herself. "I am Ernie Garcia," he responded just as confidently. She was direct and did not hesitate: "Are you a new student?"

"Yes. Well . . . new to the high school, but I grew up in Garden City," he said with a smile.

"Oh . . . I don't remember seeing you before this year," she said in a surprised tone.

"I went to school in Ohio last year." In an effort to impress her, Ernie strategically failed to mention his school was a Catholic seminary. Apparently satisfied, she finally gave her name. "Oh . . . well, I am Paulasue Patterson. I hope you like it here." Despite his initial lack of friends at the high school, Ernie responded, "I already do."

"Great! I'll talk to you later." She smiled and walked away toward a small group of girls waiting for her return.

Within a few days, Paulasue had introduced Ernie to a number of her friends, girls and boys. He soon became part of their circle and began to feel a sense of comfortable belonging. Ernie was fortunate, since that sense of fitting in is elusive for many teens in high school.

He began to join his new friends at the football games. Afterward they went to Garden City's recreation center on Main Street. Students quickly filled the small center after games, leaving only a small area for dancing to the top hits of the day. Many of Ernie's classmates did not know any dance steps and were left to stand. But Ernie drew on his Mexican Fiesta dancing experience to become a popular dance partner. The stroll, la bomba, and the twist were already in his repertoire. When the twist first became popular, the center initially attempted to stop students from dancing to the hit record, but over time, it abandoned its efforts. Just a few years earlier, the recreation center had denied access to Mexican American students. The

Latin American Club, a group of Mexican Americans organized and supported by Father George Spaeth, a local Catholic priest, led the drive to desegregate the center. The club also successfully fought for an end to the segregated balcony seating in Garden City's movie theaters.

When basketball season began, Ernie earned a spot on the team. Although he played with a great deal of intensity and effort, off the court his teammates found Ernie easygoing and fun company. He became friends with his teammates and expanded his circle of friends. He became especially good friends with Randy Bowling. Randy, also a sophomore, shared Ernie's passion for basketball, and appreciated Ernie's quickness and hustle on the court. They began to spend more time together during and after school hours when Ernie was not working. Randy's parents warmly welcomed Ernie into their home, and Luisa did the same for Randy.

Randy was particularly fond of Luisa's cooking. He thoroughly enjoyed the Mexican food she prepared for the two of them and their friends. Randy was aware that Mexican families were tagged as coming from "south of the tracks," but for Randy and the Bowling family, the differences in heritage were of no consequence. Unknown to Ernie at the time, a few students in his new circle of friends deflected to some degree any parental objections to their friendship by identifying Ernie as Spanish rather than Mexican.

It was during this time that Ernie first laid eyes on a pretty strawberry blonde in Paulasue's group of girlfriends. It was not love at first sight, but it became a bond ever so tight. Her name was Sharon Lee Cobb.

When they first met, Sharon Lee thought Ernie's smile was gorgeous. As they got to know one another, she found that she enjoyed his company and sense of humor. Paulasue's circle of friends was a popular group, but Sharon Lee did not consider herself one of the "popular" girls at school. She was focused on doing well in the classroom. When dealing with boys, she was cautious and had little self-confidence. She would not ask for a dance nor initiate a conversation in person or by phone.

During their sophomore year, neither Ernie nor Sharon Lee had a driver's license, so they spent most of their time together in group get-togethers. Their interest in one another grew over the course of parties, sporting events, and Friday night school dances. Sharon Lee liked to dance, though she was not quite as nimble on her feet as Ernie. During the school day they took advantage of the passing in the hallways between classes. When they encountered each other the two exchanged not only brief conversation but also sweetheart notes.

Over time, Ernie drew Sharon Lee out of her caution, and she became more outgoing and affectionate. But they still did not talk on the telephone. Her parents, Bob and Jimmie Ruth Cobb, insisted that she not spend significant amounts of time on the phone. Bob—a successful architect in Garden City—and Jimmie Ruth were very protective of their only child. In Ernie's initial contact with Sharon Lee's parents, they were gracious toward him. Ernie appreciated that Sharon Lee's friendship was not conditional on his living on the "appropriate" side of the Santa Fe's main line. She was at ease with him when they were together in public settings and was not concerned with the whispers of others. Most importantly, when they became close, she did not end their friendship when her parents eventually objected.

In the end, Ernie's sophomore year was quite successful. His social life dramatically improved with his new friends; he was at ease with both the guys and the girls. His place on the basketball team enabled him to pal around with other athletes. The blemish on Ernie's success was his grades—they remained poor. He continued only to get by.

In the summer that followed, Ernie found work at Garnand Furniture. He worked on Garnand's delivery truck. He enjoyed the new job, especially the out-of-town deliveries to the small rural towns surrounding Garden City. Ernie's supervisor on the truck was a middle-aged man named Mr. Healy. Before leaving Garden City for out-of-town deliveries, Mr. Healy regularly stopped at a grocer to buy bologna, bread, chips, and drinks. As soon as the truck passed the city limits, he frequently turned over the driving duties to Ernie, who had recently obtained his driver's permit and was thrilled to take control of the wheel. Mr. Healy then slept while Ernie drove them to their destination.

Ernie's second duty was to deliver caskets to the funeral home also owned by the Garnand family. The caskets were unloaded and placed into the funeral home's display room. The problem for Ernie was that the light switch for the display room was on the wall opposite the entrance. Mr. Healy always made Ernie cross the darkened room of twenty-five to thirty—presumably empty—caskets to turn on the lights. Ernie's faith and belief in spiritual beings made him apprehensive of the crossing. With a quick pace and uneasy stomach, Ernie would bump his way across the room until he reached the switch. Even with the lights on, he still felt some uneasiness in the midst of the vessels for the dead.

By summer's end Ernie began to search for part-time work to accommodate his upcoming school schedule. Before he left Garnand's, however, he learned that the bologna sandwiches Mr. Healy generously paid for were actually purchased with meal money provided by Garnand's for the two of them. Mr. Healy had pocketed the savings resulting from the cheaper sandwiches. At the time Ernie was surprised to learn that a person working alongside him would better his position at Ernie's expense. It did not sit well with him that Mr. Healy had misled him into thinking he was a generous man.

For their junior year, many of Ernie's friends enrolled in chemistry, geometry, and other challenging classes. Ernie wanted to be in their company, so he did the same. After the first week, both Ernie and his chemistry teacher knew he was unprepared for the rigor of the class, but the teacher did not suggest any solutions to help him successfully navigate the material. Perhaps the teacher felt he could not spend any extra time to teach Ernie, or worse, that he did not have the capacity to learn chemistry. In any event, the effort was not made. Instead, the teacher recommended a shop class. Ernie welcomed the suggestion to leave the chemistry class, believing the teacher was helping him. However, the shop class was full, so he was assigned to the library for an extra study hall period. He was not self-conscious about dropping chemistry; most students considered it a difficult class. More troubling and slightly embarrassing was the assignment to another study hall, often a dumping ground when academic counselors have no better solution.

Apart from the schedule changes, Ernie's junior year started on a good note. He found a job working after school and on Saturdays as a sales clerk in the men's and shoe departments of the J. C. Penney store on Main Street. This extra money allowed him to dress sharply for school. Luisa's precise pressing of Felipe's shirts had taught him that his public appearance was important. He developed a good relationship with an energetic and fast-moving department manager named Otto, a middle-aged man of German descent. Otto asked Ernie for suggestions on the style of shoes and clothes favored by the high school students and often ordered stock as Ernie suggested. Otto was flexible with Ernie's work schedule, and accommodated his requests for social and sports events just as Lefty had done.

During the basketball season, Ernie developed a close friendship with another teammate, Bill King Jr., and his father, Bill Sr. At five feet, nine inches, Ernie was a starting guard, while Bill Jr., who stood six feet, four inches, started at center. But Junior was not as fast on his feet. Ernie's game was based on quickness, hustle, and smarts. Bill Sr. attended all of their games. His constant presence made Ernie aware that no one, apart from Sharon Lee and their circle of friends, ever went to the games specifically to watch him play. Luisa was at home caring for the younger children, and Jim was working or with his friends.

Bill Sr. sensed that Ernie did not have the fatherly support that his son did, so he took him under his wing. After games and practices he often drove Ernie home and offered his praise and encouragement and criticism as needed. His comments gave Ernie confidence in his ability to play the game and a sense of his value to the team. Bill Sr. was openly critical of the coach if he limited Ernie's playing time. Many years later, Bill Jr. told Ernie that his dad had said to him, "Be assertive and a go-getter—like Ernie."

Ernie and Sharon Lee's romance grew stronger throughout the school year. They were together at every chance, especially at school events and dances. Sharon Lee frequently drove to Ernie's home on Santa Fe Street, literally crossing over to the other side of the tracks to be with him. Luisa warmly welcomed her and would insist that she stay for dinner.

During that year Sharon Lee and her mother were called into the school counselor's office. A female counselor sat both of them in her office across from her desk. Jimmie Ruth could not think of anything that required the counselor to speak to her—she had not seen any decline in Sharon's grades, nor was she aware of any discipline issues in the classroom.

Looking at Jimmie Ruth, the counselor said, "I am sure you are aware . . . or at least you should be aware, that Sharon Lee has a boyfriend, Ernie Garcia." Jimmie Ruth thought to herself, *Is that what this meeting is about?* Calmly, she answered, "Yes, I am." The counselor continued as if on cross-examination. "And are you aware that Ernie has given Sharon Lee his class ring?" At that question Jimmie Ruth shook her head, and said, "No." She wondered where these questions were leading.

"Mrs. Cobb, Sharon Lee is going steady with him!" The counselor then looked at Sharon Lee. "She leaves his ring in her locker at the end of the school day and slips it back on her finger the next morning."

Sharon Lee looked down and cringed. She had not told her mother that her friendship with Ernie had progressed to the point of going steady and a ring. When she finally looked at her mother, Jimmie Ruth was already looking at her but with no expression of anger on her face. She asked Sharon Lee, "Is this true?" Sharon Lee only nodded. Her mother then asked with a bit of skepticism, "Is it against the school rules for girls to wear a boy's ring?" The counselor, surprised at Jimmie Ruth's response, could only respond, "Well . . . no. No, it is not. But I thought you should know."

Jimmie Ruth politely but coldly ended the conversation. "Well, thank you for telling me. I will talk to Sharon Lee, and if there are any other problems, please let me know." As they walked out of the counselor's office Jimmie Ruth said to her daughter in a serious tone, but without exasperation, "I'll talk to you when we get home. Oh, and I'm going to talk to your father about this, too."

Sharon Lee was expecting the worst. But the counselor's disclosures did not have their intended effect. Rather than ending Sharon Lee's romance, her parents realized that she cared a great deal for Ernie. For her parents, the challenge was to find a way to allow her to be with him without creating undue friction between Sharon Lee and the two of them. Her parents wanted to do their best and raise their only child the right way. As part of the right way, they expected Sharon Lee to attend the University of Kansas and graduate. They feared that their daughter's romance might interfere with her successfully completing college, or worse, getting married and not attending college at all. Jimmie Ruth had completed two years of college but did not obtain a degree. She in particular did not want Sharon Lee to repeat that history. An additional worry for her parents was their belief, as in other families in Kansas in the early 1960s, that raising a child the right way did not include a marriage of mixed nationalities.

Despite their concerns, Sharon Lee's parents tentatively accepted her friendship and romance with Ernie. At the time, Tom Saffell was principal at the high school and friends with Sharon Lee's parents. Years later, Ernie thought it possible that he had kept Sharon Lee's parents informed not only about their daughter's academic progress but also about her romance with Ernie.

When Ernie was in high school and living on Santa Fe Street, Rosa was still living in the house Jose had purchased on Fourth Street. Since the mid-1940s, Jose and Rosa's oldest son, Porfirio, his wife Velia, and their three children had lived with her. In recent years, Rosa had been fighting diabetes, but at age seventy-seven the disease had caused her to weaken and become short of breath.

Perhaps her body was simply exhausted from the monumental amount of energy and emotion she expended in her lifetime. She lost infants in childbirth and fled the hardships of Mexico and its revolution. Along with her husband and her two small children, she immigrated to a country with a different language and culture. She was separated from her side of the family, except for her initial months in Kansas when her brother, Cayetano, his daughter, and her family lived in Garden City. Jose relied on her support as he performed difficult and dangerous manual labor. When circumstances allowed, she worked alongside him and her sons in el betabel. She raised six sons, feeding them, washing them, and clothing them without the conveniences of a modern kitchen and appliances. She became a widow at fifty-two, with four sons under the age of twenty.

Yet through all the difficulties, she displayed the best of humanity. She generously cared for others, nursing an infant whose mother's milk had stopped and taking in the five-year-old son of her widower cousin who was left to raise young children. Though she was by then in her early fifties, she cared for and raised the child until his father came for him after remarrying four years later. On one occasion during World War II, she responded to the shouts of Mexican American soldiers as they stood by train cars waiting to be transported to war. They longed for a meal with the taste and comfort of home. She prepared bean and egg tacos and took the meal to the soldiers where they waited.

Rosa was admitted to Saint Catherine's in mid-April 1963. Her sons who still lived in Garden City, Porfirio and Dionicio, visited her when they were not working. One of Rosa's granddaughters, Marcella, oldest daughter of Dionicio, was a nurse aide at Saint Catherine's. She visited Rosa before and after her daytime shift. Other grandchildren visited her when they were let out of school.

Rosa did not complain to her visitors that she was in pain or suffering. She laid on her side with her hands together under her cheek, as if in prayer. She told her visitors that she felt tired but otherwise was alright. Rosa understood that she might be dying and apparently was resolved not to fight death if it was near. Her appearance did not suggest it was imminent, since she spoke calmly with her guests. But on the afternoon of April 16, Rosa passed away, most likely in her sleep, of congestive heart failure. With her family at work, or in school, or tending to children, she died alone. She was buried three days later in the presence of her five surviving sons and many of her forty-four grandchildren, including Ernie. Her headstone in Garden City included Jose's name, though he, of course, was at rest in east Los Angeles.

Jose and Rosa labored mightily for their children's success. They endured many hardships and sacrifices. Their labors and hopes were rewarded, but death denied them the chance to see and share those successes that lay just beyond the horizon. Jose died before his sons left el betabel, and Rosa died before her grandchildren entered college.

The summer after Rosa died, Ernie began full-time work at J. C. Penney. When the downtown stores on Main Street closed at six, he had little to do except rendezvous with Sharon Lee when possible. He and other bored high schoolers with a great deal of time and energy were a recipe for trouble.

On one summer night, Ernie, Randy, and three of their friends—Tim Gotschalk, Bob Stalter, and Bob Hubert—jumped the fences at the zoo. They climbed onto the donkeys and a camel and rode them in their pens. On another night, Ernie and his friends absconded with a swan and took it along with them as they dragged Main in Randy's car. Of course, they were the most attention-getting vehicle on Main that night. When their swan date ended, they deftly left the swan in the vestibule of the city police station without being noticed.

On other nights, Ernie and Jim, along with Tim and Bob Stalter, drove out to the city dump just south of Garden City. They arrived in Tim's car under the cover of darkness, like commandos. Tim then aimed his headlights on the piles of garbage and illuminated the rats feasting on the garbage. From inside the car, they took turns shooting at the rats with a .22-caliber rifle. Some nights, Bob was particularly rambunctious, getting out of the car and chasing the rats without knowing if his comrades would hold their fire. The shooting gallery at the city dump was Ernie's first experience with firearms.

One night during the previous summer, three of the commandos, Ernie, Jim, and Tim, were joined by Ernie's "Hound Dog" performance partner from Saint Mary's, Terry Billinger. To relieve the boredom of dragging Main, they decided to create their own excitement by climbing atop the grain elevator at Sixth Street and the railroad tracks. Standing twelve stories high on the south side of the tracks, it was the tallest and longest grain elevator in Garden City. A ladder leading to the top was attached to the east edge of the elevator, but the first rung was fifteen feet off the ground and out of reach. The commandos were stymied but determined. They changed their mission to climbing the city's water tower near Main and Kansas Avenue. The tower was fourteen stories high, and its tank held five hundred thousand gallons of water. In the past, the tank had been a popular target of high school students who painted their class year on its side for all to see.

The commandos climbed over a chain-link fence and headed for the tower ladder. Ernie overcame his apprehension about the climb and was determined to display no fear and keep up with his older brother and their friends. One after another, the teenagers reached the catwalk that circled the tank. Their view of the city lights below was short-lived—within minutes a police car arrived. The officers used a loudspeaker to order them to climb down. Ernie backed away from the precipice and immediately began his descent with Tim following closely behind. Jim and Terry, however, were defiant. They shouted to the police that they were prepared to jump if they did not leave. Fortunately, Jim and Terry's bravado eventually melted away, and they complied with the order to climb down.

The commandos were taken into custody and transported to the police station, where they were questioned about their adventure on the tower. The police called Tim's parents to come and retrieve their son. When Tim's father arrived, the question of what to do with the young man was unresolved. The decision was left to Chief of Police Richard Rohleder. Chief Rohleder ultimately released Tim without arrest, but Jim, Ernie, and Terry, who all resided on the south side of Santa Fe's main line, and whose fathers were both deceased, were arrested and charged with trespassing. Their mothers were never called. Ernie thought Tim was released on the simple fact that his father had appeared. It was not until later in life that he realized that the difference in treatment, and lack of effort to contact their mothers, might have been related to their nationality or barrio home addresses.

Terry, Jim, and Ernie spent the night in jail in a general holding tank, in the company of a collection of drunks, thieves, and other criminals. Their breakfast the next morning consisted of scrambled eggs and potatoes served from a tin bucket. Ernie had no appetite for the meal, but Jim did. He ate his breakfast and Ernie's as well.

Luisa was worried and fearful when her sons did not come home that night. In the morning, she called Rudy Perez, who operated a gas station on Main. At the time, Ernie worked for Rudy at the station, and he had become a friend and mentor for Jim and Ernie. Luisa asked him if he knew where the boys might be. Rudy told her that he had no idea, but he would check into it.

Rudy's first call was to the police station. They confirmed that the boys were being held there. He immediately called Luisa and told her that the boys were in custody and assured her that he would get them out and bring them home. Rudy paid the $5 fines for trespassing and drove the boys home. Rudy lectured them on the way, telling them that they should feel great shame for the worry and embarrassment Luisa suffered at their hands.

Luisa was generally a mild-mannered and patient mother, but the boys felt her anger with them at this reckless escapade. She told them that she was disappointed in them—especially Ernie, who had gone to the seminary! Ernie saw the hurt in his mother's face. This was a low point for him. He apologized and vowed to himself, *never again*.

Ernie's summer of 1963 was mostly a successful pursuit of fun and good times. He began his senior year in a good place with a girlfriend and a job. He was comfortable with his friends and had a sense of belonging. But the harsh realities of the adult world began to disrupt the comfort and security he had experienced during his first two years of high school.

Ernie and Sharon Lee continued to exchange their notes at school. Over time the contents of the notes had changed from lighthearted greetings to expressions of romance and affection for one another. Sharon Lee's parents' scrutiny intensified when her mother inadvertently found one of Ernie's more amorous notes. From that point, Sharon Lee's parents' general acceptance of her romance began to fade. Around this time, Uncle Porfirio told Ernie to stay away from white girls. He had never cautioned Ernie about anything of that nature in the past. He was the patriarch of the Garcia family, so Ernie did not challenge his warning, but he wondered about the source of the sudden caution. Uncle Porfirio worked for a dry cleaning business in Garden City; perhaps someone close to the Cobb family commented to the owner, who in turn passed on the displeasure to Porfirio. Sharon Lee and Ernie's open and public romance became one of the Capulet and Montague variety, secret and forbidden. But the couple was undeterred. Among their close friends, their romance was no secret at all.

After football and basketball games, Ernie and Sharon Lee continued to meet and dance at the recreation center. The director of the center was Herman "Pop" Beringer, an older gentleman in his fifties. Ernie had seen Pop tap on the shoulders of Mexican students and tell them not to dance with students of a different nationality. Ernie was unsure if Pop's objections were personal or the result of an unspoken rule made by influential people, but Pop conducted his tapping on shoulders even if a white student had asked for the dance. Ernie thought on different occasions that Pop might tell him to stop dancing with Sharon Lee, but he never did. Ernie concluded that because of his light complexion, Pop did not realize he was of Mexican ancestry.

Pop Beringer's potential interference was not Ernie's only concern about nationality and prejudice. He also began to hear comments from other students that certain Mexican students wanted to fight him and kick his ass. Ernie was taken aback. He could think of nothing he had done that would incite a fight or call for retaliation by any student. He speculated that their animosity was the result of his many friendships with white students. He did not understand how that fact alone could lead to hostility.

Ernie was frustrated by the nationality and prejudice issues that constantly appeared during his senior year. He spoke about his frustrations with Randy and his mother, Evelyn. She counseled Ernie that he should focus on his future. If people had an issue with race or nationality, that was their problem to fix. She assured him that he should not waste his time and energy trying to resolve their problems. He took her advice to heart and tried to follow it then and in the years to come.

By this point, many of Ernie's friends had already begun their college search by joining the Explorers Club in their junior year. The goal of the Explorers was raising the interest of high school students in higher education by sponsoring trips to universities, colleges, and educational events within the state. Ernie wanted to remain in his circle of friends, and he appreciated the Explorers' sharp blue blazers and gray slacks, so in his senior year he joined as well. During the spring semester of their senior year, members of the Explorers began to submit their applications to colleges and universities. Sharon Lee and Ernie applied to the University of Kansas. They planned to attend KU together, graduate, and then marry. They understood that if Ernie was accepted, he would struggle to pay his college expenses, but they believed they would find a way.

Commencement ceremonies for the class of 1964 were held in late May. Afterward, a graduation party was held at the home of a classmate, but the gathering was no party for Ernie. It was a rude awakening. While his friends were talking about their college plans, Ernie could not join them. KU had denied him admission because of his grades. His romance with Sharon Lee, not his grades, had been his priority. Nonetheless, Ernie wanted to remain her equal and say that he too was going to college.

They devised a plan to get Ernie to KU. Ernie would complete classes at Garden City Community College to strengthen his transcript for admission to KU. Sharon Lee would go on to Lawrence, where he would visit her on weekends as often as possible. She told him she had confidence in his abilities and that she would assist him with the selection of his classes. She assured him they would eventually attend KU together. In the summer months that followed, Ernie worked full-time at Rudy Perez's gas station. He began to save money to pay for his classes at the community college and his visits to Lawrence, 340 miles away. In the face of their impending separation, the young couple spent as much time together as possible.

While Ernie was focused on the plan to join Sharon Lee at KU, events in Southeast Asia were transpiring that would impact their plans. At the beginning of 1964, the number of American troops in Vietnam had reached sixteen thousand. In August a US naval destroyer and North Vietnamese patrol boats exchanged gunfire in the Gulf of Tonkin. Congress immediately responded with the passage of the Gulf of Tonkin Resolution, which authorized an increase in troops. By the end of 1965, more than 190,000 troops were stationed in Vietnam.

6

Recruit

1964–1971

Ernie enrolled in Garden City Junior College to complete the core classes, English and history among them. He traveled to Lawrence by car or on the Santa Fe almost every weekend. When he rode the Santa Fe, he walked from his home on Santa Fe Street to the Garden City Depot, and Sharon Lee met him in Lawrence six hours later. They spent their weekends as did other KU college students, attending games and parties. One of the more memorable weekends included the KU-Oklahoma football game in October 1964. They sat near the field and saw Gale Sayers, one of KU's all-time great players. KU's Mike Johnson scored at the game's end for the KU win by a point. As fate would have it, Johnson was a graduate of Garden City High School and had been one of Jim's teammates. Throughout that fall semester, Ernie's focus remained on his time with Sharon Lee in Lawrence. His history and English grades reflected that priority. Although he wanted badly to be in college with Sharon Lee and his Garden City friends, he was putting little effort into being a better student. With his academic struggles, he did not enroll for the spring semester.

In the spring of 1965, Luisa decided to move the family to Wichita after the younger children completed the school year. She planned to keep her home on Santa Fe in the family and rent a house in Wichita. In addition to the move, Luisa made the surprising decision to work outside the home for the first time. Felipe's brothers Jesus and Guillermo had previously left Garden City and taken their families to Wichita for better work opportunities. She believed she could do the same. These were relatively bold steps for her, given her prior work history.

In late May she completed the family move to Wichita. Initially, Jim was reluctant, but he ultimately went along in order to attend drafting school. Soon after her arrival, Luisa found work in a laundry, washing and pressing clothing. The workplace was hot and uncomfortable, but she was able to support the family on her wages and Felipe's benefits. The passage of time proved her assessment of work opportunities in Wichita to be accurate. Despite a limited education thanks to her childhood labor in the beet fields, she advanced to new jobs and learned as she went, just as Felipe had done. Ultimately, she held a position as a lab assistant for the county health department.

Ernie stayed behind in Garden City to spend as much of the summer as possible with Sharon Lee. Ernie's revised plans were to join Luisa after Sharon Lee left for KU and enroll for the fall semester at Wichita State University. He was still working at J. C. Penney and part-time with Rudy at the gas station. Ernie and Randy Bowling had become as brothers, and Randy's parents had invited him to stay in their home. Ernie's move to the Bowling home left the home on Santa Fe unoccupied.

On June 16 and 17, heavy rains fell in eastern Colorado. Reservoirs and dams designed to contain excessive rainfalls could not hold the deluge. Much of the water drained into the Arkansas River and headed east across the state line with Garden City in the path of the flood waters. It was clear to Mayor Jim Cowgill and city officials by June 17 that the flood waters could reach Garden City's downtown and the homes north of the Santa Fe's main line.

The main line was on bedrock and built on slightly higher ground. Someone, perhaps the mayor or other city officials, made the decision to build a wall of sandbags on the Santa Fe main line. The rationale for the decision was not clearly stated by city authorities. However, the objective and consequences were clear: The objective was to protect the businesses and homes north of the main line by keeping the flood waters to the south. The consequences were that flood waters damaged the homes south of the main line, the city park, and the zoo. Just as important, the resulting higher flood waters in the barrio increased the severity of the damage.

At 4:00 P.M. on Friday, June 18, police cars drove up and down Santa Fe and Maple Streets with red lights flashing and loud speakers blaring. They directed the residents to vacate their homes immediately. Families gathered their most essential papers and valuables and fled their homes. They quickly made arrangements to stay with friends or relatives north of the tracks. In the meantime, city employees attempted to rescue as many animals as possible from the zoo. Some were taken to a buffalo reserve south of the Arkansas River, but many others were left behind to fend for themselves.

By 10:00 P.M. a sole police officer stood in the middle of Main Street one hundred yards north of the bridge over the Arkansas River. In the street lights, he could be seen facing the bridge with his hands clasped behind his back. As the flood waters reached his position, he retreated fifty yards northward toward the Santa Fe's main line and resumed his on-guard stance. With each new approach of the flood waters, the officer retreated another fifty yards until he reached the sandbagged main line.

By midnight, the barrio was completely dark. Its residents stood at the sandbag wall, including some who had assisted in filling the sandbags. They could hear the waters rushing through the streets and yards and barking dogs. But they could not see the damage to their homes. They had to wait to see what daylight revealed.

On Saturday morning, Ernie and Randy stood at the wall of sandbags. The morning light revealed a neighborhood in a small lake—except that the water was not blue. Instead it was green, foul-smelling, and filled with debris. The further south the houses were located from the sandbags and railroad tracks, the higher the flood waters rose in the homes.

The police barred residents from going to their homes. Later that Saturday morning a few teenagers, including Ernie, waited until the police were distracted to venture into the dirty flood water to inspect their homes. Ernie waded when possible, and swam when necessary, through the debris and stench to reach his home. Once there, he found the water line in the house two to three feet high. The frame of the home was intact, but the walls and floors were warped and ruined. Most of the pieces of furniture that Luisa had left behind were damaged as well. Ernie made his way back to the wall of sandbags and, as soon as he was able, called her to report the damage. He advised her that only a few pieces of furniture were salvageable.

Two blocks further east on Santa Fe Street, a dog had made its way onto the roof of a shed and had been barking off and on since daybreak. People on the sandbag wall repeatedly asked the police to rescue the pet. They refused. Finally, one of Ernie's friends, Lino Mesa, entered the water and made his way to the shed. Lino grabbed the dog and carried it back to the main line to the applause of the bystanders.

The city did send rescue teams to the zoo, where they found water levels in the park five feet deep. Penny the elephant and the rhinos withstood the waters. The big cats, a lion and two tigers, stood on their hind legs for nearly twenty-four hours in order to survive. Some of the smaller animals and birds that were left behind were trapped in their cages and perished.

On Sunday evening when the waters had receded, barrio residents were finally able to return to their homes, only to them find uninhabitable. Many members of the community, Mexican and non-Mexican, graciously housed and assisted the barrio families. Saint Mary's parish opened the school cafeteria and provided suppers for them. A hot meal at the end of a day spent slogging through the green, smelly mud was a small treasure for the barrio residents.

Ernie, Randy, and Randy's dad, Doc, returned to Ernie's flooded home on Santa Fe on Monday. They salvaged what items they could. Doc allowed Ernie to store the salvaged furniture in a warehouse he owned as part of his sign-painting business. Ernie was thankful for the support the Bowling family had given him over the years, but he was never more thankful than during the summer of 1965 when Luisa was in Wichita and their home flooded.

Over the next few days, barrio residents dragged the damaged furniture and debris out of their homes and into their yards. The city had directed the residents to leave the debris and trash on the curb for pickup by city dump trucks. With great effort, they carried their waterlogged couches, mattresses, and other debris to the street curb. On Monday and Tuesday, city authorities allowed members of the public to drive up and down Santa Fe and Maple Streets. Many barrio residents were annoyed at the local tourists who eagerly gawked at their plight but would not soil their hands to help.

By summer's end Ernie had joined Luisa in Wichita. Despite his poor grades at the junior college, he was able to enroll as a freshman at Wichita State for the fall semester and restart his college career to pursue Sharon Lee and a transfer to KU. He wanted the ties to Sharon Lee and his high school friends to remain intact and experience KU as they did. But their continued separation hinted at a withering of Ernie's connection to them and his life in Garden City. That hint of separation produced a sense of urgency in his efforts in the classroom. During his first semester at WSU, Ernie did improve his grades but not dramatically. Despite his increased focus in the classroom, the work and traveling continued to be a drag on his classroom performance.

Unable to be a part of KU's circle of fraternities and sororities, Ernie pledged the Beta Theta Pi fraternity at WSU. He especially wanted the experience of "pinning" Sharon Lee. The pinning rite entails a fraternity man giving his fraternity's pin to a sorority woman as a public declaration of a couple's intent to remain in a serious, committed relationship and possibly marry in the future. Eventually, in Lawrence, Ernie presented Sharon Lee with his fraternity pin. She wore the pin at social events with the belief that they would reunite at KU in time.

In the spring of 1966 Ernie again applied to KU. He was anxious when he received a letter from the admissions office. He let out a shout when the first word of the letter was "Congratulations" and immediately called Sharon Lee with the good news. Finally, after two years of struggling with grades, work, and travel, they would again be close to one another. There was one note of caution in the acceptance letter, however: he was admitted for the 1966 fall semester on a probationary status. His grades would have to improve if he were to remain at KU.

Once at KU Ernie shared an apartment with Randy, who had enrolled there as well. Ernie supported himself by selling shoes at the Royal College Shoe Shop in downtown Lawrence. With classes and work, he found it difficult to spend time with Sharon Lee and his friends "on the hill," as the campus was nicknamed. Most of them had free time after classes and went home for holiday vacations. Ernie stayed behind during school breaks to work more hours in order to pay the bills.

Ernie's first semester grades were not good, but he was able to enroll for the next semester. Halfway through the spring semester he received the envelope all young American men dreaded during those times. The return address was Garden City's local board of the US Selective Service System. The enclosed notice directed Ernie to report for induction into military service. He had been drafted to meet the demand for an increase in troops in support of the Vietnam War.

Ernie's initial responses were surprise and disbelief. He knew men were drafted, but he had given little thought to the possibility that he could be called to serve. After all, he was in college. He was aggravated by the thought that his efforts to get into KU to be with Sharon Lee would be undone.

Internally, he questioned the reasoning of the Garden City draft board. Why was he selected and not some other person? He thought, *What is the difference between my best friend, Randy, and me? We are the same age, from the same town, lived in the same house, and attended the same college—for Christ's sake!* He wondered if it was a matter of favoritism. Did the last name of Garcia suggest that he was not in college? Or was it simply God's will? In the end, he could only speculate on the reasons.

Ernie grabbed the notice and went to Sharon Lee's sorority house. As he waited for her in the sitting room, he was unsure how to tell her they could soon be separated, again. When she entered the room she was smiling. "This is a surprise, I wasn't expecting you!" They kissed as she sat next to him on the couch. She noticed immediately that his smile quickly slipped away, and his eyes did not have their usual sparkle.

Before she could ask if anything was wrong, Ernie said in a serious tone, "I got some bad news today." He held up the envelope for her to see. "I've been drafted."

Sharon Lee was not sure she understood. "What?"

As he handed her the notice, he said, "I've been drafted by the army, and I have to report in May." She took it with a look of dread on her face. She said nothing and began to read in silence. Not understanding what she was reading and not wanting to understand, she put down the notice after a few moments. Frustrated, she asked him, "What does all this mean?"

"It means I will probably be in the army a month from now."

They sat together in silence. She was devastated. He was thinking the worst—Vietnam. Each in their own mind played out the consequences of the notice. She then leaned toward him, and they embraced one another. She asked him, "Where will they send you? For how long? What will you be doing?" He had no answers. "I don't know." She tried to fight back the tears, but they escaped her eyes and rolled down her cheeks. "All I wanted was for us to be somewhere . . . a place where we could be together, out in the open."

"I know . . . me too."

After talking a short while about what was in the future, they walked to the door. Ernie told her, "We'll just have to wait and see what happens." In a tone of resignation, he said, "For now . . . for now, I'm going to go to work." She nodded, her questions unanswered, and closed the door behind him.

Luisa was saddened by the news, but she reluctantly accepted that her sons might be called to serve in the military. She was concerned for their safety and feared they might suffer as Felipe had. She and Felipe had every reason to have been angry and resentful for Felipe's fate in military service. But Felipe was always proud that he had served, and Jim and Ernie had detected his admiration for men who answered the call to military duty, both in real life and in the movies. Felipe and Luisa were among the Mexican American parents across the nation who accepted the argument that World War II military service was key to opening doors of opportunity to education, better jobs, and a voice in social and political matters. During the Vietnam War era, parents were prepared to have their sons continue on a similar path.

As for the young draftees, many viewed military service not only as a duty to country but also as an opportunity to honor and emulate their fathers who had served in World War II. Many were quite eager to display their courage and ruggedness by selecting the US Marines or Army Airborne as their preferred branches of service.

A few months before Ernie received his draft notice, Jim had joined the marines, anticipating that he was about to be drafted after learning classmates had received their notices. Jim was sent from Wichita to Camp Pendleton in California. But after two weeks in training, the results of his physical caught up with him. He was discharged because of a hernia and flat feet.

Luisa was relieved that Jim had returned home, but she tried to remain stoic when Ernie told her his news. She had avoided the heartache of Jim's serving in the military, but with Ernie, there would be no such escape.

Ernie understood that a man drafted into the army would actively serve for roughly two years, then be subject to call-up for three years. A second alternative for the draftees was to volunteer for four years of service in the army or some other branch of the military. A third alternative was to serve in the reserves for six years. The word among men facing conscription was that a two-year stint in the army would likely include a year of service in Vietnam. A four-year commitment would likely result in an assignment outside of Vietnam, possibly in a location of one's preference. A six-year commitment in any branch of the reserves would include an initial period of service of approximately one year, followed by periodic training and service for the duration of the six years. Additionally, reserves were subject to call-up for active duty as needed but less likely to serve in Vietnam for an extended period of time.

Ernie knew that some men did not serve in the military because they were conscientious objectors. Others obtained deferments or fled the country. But with the strong sense of military duty that Felipe exhibited to his sons, Ernie gave no thought to avoiding military service. Even if he had considered pursuit of a deferment, it was unlikely given his probationary status at KU. His hope was to serve in a manner that might avoid the hell of combat and allow him to return to KU. He ultimately chose to join the Marine Corps Reserves because he was attracted to their reputation as dedicated, disciplined, and rugged military men. They portrayed those qualities in their demeanor and dress. And Ernie was particularly impressed with their dress blues. After his sales experience, he appreciated the dark blue coats matched with the red-striped sky blue trousers, the shiny black shoes, and the white cap.

When Ernie told Sharon Lee he was enlisting in the Marine Corps Reserves, he again tried to assure her they would stay together: "I'll come and see you, like I always have."

"When? When exactly will you be coming back?" she asked. He could not tell her a specific date. "Probably in nine months or so. I will come as soon as I can." When they embraced to say goodbye, Sharon Lee told him, "Please, please don't take too long."

He withdrew from his classes at KU shortly thereafter and gathered his few belongings from the apartment he shared with Randy. As brothers do, they gave each other a strong embrace saying goodbye, each of them promising to take care of themselves.

Ernie went to Wichita to prepare for his departure and say goodbye to Luisa, who gave him a small gold medallion and chain. The medal was blessed with holy water and was her constant prayer for Ernie's protection in his travels. Imprinted on the medallion was the image of La Virgen de San Juan de Los Lagos (Blessed Virgin Mary of Saint John of the Lakes). The image was a gold-colored depiction of the Blessed Virgin Mary wearing a crown, dressed in a robe with hands held together in prayer.

The devotion to the Virgen de San Juan began in the mid-1500s in the village of San Juan de Los Lagos in Mexico in the state of Jalisco. A fatally injured child was taken to the church by her parents for burial preparation. The caretaker of the church, an elderly woman, placed a statue of the Virgin Mary next to the child's body, and soon the parents saw movement under the burial shrouds. When the cloths were removed they found their daughter alive and unscathed. Word of the miracle spread to all parts of Mexico, and since then people have made pilgrimages to the church where the statue is displayed. Each year in late January and early February, as many as a million people attend a festival held in San Juan to honor the Virgen, including those who arrive after miles of walking. Many completing the pilgrimage are those who prayed to the Virgen for the recovery of their loved ones from illness or injury and whose prayers were answered.

Ernie vowed to always wear the Virgen de San Juan medallion. When he left and was out of her sight, Luisa cried a great deal and began to recite the first of many, many prayers for his safety.

Ernie gathered in a hangar with other marine recruits in Kansas City on May 20, 1966. He stood nervously in the cool of late afternoon waiting to be flown to San Diego, California, for boot camp. The excitement of his first flight was diminished by his separation from his family and Sharon Lee and his thoughts of the training ahead of him.

The recruits were allowed one small bag of personal items and one call to notify family of arrival. Ernie made his brief call to Luisa, advising her of his safe arrival and assuring her that he would be safe. The recruits were then directed to wait for a bus that would take them to the Marine Corps Recruit Depot in San Diego. During the wait, Ernie's initial impression of California was that it was a pretty nice place. But the pleasure of his surroundings did not last.

Soon, the bus arrived and took them to the recruit depot. When the bus finally stopped on base, the door opened, and a frightening marine stepped on board. His uniform fit tightly on his muscular physique and a marine insignia was pinned to his round brown campaign hat. Ernie correctly surmised he was a drill instructor. The DI began yelling commands and threats to the recruits. He did not stop barking at them for the next twenty-four hours. Ernie's life was never the same after that day.

From the beginning Ernie believed he could tolerate the discipline. This confidence in his survival gave him an advantage over many recruits who struggled mightily with the mental and physical challenges. He had a core of toughness within, though his personality and earlier pursuit of good times might have obscured that quality to those who did not know him well. His early life experiences, Felipe's illness and death, and his time at Brunnerdale

Seminary with its large doses of discipline prepared him for the mental rigors of boot camp.

He had expected the yelling and screaming of boot camp, but he was surprised by its intensity. At times he experienced genuine fear and intimidation, but there were times when he did not. If his drill sergeant detected that Ernie was not sufficiently cowed, he ramped up the in-your-face yelling and screaming until he believed Ernie was sufficiently "shaking in his boots."

As the thirteen-week boot camp progressed, Ernie focused on the challenges of the day before him and tried to do all that his DI asked of him and more. During inspections by the DI, Ernie's boots had the best shine in the unit. His DI took notice and ordered him to shine his shoes as well. It would not do to have a recruit with a better shine than the DI. Ernie was pleasantly surprised that his efforts at Lefty's had led to a rare moment of positive recognition during boot camp.

If the psychology of boot camp is to persuade recruits to abandon their civilian values and implant those of the Marine Corps, Ernie was fertile ground. With each passing month Ernie adopted the corps's values: teamwork, organization, commitment, courage, and honor. He believed these values made a man a good marine and citizen. His initial disappointment in the military draft dissipated—he wanted to be a marine. At boot camp graduation he was promoted to private first class. His success left him wanting more of the same. It seemed reasonable to him that he could rise in the ranks to become a platoon sergeant and a leader. Perhaps more than he realized, he was in the grasp of the corps. He wanted to be first to wake, last to sleep, and last to eat. He was developing the desire to prepare and work in order to excel and succeed. A mental transformation was underway.

After boot camp he received orders to report to Naval Air Station Jacksonville in Jacksonville, Florida. There he attended a joint navy-marine F-8 and F-4 jet fighter school on avionics and aircraft engine maintenance. His first duty assignment, after a relatively quick promotion in rank to corporal, was a post at Roosevelt Roads Naval Station in Puerto Rico. There, he was assigned to aircraft maintenance and flight line operations. Ernie worked on F-8 Crusader and F-4 Phantom jets. The Phantoms were commonly used in the Vietnam War for reconnaissance and bombing ground targets. Equipped with air-to-air and air-to-ground missiles, the versatile jets were able to defend themselves in aerial combat and against antiaircraft ground installations.

At Roosevelt Roads, Ernie encountered a staff sergeant nicknamed Spot for the highly visible brown spot on his forehead. Spot was a no-nonsense, by-the-book marine. After every aircraft was launched, his crew met to conduct an after-action report, a review of their performance during the launch. Ernie, with his limited experience, began to assertively describe his assessment for the others. Spot barked, "Corporal Garcia, sit down and shut up. And listen. We don't want to hear your bullshit!" The sergeant's rebuke was a stunning knockdown of Ernie's attitude. It made him understand that his knowledge of operations around the F-4 was limited. The put-down was an admonition that expertise was not easily acquired. Over time, he realized that Spot slamming his comments made him a better marine, and he was grateful for the sergeant's instruction and guidance. Sadly, Sergeant Spot was killed while serving in Vietnam.

Ernie eventually became a crew chief for his squadron and was responsible for supervision of all ground movement of the aircraft and attending equipment, commonly referred to as yellow gear. He dressed in color-coded vests on the flight line to signal his responsibilities. Ernie always felt a sense of a job well done when technically advanced military aircraft took off at his signal to the pilots.

Before Ernie's assignment in Puerto Rico, he had not been off the US mainland. During his free time, he ventured into towns and cities. Curious about the people and how they lived, he strolled not only through the finer neighborhoods and shopping districts of San Juan but also through the poorer neighborhoods. Talking with the vendors and waiters, he surprised them when the first words he spoke were in Spanish. They did not expect this American-looking man to speak their language. His smile and engaging manner also helped put them at ease. One restaurant owner confided to him that he appreciated the way Ernie carried himself in contrast to some marines he had encountered, who were rude and condescending to their fellow American citizens in Puerto Rico.

While stationed in Puerto Rico, Ernie had felt the sting of bias toward Puerto Ricans. On one occasion, a marine commented to Ernie and a group of marines that Puerto Ricans were ignorant and poor and that the women were without virtue and infected with venereal disease. The marine might not have expressed his ethnic prejudice had he realized that Ernie felt a kinship with Puerto Ricans, sharing not only their language but also the heritage of mixed Spanish, native, and African bloodlines. Encountering this strain of intolerance in the corps was disappointing to Ernie. To counter the prejudice, he tried to set an example with a respectful demeanor when interacting with the local community, particularly when in a group of marines. He had many opportunities to do so, as he became a popular companion for off-duty buddies wanting to tour the largely Spanish-speaking communities.

While Ernie was away for the initial ten months of his active duty, he communicated with Sharon Lee by mail and phone calls. But the time and distance between Kansas and California and Puerto Rico had their impact on the two of them. She was in the spring semester of her junior year when he returned to KU to see her; she had begun to date another student in his absence. Even after Ernie left for the marines, she felt a lingering pressure from her parents to end her romance with Ernie. She told him that they had offered to buy her a new car and send her to Europe for a vacation. He believed their offer was conditional—though unspoken—on her ending the romance with him. She told him that she had refused the offer.

Ernie carefully considered their situation. He was unemployed and intended to return to Wichita in the short term. He had no immediate plans to enroll at KU. Even if he did so, he would be on probation and finishing his freshman year at best. If he waited to enroll until the fall semester, she would be starting her senior year while he would still be a freshman.

In the end he told Sharon Lee to take the car and vacation. He believed the divide between them had opened instead of closed. She had a new dating interest, while Ernie had a new interest in the Marine Corps. Time and events had severed their connection, and they agreed to end the romance.

On Ernie's return to Wichita in the spring of 1967, he found work at a high-fashion shoe shop named Eldon's, which was owned by Carolyn and Eldon Ewing. For the Ewings, Ernie's engaging personality and his eye for the most popular styles brought new customers and repeat sales. They soon regarded Ernie as essential to their business and accepted that he might be called to serve in the marines for an entire year sometime during the next five years. They assured him nonetheless that his job was safe and that they would await his return. He appreciated their flexibility and felt that they treated him well.

One of Ernie's calls to service was an active duty assignment to Japan in support of the F-4s in Vietnam. He was aware that the marine infantry looked down on the marine air wing, which did not face combat in "the bush" in Vietnam, but he was not deterred from carrying out his duties in a professional manner. Although his stay in Japan was brief, he became aware of the brutality of the war from the details recounted to him by marines returning from combat.

When Ernie once again returned to Wichita, he became the manager of Eldon's. He was able to help support his family by hiring his brother, Frank, and his sister, Ana. But with the draft lurking, Frank too joined the marines in 1971. He was assigned to the infantry and was sent to Vietnam, where he became a combat veteran. For Luisa, Frank's service was more difficult to accept than that of Jim and Ernie. Her prayers for Frank's safety could not temper her irritation with the military calling a third son to service. Frank was her youngest, and she knew he was to be sent to a combat zone. Her tears and prayers were far more frequent but were answered when he returned home safely.

During this time, Ernie began to experience success in his Marine Corps career as he rotated between active duty and the Marine Corps Reserves. He enjoyed a level of comfort and job security with his positions at Eldon's and in the reserves. But the long-term weakness of that comfort level was exposed in early 1971 with a visit to Eldon's by a Garden City barrio friend, Henry Avila.

Henry was two years older than Ernie and was also born in Garden City. He had been in Jim's high school class. His given name was Enrique, but his parents used the name Henry to accommodate English speakers who struggled to pronounce Enrique. He had attended Garden City's public schools rather than Saint Mary's. Over the years the Avila family had become friends with the Garcia and Ayala families. The Avila home stood where Second Street ended at a railroad spur, two blocks away from both Ernie's home and the Ayala home.

Enrique's parents were typical barrio parents, hardworking supporters of their families with dreams for their children. His mother, Jessie, was a housekeeper, while his father, Jess, worked for the city sanitation department on a garbage truck. In those times, Garden City residents used open oil drums as garbage receptacles. As the dump truck drove down the alleys, the garbage men stepped off the rear of the truck, rolled the drums to the bin of the truck, and then lifted the drum to empty the refuse into the bin. It was difficult work as there were no hydraulic lifts for the drums. These men were always in the elements—heat, humidity, cold, and always the Kansas wind.

When adults think about their childhood neighborhoods and schools, they usually remember one very smart and capable kid. That exceptional child was usually the bookworm type. He or she was often included in neighborhood games and adventures, but still everyone believed that kid's accomplishments would far exceed their own. In the Santa Fe barrio, that kid was Henry.

Henry loved to play basketball with Jim, Ernie, and the guys. But unlike the others, he had a special talent off the court: he played classical piano. In first grade, his Alta Brown schoolteachers recognized his musical potential. Since the school had no music teacher, they sent Henry to a nun who taught music at Saint Mary's. By the time he reached high school, he had already won piano competitions. He played the classical works of Chopin, Bach, and Mozart and performed live on local television. In his senior year in a recital, he performed Beethoven's "Moonlight Sonata" to a thunderous ovation in the Community Congregation Church. He also won a regional competition that led to a full-ride scholarship at Saint Mary's of the Plains, a Catholic college in Dodge City, Kansas. Even Principal Saffell, surprisingly, wrote a letter of recommendation in support of Henry's application to Saint Mary's of the Plains.

After two years in college, Henry's focus shifted. He became a voracious reader in many topics, such as history, philosophy, political science, English literature, natural science, and much more. He continued to play the piano and taught piano lessons on occasion, but his passion had become reading.

Henry's barrio friends were adept at tagging a person with a nickname that identified a characteristic or mannerism of that person. The nicknames were often humorous but still affectionate. One six-year-old boy declared that he was going to shoot Pancho Villa with his toy gun. For the rest of his long life, the gentleman was called Villa. In Henry's case his friends took note of a volume of works by the philosopher Friedrich Nietzsche resting on his coffee table and tagged him with the nickname Neech.

Ernie and Neech were good friends—barrio brothers. On one occasion when Sharon Lee was away at college, the two young men were at a Mexican dance at the county fairground building. The dance floor was dimly lit where they stood together watching the dancers on the floor. As usual,

Ernie was not content to watch, so he asked a pretty Mexican girl to dance. She accepted.

As Ernie and the young lady danced, without any warning, someone came up from behind and took a roundhouse swing at Ernie. The punch struck him with a great deal of force on the temple, knocking him to the floor. Neech helped him up and walked him into a lighted area. After looking him over, without hesitation, Neech told him it was time to go. The blow to the side of the head later developed into a nasty black eye. Ernie always believed that the assailant was a young, envious Mexican teen who might have been frustrated at the sight of Ernie enjoying himself with a Mexican girl. Perhaps the teen was resentful that Ernie had a white girlfriend and felt that he had no place at a Mexican dance with one of "our girls."

On that winter day in 1971, when Neech stopped to say hello to Ernie at Eldon's, he was a graduate student at KU. After a short chat with Ernie, he asked him a question. "Hey, bro, are you going to sell shoes all your life?"

The question surprised Ernie, and he was not prepared to respond. "Why don't you go back to school?" Neech suggested. Ernie explained, "Look, Neech, my grades aren't that good." Neech seemed unconcerned with his response. "I know people who might be able to help." Ernie shrugged, unconvinced. Before Neech left the store, he said to Ernie, "Give it some thought."

"Yeah, I will."

Ernie appreciated Neech's concern for him. In the weeks after his visit, Ernie deliberated a great deal over his offer. His ties to Garden City had been cut: Luisa and his siblings were living in Wichita. His grandfather, Chalio, had passed away in the summer of 1970 at age eighty-three. Both his romance with Sharon Lee and his friendship with Randy had been interrupted while they were at KU and he was on active duty in the Marine Corps. Later Randy attended optometry school in Tennessee, putting even more distance between them.

Neech's comment about selling shoes left Ernie unsettled. His question was on point; what was Ernie's future? In Wichita he was pleased with his position as a manager, and in the Marine Corps Reserves he had reached the rank of sergeant. He considered the corps a solid fallback position. But still, neither Eldon's nor the corps was the same as a college degree.

While Ernie often took matters to the edge, he was not reckless with decisions regarding his future. After all, he was not the one who jumped out of the car and chased rats while others might be shooting, nor did he threaten police with a jump from the city's water tower. Ernie sensed that he had little to lose and much to gain—but he was hesitant, given his prior unsuccessful attempt at KU. However, he did feel some assurance that Neech would look out for him and guide him along the way if things became difficult, just as he had done when Ernie was assaulted at the Mexican dance.

In the middle of the summer of 1971, he decided to call Neech in Lawrence and ask a question. When Neech answered, he was surprised to hear Ernie's voice.

"Hey, Neech, this is Ernie. How ya doing, bro?"

"Doing good, doing good." Neech detected an unusually serious tone in Ernie's voice.

"Neech, I got a question for you."

"Yeah, sure. Go ahead," Neech answered, ready to provide information about KU. Continuing his serious tone, Ernie asked, "Do you have any chorizo in your fridge?" Neech thought he had misunderstood. "What? What did you say?" Ernie slowly repeated, "Do you have any chorizo in your fridge?" Neech paused. He had heard correctly. He was so taken aback he could not think of anything to say other than, "Uh . . . no."

"Well, you better go out and get some because I will be there in a week!"

After realizing they would be eating breakfast together while attending KU, Neech laughed and was pleased with Ernie's decision. And he was amused that he had allowed himself to be made the straight man in Ernie's humor.

7

Gateway to the Senate

1971–1977

The summer passed quickly, leaving Ernie's renewed pursuit of his KU degree just days away. He readied himself, knowing that if he failed again, he might never have another opportunity. Neech's provocation had led Ernie to reflect on what he valued most. He wanted a successful career in a field that paid well and allowed him to comfortably support himself and a family. He concluded that a degree from KU, which had eluded him once before, was the key to experiencing the success he wanted in life.

With Ernie's community-centric upbringing and awareness of the financial hardships of friends and family, he also wanted his career to contribute to the well-being of the people in his community, particularly the Hispanic community. Though his attention in the late 1960s focused on his pursuit of Sharon Lee and military service, through the power of television, he became aware of the battles fought across the country by black Americans during the civil rights movement. Albeit at a distance, he saw the struggles of Cesar Chavez and the United Farmworkers against California wine growers; he also witnessed the Mexican American students who walked out of their high schools in Los Angeles in 1968 demanding changes in the schools.

It is unlikely that the activists in the South and in California believed the ripple of their sacrifices might reach the small towns of Kansas and the heartland. But they did. Mexican Americans organized and engaged in the political process. In Hutchinson, Kansas, Jim P. Martinez was elected to the city council in 1969 and served as mayor in 1970. Ernie's uncle Dionicio was elected to Garden City's city council in 1971 and served as mayor in 1973.

With a new motivation and awareness, Ernie met with Dr. Kenneth Martinez in the Education Department at KU. Neech had arranged the meeting in preparation of Ernie's arrival. Neech regarded Martinez, who had a PhD in curriculum and instruction, as particularly capable of assisting Ernie. After discussing Ernie's background, his interests, and his transcripts, Martinez suggested potential programs that might be compatible and that might utilize the credits he had previously earned. Ernie was receptive to his suggestion of a social work program. Together they plotted a course of classes leading to a bachelor's degree. Martinez then walked with him to the admissions office at Strong Hall in KU's Administration Building, where he introduced Ernie to the registrar and director of admissions. Under Martinez's guidance, Ernie reapplied and was eventually admitted, again on probationary status.

Ernie needed to devote most of his time to his studies to improve his grades, but he still required a part-time income to pay for his basic needs. To address his financial situation, Martinez took Ernie to the Institute for Social and Environmental Studies in Blake Hall. There they met with the Political Science Department chair, Dr. Herman Lujan, who was of Hawaiian and Spanish descent. After an interview with Lujan, Ernie was offered a position as a research assistant. His duties did not entail the design or evaluation of the research projects; instead he gathered and organized data and information. The hours were flexible and did not tax his study time, making the job ideal.

As Ernie devised his new plans to earn a college degree, he remained active in the Marine Corps Reserves. He reenlisted and seriously began considering a career in the corps. To enhance his opportunities for advancement, he changed his military occupational specialty from the air wing to the infantry. Promotions were more likely and frequent in the infantry because of front-line active duty assignments that often involved danger and high risk. He understood his education remained vulnerable to a call to serve, particularly if some military crisis erupted that required an immediate military response involving ground troops. But he suppressed any anxiety over the possibility of a deployment interfering with his plans.

Before fall classes began, Ernie returned to Wichita, in part to thank the Ewings for the opportunity they had provided him at their shoe store. He met with Eldon and told him he was leaving to return to KU. Surprising Ernie, Eldon responded that managing his store was a good job for Ernie and suggested that returning to KU was not a particularly wise move. Having thought Eldon would wish him well at KU, Ernie was stung by his response. Beginning with Lefty's and with every job thereafter, he and his employers had always parted with the hope and promise of something better for him. Not this time. Eldon's response made Ernie cautious of those who might sacrifice his future if it was in their benefit to do so.

Until Ernie could find his own place, Neech invited him to share the rooms he rented in an old drafty house on the corner of Nineteenth and Kentucky Streets in Lawrence. The rooms were small but were enough to accommodate both of them for the short term. When they became roommates, Neech introduced Ernie to classical music. It was unavoidable, living in the same house. During cold, snowy days that winter, Ernie put aside the Santana *Abraxis* album. Instead, as he studied, he listened to Erik Satie's "Gymnopédie No. 1" and similar works, drank hot tea, and tried to keep warm.

Neech's influence went far beyond an introduction to classical music. He mentored Ernie, offering study habits and techniques, suggestions on reading materials, and editing on writing assignments. Neech's mentoring, matched with Ernie's marine-generated discipline and desire to acquire academic credentials, put Ernie in position to succeed. He wanted a level of success beyond what Luisa and Felipe had been able to achieve and beyond the expectations of those who might have discounted his potential. The match proved effective, and as Ernie's grades improved he was removed from probationary status.

While Neech provided quality assistance and guidance for Ernie's studies, the same cannot be said for the accommodations in his small apartment. Neech was the consummate graduate student bachelor, with minimal furnishings, beanbags for chairs, an air mattress, plastic utensils, and paper plates—and when the supply of paper plates was exhausted, the underside of Frisbees proved a durable substitute. The prized item in the furnishings ensemble was a stereo for classical music. The food items on hand and in the fridge were basic—beans and tortillas, cereal and milk.

Neech allowed Ernie to sleep in the only bedroom, which was very small and had enough room for only one bed with an old mattress. Neech, meanwhile, slept on the air mattress on the living room floor. Ernie thought the arrangement was quite generous of his friend. But after the first rain seeped through the window and onto the bed, Ernie realized Neech had gotten the better end of the deal. This time, the humor was at Ernie's expense.

The following spring Ernie received a call from his cousin Steve Garcia, son of Porfirio. Steve was four years younger than Ernie and was serving in the army in Germany. Steve explained that his military service was about to end and that he was considering enrolling at KU. He wanted Ernie's opinion about the difficulty of the classes and his chances of success. Without hesitation, Ernie replied that he was confident that Steve could successfully complete the courses. Traveling directly from Germany to Lawrence, Steve joined Ernie and Neech just before the start of the 1972–1973 school year. The three of them combined their resources and rented a two-bedroom apartment. Compared to the apartment on Kentucky, this one, with a couch and no leaking windows, was luxurious. The barrio trio lived together for the next two years.

During this period Ernie's military service did not significantly interfere with his studies. He was not called to active duty for any extended length of time, though he was deployed on several classified special operations in Southeast Asia. His absences were brief and allowed him to continue to thrive academically and complete the coursework for his degree. He made the dean's honor roll and graduated in May 1974 with a degree in sociology. Ten years had passed since high school, but with his resilience and the support of others, he reached his goal. He learned that success in education—as in the Marine Corps—was within his reach, and he intended to pursue more. Having tasted success, he promptly applied to graduate school, was accepted, and began a master's degree in social work.

During his undergraduate years, Ernie began to hold better employment positions in the university system. After earning his bachelor's degree, he worked as an assistant dean of men in Strong Hall. His position introduced him to many people in various walks of university life. His duties included addressing issues involving students, veterans, university police, and others on campus. He traveled around the state to educational and political events with Chancellor Archie Dykes to promote the interests of KU and to recruit potential students. Most of these events were more informal meet and greets, but on occasion Ernie addressed the assembled participants. These public events enabled Ernie to develop confidence in speaking before an audience. Once Ernie was in graduate school, his fellow master's program classmates recruited him to run as their representative in the student senate. Ernie was elected and for the first time felt he had a seat at the table of government. Though it was a small table and a small government, it was a sample of making a difference.

Ernie's office in Strong Hall was comfortable, and with his engaging personality, he was well suited to an open door policy. He was willing to speak to any person needing help, student or otherwise. One afternoon in early 1974, Ernie began to hear small bits of a conversation in the adjacent housing assistance office. His colleague was speaking with a woman with a strong Spanish accent. Ernie noted that her accent was likely not from Mexico nor Puerto Rico. He guessed that it was South American. From what Ernie was able to understand, the woman was indeed seeking housing assistance. But she and Ernie's colleague could not effectively talk to one another. Because Ernie wanted to help, and because he was curious about the woman, he walked over to the office, where his colleague accepted Ernie's offer of assistance.

The woman was a pretty brunette with shoulder-length hair. She and Ernie exchanged introductions in Spanish. Her name was Ana Maria Graneros, she had a master's degree in bilingual education, and she was a visiting professor from Argentina. Ernie learned that her housing issue could not be resolved immediately and that she would return to discuss the matter in the near future.

Ernie found Ana Maria quite attractive, but she found him quite arrogant. After later exchanges her view softened, and she did find him helpful. And she also found him handsome and charming—so much so that they began a whirlwind romance and married in August in Lawrence.

Ernie's marriage to Ana Maria broke up the Santa Fe Street barrio trio in Lawrence. Neech and Steve continued their studies but now lived separately. However, they were not left totally isolated. As class schedules and campus events permitted, they interacted with other students of Mexican ancestry, including a few more students from the barrio who had also made their way to KU. One campus organization, MECHA (Movimiento Estudiantil Chicano de Aztlan—Chicano Student Movement of Aztlan), arranged icebreaker events at the student union. It also promoted academic activities and acquisition of resources for the students, such as discounted texts and materials, tutoring, recruitment and placement events, and appearances by guest speakers. Though there were varying degrees of participation in MECHA's more formal activities, the students of Mexican heritage shared and supported a common objective—getting through the university system with a degree.

Ana Maria was born and raised in the city of Salta, the capital of Salta Province in northern Argentina. Salta Province is situated in rugged mountains and bordered by Bolivia to the north. Three months after Ernie and Ana Maria were married, Ana Maria's father died in Argentina. The newlyweds were unable to make immediate travel plans, but they traveled to Argentina a few weeks later to spend time with her mother, Juana. To reach the city of Salta, Ernie and Ana Maria flew into Buenos Aires and took a connecting flight.

When Ernie and Ana Maria arrived in Salta, Argentina's military was on alert for insurgents and guerrilla fighters. For decades revolutionary militias opposed to Argentina's rulers had operated in the far northern reaches of Salta Province. With good reason the military commanders and elected presidents in power were vigilant against rebellions and revolutions. They sent military personnel and materials to these northern areas to pursue and eliminate any rebels through political imprisonment and murder.

One of the rebel groups was the People's Guerrilla Army, a militia trained and armed in Bolivia, approximately three hundred miles north of Salta. The guerrillas, fifty in number, crossed from Bolivia into Salta Province in the early 1960s. However, the rebellion they hoped to ignite did not win popular support, and eventually the guerrilla militia was driven back into Bolivia. One of the founders of the People's Guerrilla Army was Ernesto "Che" Guevara. He had been a target of the US Central Intelligence Agency since his participation in Fidel Castro's 1959 rise to power in Cuba. Eventually, Guevara was hunted down and killed by Bolivian military forces in the jungles of Bolivia in October 1967.

As Ernie and Ana Maria neared the city of Salta, their vehicle was stopped at a military checkpoint. A guard with an automatic long gun slung over his shoulder demanded their identification papers. Ana Maria produced her Argentine identification, and Ernie produced a US passport. He explained in Spanish that he and Ana Maria were married. She added that they had come to Salta to visit her mother. The guard demanded to see their marriage license, but they did not have one with them.

For an instant, Ernie was fearful and disbelieving of their situation. The armed guard ordered Ernie to exit the vehicle. Ernie's military experience enabled him to recognize the guard's actions and methods. Complying with the order, Ernie stepped out slowly without sudden movement, remaining calm and offering no resistance. As the guard patted him down for weapons, Ana Maria could only observe from her seat in the vehicle. When a senior officer arrived, he questioned Ernie. His answers to the officer were the same as those he had given to the guard.

Apparently, Ernie had a strong resemblance to a leftist rebel. Ernie's appearance when he arrived in Salta was typical for the era. His black hair was long, nearly touching his shoulders, and parted in the middle in the style of early 1970s rockers like David Cassidy of the Partridge Family. He also wore a mustache and a neatly trimmed beard that grew out of his sideburns, apparently in the style of Che Guevara. Ernie's appearance caused the problem—the officer thought perhaps Ernie was a member of Guevara's old militia or a member of the CIA. After some discussion outside of Ernie's hearing, the officer escorted them to Ana Maria's mother's house and told Ernie that he was not to leave the house for any reason. He was effectively under house arrest.

In the days that followed, a military vehicle regularly patrolled the street in front of Ana Maria's mother's home. Ernie called Jim in Wichita and asked him to notify the US embassy in Buenos Aires. The embassy contacted Ernie and advised him to find a way back to the Buenos Aires airport as soon as possible, in any way possible. After several days they were able to secure seats on a plane to Buenos Aires. They arranged for an acquaintance to drive them to the airport outside of Salta. As they drove, they tried to remain at ease, though they feared military personnel might stop or pursue them. However, they were able to board the plane without incident. They spent several more days in Buenos Aires before they boarded a flight to New York. Ernie never returned to Salta and from that day forward remained cautious when he was on foreign soil, particularly in South America.

A few days after Ernie completed his master's program in the spring of 1975, Ana Maria gave birth to their son, Felipe Jorge Garcia, named after his grandfathers. Ernie was overwhelmed with the love and affection he felt for his baby boy. He had been unaware of the emotions he held within. Holding baby Felipe rekindled thoughts of his father's efforts to provide for his family despite his poor health. He wished that his father could have held baby Felipe—just once.

As part of the coursework for his program, Ernie had completed a field internship. He had a choice of several assignments and chose to work in the Hispanic community in Topeka. He helped senior citizens struggling to obtain services such as assistance with tax returns and access to medical services. Although his work in Topeka as an advocate for seniors gave him a sense of helping those in need, he nonetheless believed that as a program administrator his efforts would be more productive. As an administrator, he could determine the types of services to be delivered to the community and ensure that the services were properly delivered to the greatest number of people. With that objective in mind—and brimming with confidence and a can-do attitude as a result of both Felipe's birth and earning his master's degree in social work—he set his sights on a master's degree in public administration and began the coursework in the fall 1975.

A year later, two more cousins, sons of Dionicio from Garden City, joined Ernie and Steve in Lawrence to begin their studies at the university. If Jose and Rosa had been told, as they stood at rest in el betabel, that four of their grandsons would attend the University of Kansas at one time, they would have been in complete disbelief. But there they were, in Lawrence, at KU. The *primos* were the living dreams of their fieldworker grandparents and parents. Each of them eventually earned a KU degree.

While the mood in Lawrence in September 1976 was relatively lighthearted, some sad news arrived from Garden City. Lefty, Ernie's boyhood mentor and supporter, had passed away at the age of sixty-one. Ernie had known Lefty as a good and decent man who helped fill the void after Felipe's death, when he had no obligation to do so. Ernie prayed that Lefty would rest in peace for all the good that he had done.

Later in the school year, as part of the public administration curriculum that focused on the management and leadership of government, Ernie completed an internship in the office of Kansas governor Robert Bennett. His primary duty was conducting budget reviews in the Division of State Planning and Research. These reviews included an analysis of contracts with the state. Although Ernie was not particularly interested in the mechanics of securing funding or generating budget numbers for the accounting of government-funded programs, his primary goal remained the same: the administration of programs in the most efficient and effective manner. While at the state capitol, he established a rapport with members of the governor's staff, and on occasion conversed with the governor himself. What Ernie did not realize, as he completed his somewhat dry budget analysis, were the impressions he left with the governor and his staff. Those impressions would soon dramatically alter Ernie's life experiences.

As Ernie's graduate studies drew to a close, he began searching for employment that utilized his education in social work and public administration and his experiences in the Marine Corps and serving members of the public. He applied for a position as an aide in the Wichita office of Democratic congressman Dan Glickman, who was elected in November 1976. He was disappointed when Glickman's response was a form rejection letter. Ernie thought his ties to Wichita, military experience, and education might warrant at least an interview with the congressman's staff. Shortly after this rejection, however, Senator Robert Dole of Kansas, who was in his second term, met with Governor Bennett and told the governor that he needed a staffer in Washington, DC. The senator stated his preference for a military veteran from southwestern Kansas. The governor responded that he knew just the man.

Senator Dole was from Russell, Kansas, a small town 165 miles from Garden City—thus his preference for a staffer with similar roots from the part of the state that was his home. The senator's preference for including veterans on his staff was in part due to his belief that there was a need to consider their concerns and recommendations on the issues of the day. Additionally, his military experience in World War II put him at ease in their company.

Soon after Senator Dole's conversation with Governor Bennett, Ernie received a phone call from Bill Wohlford, the senator's chief of staff and an attorney from Wichita who was raised on a Kansas farm and had played football for KU. He told Ernie that the senator wanted to meet with him in Kansas City. The senator was scheduled to speak at a political function there, and Ernie was to meet with him after the event. Ernie was shocked, thrilled, and honored all at once—especially because he had not initiated the contact.

Ernie's priority when Wohlford called was finding employment, quickly, in order to support his wife and newborn son. Similarly, his prior application to Congressman Glickman's office had been more of economic necessity, though his duties would include assistance to constituents. He did not have a lifelong dream of working as a politician's aide. But the financial pressure enabled Ernie to reason that although working as a Senate staffer was a step removed from program administration with public contact, a senator's impact on the community and the number of constituents served vastly exceeded that of a program administrator. Ernie's political views might not have been perfectly aligned with those of Senator Dole at that time, but the fact that the senator sought him out lessened his uneasiness about working for him. In the end, he concluded that in his circumstances, the possibility of working for the senator in Washington could not be ignored. Ernie realized he did not have a full grasp of the nature of the work as a legislative aide in Washington, DC, but he sensed the experience would provide opportunities in the future. He accepted Wohlford's invitation to meet with the senator.

Ana Maria and baby Felipe accompanied Ernie to the hotel where the senator was speaking. They waited together in the lobby. Ernie was still sporting long hair and the beard, but he did wear his first suit. Aunt Kay had purchased it for him for his master's graduation ceremony. His shoes, of course, were polished to a brilliant shine.

The senator finally emerged with his entourage. After introductions, Ernie and the senator spoke briefly. Their conversation included Ernie's KU education and military service. Their meeting soon ended and the senator was whisked away. Ernie did not believe anything would come of their meeting since it had been so brief and the senator noncommittal. Within a week Wohlford called Ernie again. He said that the senator had asked if Ernie would be willing to travel to DC for a second interview. Ernie was taken aback. His first thought was: *Wow!* His second: *Of course I'll go!* His third: *How am I going to get there? I'm broke.* Wohlford resolved the problem when he advised that the senator's office would send him an airline ticket.

Ernie cut his hair, shaved off the beard and mustache, and wore his suit for the interview. He asked the senator's representatives if he would be permitted to complete his coursework for the master's in public administration, and he reminded them that he was still subject to call-up by the Marine Corps Reserves. The representatives assured Ernie that neither of these concerns was an issue. At the conclusion of the interview they told Ernie that he would be advised of the senator's decision within a week.

Wohlford subsequently called Ernie and offered him a position with a salary of $18,500 per year. Ernie thought that amount a considerable sum, but in reality it was virtually nothing in Washington. He realized that initially his family would be living paycheck to paycheck, but he was confident at that moment that the opportunity would prove far more valuable in the future. In accepting Senator Dole's job offer, he took the same approach as Jose and Felipe: follow the work, and learn as you go.

Pedro Garcia with Othello, ca. 1915

Children of Pedro and Merced Garcia, ca. 1920. Standing, left to right: *Paula, Benjamin, Augustine, Jose, and Juana.* Seated: *Guadalupe and Maria (mother of Manuela Cegarra-Rodriguez)*

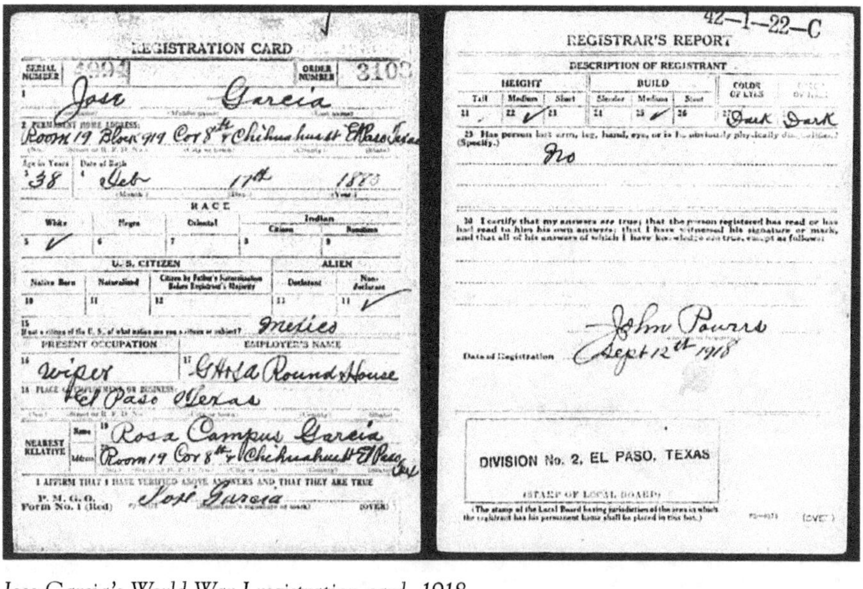

REGISTRATION CARD

SERIAL NUMBER 4994 ORDER NUMBER 3103

1 Jose Garcia

2 PERMANENT HOME ADDRESS: Room 19 Block 919 Cor 8th & Chihuahua st El Paso Texas

Age in Years 3 38 Date of Birth 4 Feb 17th 1880

RACE

White 5 ✓

U. S. CITIZEN / ALIEN Non-declarant 11 ✓

15 If not a citizen of the U. S., of what nation are you a citizen or subject? Mexico

PRESENT OCCUPATION 16 wiper EMPLOYER'S NAME 17 GH & SA Round House

18 PLACE OF EMPLOYMENT OR BUSINESS: El Paso Texas

NEAREST RELATIVE Name 19 Rosa Campus Garcia Address Room 19 Cor 8th & Chihuahua st El Paso

I AFFIRM THAT I HAVE VERIFIED ABOVE ANSWERS AND THAT THEY ARE TRUE

P. M. G. O. Form No. 1 (Red) Jose Garcia (OVER)

42—1—22—C

REGISTRAR'S REPORT

DESCRIPTION OF REGISTRANT

HEIGHT Medium 22 ✓ BUILD Medium 25 ✓ COLOR OF EYES 27 Dark COLOR OF HAIR Dark

29 Has person lost arm, leg, hand, eye, or is he obviously physically disqualified? (Specify.) No

30 I certify that my answers are true; that the person registered has read or has had read to him his own answers; that I have witnessed his signature or mark, and that all of his answers of which I have knowledge are true, except as follows:

John Powers

Date of Registration Sept 12th 1918

DIVISION No. 2, EL PASO, TEXAS

(STAMP OF LOCAL BOARD)

(The stamp of the Local Board having jurisdiction of the area in which the registrant has his permanent home shall be placed in this box.) (OVER)

Jose Garcia's World War I registration card, 1918

Rosa Garcia, holding a child, and Jose Garcia, ca. 1915

Palm Sunday dust storm, 1935 (Kansas State Historical Society)

Jose Garcia topping sugar beets, ca. 1935

Jose Garcia's headstone

MEXICAN BEET WORKER DEAD

Joe Garcia, 56, Mexican and former beet field worker in the Garden City area, died Monday at Los Angeles, Calif., relatives here were informed today. Funeral services for Garcia, who lived here more than 20 years, will be conducted Saturday at Los Angeles. He left for Los Angeles a month ago. His wife and six sons, five of whom live near Garden City, survive.

Obituary for Jose Garcia, February 1938 (Courtesy Garden City Telegram*)*

Rosa Garcia with sons, ca. 1945. Standing, left to right: *Guillermo, Jesus, Miguel, and Dionicio.* Seated: *Porfirio, Rosa, and Felipe (Conard Studios, Garden City, Kansas)*

Family of Felipe Garcia, ca. 1954. Left to right: *Felipe, Francis, James, Ernest "Ernie," Alvina, and Luisa*

Rosalio Ayala with daughters Luisa, left, *and Catalina,* right, *ca. 1928*

Ernie Garcia, US Marine, 1966

Felipe Garcia's home on Santa Fe Street

Finnup Park entrance after the June flood, 1965. View to the south from Santa Fe main line. (Finney County Museum)

Rosa Garcia and granddaughter Olga at Fourth Street home, May 1962

Ernie Garcia with Senator Robert Dole

Ernie Garcia with Pope John Paul II

Ernie Garcia escorting President Ronald Reagan to a State of the Union address, February 1986

Ernie Garcia, Senate sergeant at arms, at the Capitol building

Ernie Garcia escorting President Miguel de la Madrid of Mexico

Ernie Garcia (holding helmet) *in Iraq, 2004*

Ernie Garcia, US Marine, June 2006

Ernie Garcia's marine retirement ceremony, 2006

8

Making the Grade

1977–1979

Ernie rented a large U-Haul truck for the move to DC. After backing the truck into the loading dock of a local business, he drove his small, sporty, and very used Porsche onto the ramp of the dock, and then into the truck. He then loaded the family's belongings around the car. On a cold March evening, Ernie, Ana Maria, Felipe, and Ana Maria's mother, Juana, who had come to the United States to help with Felipe, squeezed into the cab of the U-Haul. Sitting tightly bunched on the bench seat, they set off for DC.

Ernie was not aware of the risk his new position carried until he was completing the employment paperwork. He realized, for the first time, that he had been hired on a probationary basis and not as a regular hire. Wohlford did not mention probationary status during their exchanges. Ernie submitted the paperwork despite his concern. He decided to ask Senator Dole's senior administrative assistant, Claude Alexander, about his status. Alexander was born and raised in Ulysses, Kansas (population three thousand), in the southwest corner of the state, about an hour's drive from Garden City. Alexander graduated from Ulysses High School, attended West Point, and later became an army airborne ranger.

Trying to find the right moment, Ernie waited a few days before approaching Alexander. Ernie stepped over to his desk, and in an inquisitive, rather than intense or angry tone, interrupted Alexander. "Excuse me, sir. If you have a moment, I have a question regarding the employment papers I completed." Alexander, still holding a pen in his hand, turned his chair toward Ernie, sat expressionless, and responded, "Sure. How can I help you?"

"Well, sir, I noticed on the forms that the probationary box was checked. No one has ever mentioned anything to me about a probationary period. Am I on probation?"

Alexander paused, put down his pen, and looked at Ernie. "Look, Ernie, I'll be direct with you. They wanted to make sure you could cut it." He continued bluntly, "If you don't, you're gone."

It was Ernie's turn to pause. He finally responded, "Oh. I see. I wasn't aware of that. Well, thanks for letting me know." Frustrated, Ernie tapped the file he was holding into the palm of his other hand as he returned to his desk in the cubicle. Alexander's responses were intimidating and at the same time irritating. Ernie had little experience working with politicians and legislators, and he understood that he might not be as prepared to perform as well as his coworkers. They were graduates of prestigious colleges such as Harvard, Duke, and West Point. Ernie loved KU, but he knew that, with or without good reason, KU did not evoke the confidence in others as did the elite schools and military academies. He now understood that "they" had doubts, but why? Was it his KU education, his heritage, or both? He wondered if the two other individuals of color in the office were required to complete a period of probation as well. In the end, he realized an answer was not forthcoming, and he turned his focus to the work at hand.

Toward the end of his first day, Wohlford placed a foot-high stack of papers on his desk. He told Ernie the papers were Senator Dole's recent speeches and policy papers. Without offering any guidance, he instructed Ernie to read them so that he would understand the senator's position and delivery on the issues. Wohlford was strict in his methods, but Ernie was accustomed to that approach through his marine experience. He spent most of the next few days at the office reading. The materials covered a broad range of topics, many of them unknown to him. He was overwhelmed. Some topics and issues were described in great depth and detail; others had little supporting background. He asked himself how he possibly could remember all of this information. The thought of returning to Kansas entered his mind as he considered whether this position—and a probationary one at that—with Senator Dole was in line with his career goals.

At this point of doubt, he again relied on his Marine Corps experience and his upbringing. He told himself he had a mission to complete. He needed to focus on the day before him and do more than was asked. Ernie became one of the few staffers who regularly arrived early at the office—

many mornings he was the first to arrive. He also stayed late every evening as he worked through the stack of speeches and policies. Although reluctant to expose his limited knowledge of the issues, he frequently asked questions of his cubicle partners, Alexander and another aide, Jack Nutter. Nutter had earned a law degree from Georgetown University and was a principal staff member for Senator Dole on the Senate Finance Committee. He was highly respected in the finance arena by Dole and other senators.

Alexander took note of Ernie's effort and commitment. Sharing the same legislative subjects—armed services, veterans' affairs, foreign affairs, disability issues, and general Kansas issues—he soon began to take Ernie under his wing. Ernie discovered that Alexander, like Wohlford and the senator, had a strong empathy for military men. Particularly helpful to Ernie was Alexander's knowledge of the law-making process and procedures, Senator Dole's legislative interests, and office procedures. His willingness to pass on that knowledge smoothed Ernie's way to becoming an effective aide.

Within six months Ernie was able to prepare summations on pending legislation and present the materials in a format suitable to the senator. Alexander began to delegate more and more of the work to Ernie. He was taken off probation and given a raise to $25,000. While the pay raise was certainly needed, Ernie's sense of accomplishment was far greater when Alexander and Nutter began to ask for his opinions on different legislative matters.

Ernie began to see that his colleagues were not all-knowing wizards. They had knowledge and skills in particular areas but little or none in others. He began to realize that they put their pants on just as he did. Well . . . almost all of them. One of his colleagues, a brilliant Harvard Law graduate with a PhD in economics, was an unusual character. His appearance was odd, his hair was always mussed, and his clothing disheveled. He had a heavy beard and thick glasses. In the winter he wore two pair of pants at the same time, presumably for warmth. Outside of his advisory role, he was quite socially awkward. But in his academic role as an economic advisor, he was unmatched. Despite the inelegance, Senator Dole did not hesitate to rely on his knowledge and counsel.

About the time Ernie's confidence level was rising, he was notified that Senator Dole was about to offer an amendment to a bill under consideration by the Senate. Ernie had prepared the amendment and accompanying statement for the senator. Nervously, he gathered his files and took the

Senate subway from the Dirksen Senate Office Building to the Senate side of the US Capitol. Senator Dole was preparing to speak on his amendment, and he wanted the information in the file to be immediately available.

On reaching the Senate chamber, Ernie took a seat along with other Senate staffers on a brown leather couch against the back wall. When the senator began his remarks, he motioned to Ernie to join him at his Senate desk. Ernie was still seated with the file containing the amendment and accompanying statement. He held the file under his arm as he rose from the couch. The folder was an open expandable type, so as the weight of the contents shifted, it fell from his hold. All of the papers emptied from the folder and slid across the floor like a dropped deck of cards.

There was dead silence in the chamber. Ernie immediately got to his hands and knees and attempted to gather the paperwork. The other Senate aides looked on in disbelief, and then they fought to hold back laughter. Ernie glanced up and saw Senator Dole looking at him with a serious, waiting expression. Soon other senators turned to see what was delaying the proceedings. After what seemed to Ernie and Senator Dole like an eternity, Ernie was able to gather the papers. With the folder in hand, he took his seat on a small chair next to Senator Dole's larger chair and desk. The senator barely acknowledged him. Ernie was in agony with embarrassment as he asked himself how he could have blundered so. He wanted to hide. He was sure he would lose his job at the day's end.

To make matters worse, Ernie was scheduled to accompany the senator that evening to a dinner with members of the banking industry from Kansas. When Senator Dole spoke at the dinner that evening, he expressed his pleasure at meeting with the bankers. He added that it was an honor to represent them, and he assured them that he and his staff were eager to help in any way possible. The senator then said he wanted to introduce one of his staffers who would be able to assist them. At that point he introduced Ernie. The senator went on to say that Ernie and the rest of his staff were good and capable people, that he had confidence in his staff, and that he appreciated all their work for him and the people of Kansas.

The senator had reason to be openly critical of Ernie on that day. Instead, his comments at the dinner were his way of saying, "That's all right, kid. Keep your head up. I appreciate your work." Ernie began to understand that Senator Dole was not a man eager to express his sentiments directly. The senator was not looking for buddies, just dedicated staffers.

Toward the end of Ernie's first year, Wohlford assigned Ernie a policy paper for Senator Dole. Ernie had learned that the senator initially wanted an assessment of the issue at hand, followed by the available options, including the pros and cons of each option. Then the senator wanted the personal recommendation of the policy writer and the rationale for the recommendation. Ernie immediately went to work, and when he completed the paper he believed the final product was one of his better efforts. With some confidence, he submitted it to the senator. Not only did the senator reject it, but he did so with a big red check mark covering the entire document. All of the staffers understood the big red check mark to mean, "I don't want to hear it!" The senator never offered explanations for his rejections. Ernie felt disappointment, but six months later in a speech, Senator Dole used some of Ernie's rejected recommendations. The senator never spoke to him about the recommendations, but his use of them confirmed for Ernie the value of his work for the senator. He felt a sense of worthiness as a Senate staffer and began to believe that, just maybe, he was on par with his colleagues.

In the late fall of 1977, Wohlford asked Ernie, "How is your Spanish?" Ernie responded, "It's not perfect, but I can carry on a conversation." Wohlford replied, "Good, because you are going to Panama with Senator Dole."

During that time, the Senate was debating ratification of the treaties that had been signed in September of that year transferring control of the Panama Canal back to Panama. Senator Dole was part of a group of senators who were to conduct a fact-finding mission to Panama. Among those accompanying Senator Dole were Senator Paul Laxalt of Nevada and Senator Dole's foreign affairs advisor. The senator invited Ernie as a defense advisor. The invitation signaled to Ernie that after nearly a year as a staffer, he had earned the senator's confidence.

The mission's agenda was all business, no sightseeing nor shopping. The senators, their staffs, and the civilians included in the mission were to be housed in army barracks. In late December, the senators and staff met with the leader of Panama, General Omar Torrijos. At their meeting, the senators and the general sat at a table across from each other. General Torrijos spoke only Spanish, so official interpreters were required. When Dole was not speaking, he wanted Ernie to interpret the discussion. Ernie did so quietly for both Senator Dole and Senator Laxalt.

At one point General Torrijos noticed Ernie whispering to Senator Dole. The general stopped speaking, looked at Ernie, and asked in Spanish, "Who are you, and where do you come from?" Ernie—wearing a traditional Central American white guayabera, an open-necked shirt with two breast pockets and two hip pockets—stood up and answered in Spanish, stating his name and that he was Senator Dole's assistant. Ernie also explained to the general that he was a US citizen of Mexican heritage.

General Torrijos paused for a second; then, he nodded slowly, still looking at Ernie. The general apparently had accepted Ernie's response and resumed his discussions with those at the table. Ernie took some satisfaction in seeing that the general had been a little unnerved by his presence. Perhaps the general thought the senators had brought a representative from another Central American country. Ernie hoped that the exchange demonstrated to Senator Dole that he was able to be direct yet respectful when addressed by a foreign head of state.

In the succeeding months, Ernie and other US officials returned to Panama for follow-up meetings with General Torrijos. Senator Dole's foreign affairs advisor asked Ernie for his recommendation and input on the treaties. Ernie responded with information regarding the capability and readiness of US military forces in the event of an attack on the canal while under Panamanian control. Ultimately, in March and April 1978, the treaties were ratified by the Senate, with Senator Dole voting against.

Ernie completed his first year with Senator Dole shortly after his work in Panama. At that time he was given another increase in salary. His salary had increased by more than 70 percent in the course of a year. Along with all his efforts for the senator during the year, Ernie completed his requirements for his master's in public administration from KU. Ernie's colleagues had grown more at ease with him by the end of his first year. Perhaps his completion of his master's in public administration and his continuing military service had an impact on their view of him. In any event, Ernie enjoyed a higher of level of camaraderie with the other aides.

Often that camaraderie included large doses of humor. In the days before computerized cut and paste, it was common to use a utility knife with a fine sharp blade for editing. The editor literally cut paragraphs and articles from papers and magazines and pasted or taped them to a clean page. For amusement, Alexander, a wounded and highly decorated Vietnam War veteran with a wooden leg as a result of his injuries, would occasionally slam his utility knife into his wooden leg in an area that would have been his quadriceps muscle. Alexander had the responsibility of training and assigning work to young interns working in Senator Dole's office. On one occasion, two new interns approached Alexander at the cubicle. Alexander remained seated as he described in all seriousness the nature of the work they were to complete. As he reached the conclusion of his presentation, he raised his voice and said forcefully, "Remember, you must do your best work!" As he made the declaration, he raised his hand holding the knife and brought it down on what the interns believed was his thigh. He then said, "Now, are there any questions?" The interns were horrified at the protruding knife. They shook their heads "no" and quickly walked away. When they were out of sight, Ernie, Alexander, and Nutter could not stop laughing.

Some of the humor involved an unsuspecting Senator Dole. Alexander was a zealous cigar smoker and often invited Ernie and Nutter to join him for a smoke in their cubicle. At that time smoking was permitted everywhere, including in office buildings. As the trio enjoyed their cigars, the senator approached their doorway to discuss an issue with them. They rose to their feet, showing the proper respect for the senator as he entered. The discussion proceeded in a serious tone for some time with Ernie standing next to the senator. As he did so, the ash on the end of his cigar was getting extremely long. Ernie flicked the end of the cigar to knock the ash into a trash can. But flicking the ash in such a manner was not the equivalent of shooting hoops in the back yard. Ernie's shot went astray, and the ash landed on the senator's pant leg.

Once again, Ernie was mortified. Should he reach over and swipe the senator's leg? Should he apologize? Which should he do first? Before he could reach a decision, the senator reached down and brushed off the ash. The senator, always holding his responses in reserve, awkwardly continued the discussion without interruption. Ernie said nothing and tried to carry on as though nothing was amiss. Alexander and Nutter did all they could to keep from bursting out with laughter. They waited until the senator walked away.

Despite the occasional awkward moment with Senator Dole, Ernie learned the process of guiding a proposed bill through the Senate and making it law. In his second year, at the last moment late on a Friday night, the senator directed Ernie to immediately draft an amendment to a foreign aid bill that was nearing passage in the Senate. Ernie called Alexander, now his mentor, and asked for guidance. He was direct with Ernie and to the point: "Find a copy of today's *Washington Post* and read the article on Mozambique. You ought to be able to find material to draft an amendment for the senator."

Ernie followed Alexander's direction and determined that the House of Representatives had restricted direct foreign aid to Mozambique. Senate Democrats wanted to allow the president to waive that restriction in the national interest. Ernie drafted a proposed amendment that would eliminate the president's power to waive the restriction. Ultimately, the Democrats prevailed and defeated the proposed amendment. Ernie was disappointed in the result but nonetheless pleased to have participated in the process by preparing the senator's amendment on a moment's notice.

One of Senator Dole's successful legislative efforts to which Ernie contributed was the opposition to President Jimmy Carter's attempt to downsize the KC-135 air-refueling tanker fleet. The Stratotankers, as they were known, were used to refuel military aircraft in the air. The tankers were important to the Kansas aviation industry—a squadron of the planes had been based in Wichita for a number of years. Boeing produced them and was redesigning the engines for the tankers. Boeing wanted the contract for redesign in Wichita, but other interested parties argued for a contract for an entirely new engine design to be produced outside of Wichita. Senator Dole and his staff led an initiative that ultimately secured the funding for the contract with Boeing and kept the jobs in Wichita.

It seemed that every time Ernie experienced a significant success, some minor pursuit of humor with the guys in the cubicle resulted in an awkward moment with Senator Dole. The two of them often rode the Senate subway from the Dirksen Building to the Capitol. On one occasion, Ernie sat next to the senator with his arm draped across the back of their bench seat. Upon arrival at the Capitol, Ernie began his exit off the subway car. As he removed his arm from the back of the seat, his hand struck the back of the senator's head and caused him to lunge forward. The senator reacted by simply taking his left hand and straightening his hair in the area where Ernie had hit him. Ernie's inadvertent swat and the senator's response happened so quickly that Ernie had no time say anything, let alone apologize. Without saying a word to Ernie, the senator also rose and exited the car.

Ernie was again devastated, but it was far from over. He did not leave well enough alone. On his return to the cubicle, he began to recount the event to

Alexander and Nutter. Before they could finish their laughter, they saw the senator coming up behind Ernie approaching their cubicle. Ernie continued to recount the event to evoke more laughter. But suddenly Alexander and Nutter sat motionless, without laughter and with serious expressions instead. Ernie turned and saw Senator Dole standing directly behind him. Once again, Dole remained stoic and said nothing. Again, Ernie wanted to die of embarrassment. He was certain he would be told to pack his bags.

Ernie sometimes wondered why Senator Dole had not disciplined him or made mention of his antics. He believed that the senator appreciated his staffers' work and in general cared for the well-being of those who worked for him. It seemed that the senator dealt with his staffers as he would command a small platoon of men. The senator at times pushed his people hard and without any expression of approval or gratitude, but so long as the staff completed their mission, he did not comment on their antics because the troops needed downtime.

A few months later, Ernie saw another side of Senator Dole. He had the opportunity to accompany the senator to Italy as part of a congressional delegation, referred to as a CODEL. The senator led the CODEL and decided to take an unscheduled side trip. The delegation and staff members climbed aboard their bus and headed out to an unknown destination. Some members of the delegation whispered to Ernie that the senator might want to go to the place where he had been wounded in World War II. When they stopped, they lingered as tourists do. Ernie did not know their exact location and was unsure why the senator had directed the bus to stop. Without explanation the senator said to Ernie, "C'mon, let's go."

The senator took Ernie to a hill outside of Castel d'Aiano. The two of them climbed the hill with the senator leading the way. When the senator stopped, Ernie remained two or three feet behind him. Ernie realized they were on the hill where the senator had been wounded.

In April 1945 the twenty-one-year-old Dole and members of the US Tenth Mountain Division were pushing retreating Germans out of Northern Italy toward their homeland. The mountainous terrain allowed the German army to inflict heavy casualties on pursuing American forces. The battles were fiercely fought, though victory in Europe was less than a month away. On April 14 in the steep hills near Castel d'Aiano, Italy, members of the Tenth Mountain Division attacked the Germans who held positions on higher ground. A frontal assault against an enemy holding higher ground is often a lethal tactic for the attackers. The Americans were under heavy fire when shrapnel from an artillery shell ripped through the right shoulder of Lieutenant Dole and hit his spinal cord. Other men fighting alongside him were killed by the gunfire and shrapnel. The medical personnel treating the future senator did not believe he would survive his injuries. But he did recover, though he lost the use of his right arm.

Remembering the suggestion of delegation members to give the senator some space, and knowing the senator was very private, Ernie left him alone with his emotions. Senator Dole was initially quiet, in prayer. After two or three minutes, without a word, he turned and left with Ernie following. They never spoke about their time on the hill.

On their return to Washington, Ernie continued his work on legislative matters. His assignments included an analysis of every funding bill that was related to an area of interest to Senator Dole. Ernie typically analyzed bills dealing with farm subsidies, the cattle industry, and Occupational Safety and Health Administration regulations covering agricultural operations.

In mid-1979, the senator, with every confidence in Ernie, offered him the directorship of his state office in Topeka, the state capital. Ernie saw this promotion as a stepping stone for his career and his family's future. His duties as director included networking with key party figures in the state and responding to constituent issues. Accepting the senator's offer, he moved back to Kansas. He bought a house in Lawrence, thirty-five miles from Topeka.

At that time, the political winds were again shifting across the country. Ernie could not have surmised that his time on the stepping stone in Topeka would be short. Soon he would be swept back to DC.

9

World Emissary

1980–1984

In November 1980 Ronald Reagan was elected president. Soon thereafter, Senator Dole's office called Ernie back to Washington to help manage the change in presidential administrations. He remained on the senator's payroll while loaned out to the Reagan transition team. By the time he returned to DC, the transition team was moving swiftly to put its people in place to take control of the levers of power. Ernie worked with the team in Washington until February. He then went back to Lawrence to resume his duties as director of Senator Dole's state office.

Within two weeks the senator called Ernie. After they greeted each other, Senator Dole told Ernie that Elizabeth, his wife, wished to speak with him. Ernie could only speculate about the reason for her call. She had become part of the new administration and was serving in the position of assistant to the president for public liaison. After a quick hello, Elizabeth said to Ernie, "On behalf of President Ronald Reagan, I am authorized to offer you a job at the White House, if you are willing to accept."

Ernie was in disbelief. He asked Elizabeth to repeat what she just said. She did so, and he had understood her correctly. Ernie's thoughts quickly turned to his ties to Senator Dole. The legislative staffers' unwritten code of conduct provides that staffers shall not abandon the congressman who brought them to Washington. A staffer may work for another politician only with the blessing of the original sponsor. Ernie asked Elizabeth directly, "What about the senator?" She responded that he thought the new job for Ernie was a great idea. For a moment Ernie felt a little disappointment, as he wondered if the senator was trying to get rid of him. But then he said, "Yes," to Elizabeth.

Ernie hung up the phone and told Ana Maria. They had lived in their new home in Lawrence for only nine months. Since he was required to report in two weeks, Ana Maria and Felipe were unable to accompany him on such short notice. They stayed behind to allow Felipe to complete his school year while Ana Maria managed the sale of their new home. Ana's preference was to remain in Lawrence, her first and only home within the United States, except for the hustle and bustle of Washington, DC. In Lawrence she had devoted her time to Felipe's care, renewed her prior KU friendships, and enjoyed Ernie's family in relatively nearby Wichita.

Neither Luisa nor Ernie's siblings were overly inquisitive about the details of his new responsibilities in DC. There were no parties in celebration or fanfare about his appointment. They just wanted Ernie to be happy and for his family to do well. While Luisa was pleased with Ernie's new position, she was more concerned about the strain on Ana Maria and Felipe.

Ernie believed that although another cross-country relocation and his absence were stressful for the family, the resulting career opportunities and benefits made the hardship reasonably acceptable.

In Washington Ernie moved into an apartment with Senator Dole's press secretary, Bill Katz, who provided Ernie with sleeping space on the floor. During his time with the senator, Ernie had reached the rank of gunnery sergeant and had received extensive infantry training in the Marine Corps Reserves. A floor to sleep on was a comfort compared to his recent field accommodations. In his new job, he was assigned an office in the old Executive Office Building on the west side of the White House. It was a beautiful office with fifteen- to twenty-foot ceilings and a fireplace. His title was special assistant to the president for public liaison, and Elizabeth Dole was his immediate supervisor. The Public Liaison Office acts as the go-between for the president and various interest groups in establishing an image of an accessible White House. Ernie's initial areas of responsibility were congressional and public affairs, but over time his primary activity became interacting with individuals and organizations attending meetings and conferences. His ability to put people at ease, along with his dapper appearance, was ideal for leaving a positive impression with visitors to the White House. The distance between Ernie's office next to the White House and his grandfather Jose's "office" in the Dust Bowl betabel was far greater than the actual miles. To most observers, the difference was, frankly, unbelievable.

In the initial weeks that followed, Ernie reveled in the excitement of his new position, but soon those private joys diminished while the logistics of getting Ana Maria and Felipe back to Washington ran their course. Ernie was unable to return to Lawrence, leaving Ana Maria with the task of listing and negotiating the sale of the home they had purchased less than a year earlier. Despite a lack of knowledge of real estate transactions or a complete command of English, she completed the sale of the house in good order. Finally, at the end of Felipe's school term, Ernie returned to Lawrence and once again drove a loaded U-Haul to Washington. This time, however, Ana Maria and Felipe were able to fly on a private plane to Washington from Wichita. Ernie waited for them at Washington National Airport. There, he met them in an emotional reunion on the tarmac.

A few months after Ernie began his duties with Elizabeth Dole, James Baker, the president's chief of staff, called Ernie and told him he was needed at the West Wing of the White House that afternoon. Baker was a retired marine colonel and shared Ernie's affection for the corps. Ernie had interacted with him on several occasions, and they got along well. Ernie dutifully responded that he was available.

Ernie went to the White House and waited outside of Baker's office. After a short time, Baker walked out of his office and said to Ernie, "C'mon, we're going to go see the boss." Ernie wondered for a second if Baker was taking him to see Elizabeth Dole. As they walked down the hall, he realized they were walking toward the president's Oval Office. They stopped at the door where Baker told Ernie, "Wait here," as he entered the office. As he stood alone outside the door as ordered, Ernie thought, *Oh my God, I might be meeting with the president!* A short while later, Baker walked out and said, "Come on in, Ernie."

When Ernie walked in, he saw President Reagan standing at his desk. With a firm marine voice Ernie said, "Good afternoon, Mr. President." He still did not know why he was meeting with the two men. "Sit down, young man," said the president. Ernie sat in a chair on the side of his desk. "I don't know if Jim told you what we're doing here, but uh . . ."

Baker interjected, "No sir, I did not tell him. I thought I'd let you."

The president said, "What I'd like to do . . . is do a public introduction in Spanish. I need your help. I need to be able to say something in Spanish."

"The president will be meeting with the president of Mexico," explained Baker.

Ernie's first thought was, *What the hell have I gotten myself into? Here's the most powerful leader in the world asking me for help!* He gathered himself and sharply responded, "Yes, sir!"

"Good. Well, work on it for me."

Ernie left the Oval Office and immediately began thinking of a suitable introduction. Although he spoke Spanish fluently, his Spanish was not perfect like Ana Maria's. Pushing his doubt aside, he concluded that perfection was not required, as the president and Baker did not know Spanish and would be unaware of minor errors. The greeting would be very short, so the likelihood of a major presidential faux pas would be small. He charged ahead with the assignment. By the end of the day, he sent to the president a draft of a brief three-sentence greeting.

The next day, Ernie returned to the Oval Office. The president greeted him, "Hey, Ernie, how are you?"

"I am doing fine, sir."

The president invited him to sit down.

In his draft, Ernie had included a phonetic version of the statement so that the president could pronounce the words correctly in Spanish. He waited with positive anticipation for the president to begin speaking. After hearing the president say the first sentence of the statement, his assessment was: *This is not good . . . at all.* But he allowed the president to proceed and complete the greeting.

When Reagan finished speaking, he said to Ernie, "Well, what do you think?" Ernie thought, *Geez, how do you tell the president, a former actor, that his performance was poor?* Ernie relied on his ability to put people at ease. So he replied, "Mr. President, with a little more practice, I think we're going to be fine." The president responded, "You'd make a good politician. I didn't do very well, did I?"

He tried to soften the landing for the president. "Well, sir, with a little more practice . . ." Before Ernie could finish, the president looked at Baker and said, "I don't think this is going to work." Taking note of Ernie's concern, he asked, "Why not just a one-liner?"

Ernie jumped at the solution to the dilemma. He wanted to allow the president to save face, so he responded, "Mr. President, we can do whatever you want." He revised the greeting to "Buenas tardes, y bienvenidos."

Sometime later at a luncheon in California, President Reagan toasted President-Elect Miguel de la Madrid of Mexico. He began the toast with the words, "Buenas tardes, and welcome."

Ernie's assessment? That was close enough, Mr. President.

Six months after Ernie began working in the old Executive Office Building, his secretary advised him that Senator Dole's secretary was calling. His first thought was, *This call cannot be good.* When he took the call, the senator was on the line and asked him, "How are you? Tired of that place over there yet?" Ernie, glancing around at his beautiful office, thought, *Oh shit, this is not good.* But he responded, "No, Senator, I'm fine." Senator Dole then replied, "Ernie, I think there is something else for you."

He waited for the shoe to drop.

"There is a spot over at the Pentagon where I think you would do really well." The senator did not immediately specify the nature of the "spot." He then gave Ernie the names of contact persons for the unidentified job.

Ernie was slightly disappointed; in his mind a change from the White House to the Pentagon was a step down. But he called the Pentagon as the senator directed. He spoke with Marybel Batjer, an assistant to the secretary of defense. She advised him that he was being considered for the position of deputy assistant secretary of defense. The secretary of defense divides the different responsibilities of the office among assistants, and each assistant has several deputy assistants who work to complete the assistant's duties. In this position, Ernie's primary responsibility would be to analyze every piece of proposed legislation in the Senate involving the Department of Defense. He would then prepare a report and summary that would be available for review or reference by Defense Department staff or the secretary himself. Batjer told Ernie that the secretary of defense had reviewed his résumé and that Senator Dole had highly recommended him.

Ernie felt he had no option. A staffer does what his senator wants him to do. A refusal would likely torpedo future advancements, so he accepted. Batjer told him that in a couple of days someone would be at his office with the paperwork to complete the change. Two days later, a Department of Defense representative arrived at Ernie's office with papers. The representative told Ernie that upon his signature, he was to report to the Pentagon the following day.

Early the next morning, Ernie began to gather his personal items and leave his beautiful office. As he did so, his White House secretary entered and said, "Mr. Garcia, someone is here from the Pentagon for you." He responded, "Show them in, please." A black gentleman entered and introduced himself. He told Ernie that he had come to help him pack and then drive him to the Pentagon. Ernie was grateful for the help and said to the gentleman, "Thanks, that would be great. What did you say your name was?" The gentleman answered, "That's okay, Mr. Garcia. I'm really referred to as Cool Breeze." Ernie thought, *Okay, this might be good.*

When the two of them had loaded Ernie's belongings into a Lincoln Continental, Cool Breeze asked, "You ready to go?" Ernie answered, "Yeah. I'm ready," and walked around to the front passenger door. Cool Breeze said, "No, sir. You sit in the back, on the right side."

Ernie objected, "Nah, nah, that's senator stuff. That's not me." Cool Breeze explained, "Well, I'm going to get my ass in trouble if you don't get in the back seat."

"You're kidding me!" Ernie said in disbelief.

"No, I'm serious."

Finally convinced of Cool Breeze's duties, Ernie complied.

Cool Breeze drove Ernie over to the Pentagon, directly to the front entrance, and said, "I'll bring all the stuff in. There is somebody here who will take you to your office." Ernie did as Cool Breeze directed. He met an aide who was waiting to show him to his new office. As he followed, he looked around and noted the unending hallways and many men and women smartly dressed in uniforms. Civilians and military personnel scurried through the maze of office doors. Ernie thought, *I miss the White House already.*

Led by the aide, he passed through a number of corridors before arriving at his new office. The aide escorted Ernie into his office. It was just as big as his office in the Executive Office Building and had a conference table and a large desk. The office was located near the office of the secretary of Defense, Casper Weinberger. Ernie reconsidered his initial displeasure at his new surroundings. *This ain't all that bad. Not bad at all.*

At first glance, Ernie's new job description suggested a position with sleep-inducing analysis of hundreds and hundreds of pages of proposed laws and budgets. Despite the less-than-invigorating content, he was able to complete the written analysis as required. In so doing, he made personal contact with many senators, interacted with many of their staffers, and became part of a network of staffers and agency officials at the Pentagon and at the Capitol. People in the network relied on one another for the information and assistance to complete their duties. Ernie's ability to smoothly navigate the Senate network would pave the way for future opportunities.

While working for Senator Dole and the White House, both Ernie and Wohlford wanted to stop or minimize Ernie's active duty with the Marine Corps Reserves. But his Pentagon supervisor found that Ernie could be called to active duty and special assignments despite his position as a deputy assistant. Ernie was in a position to complete his Pentagon duties with the insight and access of an active marine rather than of a civilian outsider. This dual capacity was an advantage unavailable to most Pentagon officials. His firm grasp of military lexicon and nomenclature kept him from being overcome in military briefings, and he could also avoid being excluded from discussions of policy and strategy, whereas a civilian, knowingly or unknowingly, might receive filtered information. On many occasions, Ernie left DC on assignment in a suit and tie as a civil deputy assistant, but on arrival he was the equivalent of a three-star general. At times, the reversal of roles was a little awkward as marine officers saluted him. But his ability to change roles became Ernie's passage to every continent and dozens and dozens of countries across the planet.

In 1983 the Pentagon sent Ernie to meet with officials of a Cambodian refugee camp. When his official duties ended, he walked through the camp to see the people without the presence of those in charge. He found the camp, like most other refugee camps, crowded, with poor sanitation, and the people suffering. The refugees were mostly Cambodians caught in the battles between former communist allies Vietnam and the Khmer Rouge in Cambodia. But there was a large group of Vietnamese refugees in the camp as well.

A Vietnamese woman approached Ernie. Alongside her was a girl about eight or nine years of age. To Ernie's eyes the child was clearly Asian American in appearance. The woman asked Ernie, "You 'merican?" Ernie nodded, and said, "Yes." The woman pointed to the girl and said, "Daddy 'merican. You help?"

"I will try. Okay?"

The woman nodded her head. Ernie took her name and other personal information and gave her his Department of Defense business card. He pointed to the card, then himself, and said, "My name. My address." She took it from him, looked at it, and replied, "Okay. You try."

Before Ernie left the camp, he spoke to camp officials about the mother and her child. He asked to verify that the woman and her child were properly registered with the camp. They were. On his return to Washington, he contacted a woman at the State Department about the woman and her child and asked if the woman's case could be evaluated. He never received a response from the State Department.

Two years later, Ernie received in his mail what appeared to be a large greeting card. He had no idea who might be sending it. He opened the envelope and found an elaborate Christmas card. Included was a note of thanks and appreciation. The card was from the woman he had encountered at the refugee camp. She wanted Ernie to know that she and her daughter had been allowed into the United States. More Christmas cards found their way to him in the years to come. The woman sent another card when her daughter finished high school, and then another when she graduated from college. The intricate cards and notes of thanks slowed to a stop after the daughter married.

Ernie never had the opportunity to again meet the woman and her daughter. He was content simply knowing he was part of the effort that improved the lives of two people left in the wake of war. The woman and her child shared a common journey with Ernie's ancestors. Like Pedro and Jose, they had escaped the hell of war for a secure life without want.

In January 1982 Ernie traveled to Italy at the invitation of the chairman of the House Judiciary Committee, Peter Rodino. Representative Rodino and a CODEL consisting mostly of members of Congress of Italian descent were to meet with Pope John Paul II. At the meeting, Ernie, along with ten to fifteen others, sat in the pope's office anxiously awaiting the entry of His Holiness. All stood when Pope John Paul entered. Ernie was able to maneuver to a position near Rodino and the pope where he could hear them converse in Italian. Shortly after the pope's entrance, Ernie and the other members of the delegation were individually introduced to him. Pope John Paul was a little surprised that most of the Italian delegation did not speak Italian but graciously accommodated them by addressing them in English.

Throughout his high school and college experiences, Ernie's Catholic faith had remained strong. An opportunity to see the pope in person was a highlight in a Roman Catholic's life. To actually be in the immediate presence of the pope was as close to God as a man of Catholic faith could be. Ernie considered his papal visit a blessing, and it reaffirmed his faith.

As Ernie traveled from country to country, he was in the company of other marines and military personnel. One of those fellow travelers was General Paul X. Kelley, commandant of the Marine Corps. Ernie easily made conversation with the general, who was of Irish descent. Over the many trips, Ernie learned that they shared a strong Catholic faith and a love of the corps. On a trip to Europe, General Kelley asked Ernie what he intended to do about his future in the corps. He responded that there was one thing he had not accomplished, and that was to become a Marine Corps officer.

Ernie was initially content as an enlisted marine executing orders from his superiors. But with more experience in the corps, he believed he had the knowledge and skills to sit at the decision-making table, generate the orders, and oversee the proper execution of those orders. He had developed the ambition to lead men, including leading them onto the battlefield if called upon to do so. The general asked Ernie his age. When he replied that he was thirty-five, the general said he would have someone talk to him.

A few days after returning from Europe, Major Robert Magnus, who would later become a four-star general and serve as assistant commandant of the US Marine Corps, visited Ernie at his Pentagon office and brought with him the required paperwork for a commissioned officer. Ernie completed and signed the paperwork then and there. Two weeks later, a general swore Ernie in with the rank of second lieutenant—the lowest officer rank in the Marine Corps. With the recommendation and approval of General Kelley, Ernie later reported to Officer Candidate School at Quantico, Virginia, as do most marines who become commissioned officers. Due to his responsibilities as a deputy assistant to the secretary of defense, he completed Officer Candidate School in phases.

It was not uncommon to rise to the rank of first lieutenant within a year of becoming a second lieutenant, and Ernie did so. With this relatively quick advancement, he set his sights on becoming a captain. He began to complete courses and activities that put him in the pool from which captains were selected. High scores in his coursework made him eligible for selection.

In mid-1982 Ernie was in his Pentagon office when his secretary entered with a message. "Congratulations, Mr. Garcia."

Ernie was surprised. "For what?"

"You are a captain in the United States Marines."

Ernie thought, *This cannot be–a dream come true!* He was pleased that his efforts were rewarded and had kept his career on an upward trajectory. But it was not a matter of simply accumulating high-ranking officer insignia. More importantly, the corps had demonstrated confidence in his leadership abilities by placing in his hands the well-being of other marines. Captains are regarded as the officers with the primary responsibility for the care and training of the marines under their command. They instill in their troops the values of service with honor, courage, and commitment. The training included preparedness for battle so that they survive combat. Ernie's promotion to captain left him with an even greater sense of duty to the safety of the men under his command and a determination to meet his new responsibilities.

In March 1983, Ernie traveled to Hong Kong with a CODEL sponsored by Congressman Charles Rangel, the chairman of the Select Committee of Narcotics and Abuse Control. His CODEL was a fact-finding mission on drug trafficking and interdiction in Southeast Asia. The CODEL met with Hong Kong officials and US embassy personnel. The local officials briefed the delegation on the actions taken to address the trafficking of narcotics.

Ernie accompanied the CODEL as the Department of Defense legislative affairs representative. Particularly after the Vietnam War, the military recognized the importance of "winning the hearts and minds" of the local military and civilians in the areas of US military operations and interests. Ernie acted as a liaison and helped open the lines of communication and cooperation with the host country. Once again, his ability to engage people and set them at ease served him well.

After the briefings in Hong Kong were concluded, members of the CODEL toured a number of historical sites. The highlights included a visit to the Great Wall of China. The enormity of the Great Wall, its structure and branches extending well over ten thousand miles and built over centuries, was difficult for Ernie to imagine. It was also difficult to imagine the son of Mexican farm workers from Santa Fe Street in Garden City walking on the Great Wall, one of the wonders of the world.

The following month, Ernie traveled to Peru with another CODEL sponsored by Congressman Rangel and addressing drug trafficking. The focus this time was on Peru and its neighboring countries, particularly Bolivia. Ernie's ability to speak Spanish was particularly helpful in meeting with the local government officials. After meeting with community leaders, Ernie traveled to the Inca ruins of Machu Picchu. His hike to the site, nearly eight thousand feet above sea level, left him breathless, as did its setting high in the Andes. The views were unlike anything he had ever encountered. He tried to imagine the physical effort required at that high altitude to construct the complex of stone walls and terraces. He left inspired by its beauty and by the native people who built it.

The events of 1983 that sent Ernie abroad continued to the end of the year. On October 25, 1983, US military forces led the invasion of the Caribbean island nation of Grenada. Within two months, all resistance to US invading forces was subdued. The American military ousted Grenada's military head of state, General Hudson Austin, and replaced him with a temporary leader until elections were held. At year's end, Ernie participated in a fact-finding mission sent to assess the progress of the military and civil authority after the temporary government was installed on the island.

In 1984 Ernie returned to Europe, again in the company of Representative Rodino on a CODEL to the Vatican. This time Ana Maria traveled with him. As he had previously, Ernie stood next to Rodino as the delegation waited for Pope John Paul II to make his entrance. Everyone stood when the pope entered, and he again greeted Rodino in Italian. Ernie was ready for John Paul's individual greeting with each member of the delegation. When the pope reached out to greet him, the pope spoke in Italian. Ernie responded with the few words in Italian he knew. John Paul looked at his visitor's name tag and asked Ernie if he spoke Spanish. He answered in Spanish that he did. They proceeded to converse in Spanish for a few minutes and delay the introduction of the others waiting in line. Rodino was pleased that Ernie was able to carry on a conversation with the pope in a language other than English. Later, other members of the delegation, surprised at their conversation, asked Ernie, "What was that all about?"

A photograph was taken of the delegation with John Paul. Ernie and Ana Maria stood behind the pope on either side. While waiting for the picture to be taken, Ernie felt a swell of emotion. He was overwhelmed with the thought that he could be so fortunate as to be so close to the pope for a second time. As they waited for the photographer to align the delegation members, Ernie felt compelled to slowly reach out and gently touch John Paul's cassock. Perhaps Ernie subconsciously recalled from a religion class at Saint Mary's the story of an ill woman touching the robe of Jesus in order to heal. Or perhaps it was instinctive, as some have suggested that touching is the essence of humanity. In any event, it was an act of faith for the former seminarian.

John Paul ended the gathering with his personal blessing of all in attendance. Ernie would see the pope a third and fourth time but only from a distance, once in Italy and once in the United States.

Not all of Ernie's assignments and missions were filled with incredible vistas and pleasantries. When he traveled for the Department of Defense to foreign countries engaged in armed conflict, whether as a civilian or military representative, the department provided an armed security detail. When he traveled on invitation of a CODEL as a defense expert, the security was the responsibility of the CODEL sponsor, particularly when traveling to El Salvador, Honduras, Nicaragua, Colombia, and Afghanistan. Whether traveling by Pentagon directive or CODEL invitation, Ernie and his fellow travelers usually hitched a ride on the first available military aircraft. Travel by commercial air transport was infrequent.

The assignment to Afghanistan was particularly difficult. Ernie's three-week stay was under high security. He and other Pentagon officials were sent to meet with members of the Mujahideen, the local Islamist insurgent militias fighting the Soviet Union. They were taken by helicopter to the meeting place in the mountains at Khyber Pass. Ernie's anxiety level rose considerably when he saw the helicopter that would transport him and his party. The helicopter was Russian made and had been captured by the Mujahideen. His worry was straightforward: *These guys are fighting Russians, and we are arriving in a Russian helicopter.* He received no assurances that the locals were able to distinguish his helicopter as a friendly. When the helicopter landed, Ernie saw no one. But as soon as the rotor blades stopped, numerous Mujahideen appeared from behind the mountainside rocks and brush.

As the meeting began, the Mujahideen offered their guests an assortment of indescribable food on a long table. Ernie dutifully nibbled at the food. Before the meeting, he had been advised that if offered food and drink, he should accept. He declined water but did accept an Orange Crush in a glass bottle that appeared to have been used more than once. He took some comfort from the bottle's being capped. Although it was a positive meeting, Ernie and his companions departed as quickly and gracefully as possible. His group had no planned sightseeing excursions after the business of this fact-finding mission.

While travel was a significant part of Ernie's duties, he had many domestic responsibilities at the Pentagon as well. He appeared before several Senate and House committees as a witness or in support of other witnesses on a variety of issues. He also met with guests, dignitaries, and supporters of Senator Dole. When Ernie's family and friends from Kansas traveled to DC, he welcomed them and took them on mini-tours of the Pentagon.

One of the Garden City visitors was Earl C. Brookover. He owned a successful cattle feedlot operation and was a man of influence in the community. Ernie and his siblings had met members of the Brookover family through Aunt Kay, who worked as a nanny and housekeeper for the Brookovers for forty-one years. On one of Brookover's trips to DC, in 1984, Ernie led him on a quick tour of Secretary Weinberger's office and gave him a set of Department of Defense cufflinks as a token, for which Brookover was quite appreciative.

Later that year in the summer, Garden City High School's class of 1964 held its twentieth reunion. Ernie and Sharon Lee had not spoken to one another since they parted at KU in 1967. Independently, they both planned to attend, and each hoped they would have the chance to speak with one another. They arrived in Garden City not knowing if the other would be present. At the early reception, they found each other and politely embraced. Very quickly they were in easy conversation as they had been in the past. They updated each other on their families. Sharon Lee knew Ernie was working in DC but few other details. She was married but had filed for divorce and was now living in California with her daughter and son. She had become a teacher after earning a master's degree at Kansas State University. During the class reunion they gathered with their high school friends, enjoying the time with those they were close to. By the reunion's end, Ernie and Sharon Lee agreed to stay in contact.

A few months later, in November, congressional and presidential elections were held. The Republican Party retained control of the Senate and elected Senator Dole as its majority leader. Those election results opened the door to an opportunity that would take Ernie out of the Pentagon.

10

Sergeant in Peace, Captain in War

1985–2000

On a late afternoon in March 1985, Senator Dole's senior assistant called Ernie at his Pentagon office. She informed him that the senator wanted to speak with him in person. Once again the senator's call led Ernie to think, *Oh boy, what have I done now?* He sensed that his life was about to change. The only question was whether the change would be good or bad.

As the new Senate majority leader, the senator had the privilege of nominating his candidates to several offices in the Senate. At their meeting that evening, the senator offered Ernie the position of sergeant at arms for the Senate, the chief law enforcement officer of the Senate chamber. Senator Dole told Ernie that he wanted him to first serve as the deputy sergeant at arms until the sitting sergeant was able to vacate his position. The senator further explained that if Ernie served as the deputy, he would be in a better position to make the transition to sergeant at arms.

Ernie was again taken by surprise by the senator's offer. He thought, *You're kidding! This can't be true!* He simply had no innate sense nor engrained notion that promotions in his military or government service were to be expected or available as a matter of course. Ernie always appreciated the chance to rise in the ranks and advance his careers, but he viewed new opportunities as the result of both effort and good fortune. He never felt he was entitled to advancement, nor did he feel that any promotions he received were past due. He always expressed gratitude to those who provided the opportunities. He immediately accepted the senator's offer and thanked him.

After four years as a legislative aide and four more monitoring Senate legislation for the Pentagon, Ernie was confident he would be able to effectively manage the legislative operations of the Senate. He was on a first-name basis with many staffers and senators, and he knew the names of the maintenance crews, secretaries, shop clerks, security officers, and members of the press as well. His challenges as the deputy were the budgetary and bureaucratic details of the office.

On May 16 Senator Dole entered into the congressional record a resolution to elect Ernie as the Senate deputy sergeant at arms. The senator supported the resolution by noting Ernie's "enviable record of public service." He described Ernie's dedication, patriotism, loyalty, and integrity as of the "highest caliber." He added that Ernie was "worthy of the responsibility this body would entrust to him." Ernie felt a great sense of satisfaction and worth with Senator Dole's comments. He knew the senator was cautious and slow to personally compliment, so he was especially appreciative that the senator did so in such a public forum.

His nomination to serve as sergeant at arms required confirmation by the full Senate. After a few weeks as the deputy, his nomination was set for a vote on June 3. Ernie's Senate floor privileges ensured that he would be present for the discussion and vote. He took a position at the back of the Senate chamber to observe the proceedings—the same area where he had dropped Senator Dole's papers years before.

Senator Dole began by calling for Ernie's nomination to be brought before the Senate. Ernie was certain his nomination would be approved, but he was concerned there might be objections. Strom Thurmond, the presiding officer of the Senate, asked if any senator wanted to speak on the nomination. After several senators made supportive comments, he then called for a vote. Ernie's concerns were unfounded: the vote was unanimous. With the Senate's vote, he became the thirty-ninth US Senate sergeant at arms and the first Hispanic American to serve in the position.

Moments after the vote, several senators, Republicans and Democrats alike, spoke to Ernie and congratulated him. One in particular, Senator J. James Exon, a Democrat from Nebraska, approached Ernie. He put his hand on Ernie's shoulder and in a hushed voice said, "How did you ever become a Republican? I thought we had all of you folks in our party." In the moment, Ernie did not give much thought to Senator Exon's comment. But when the excitement of the moment subsided, he considered Senator Exon's words and thought they reflected a mistaken assumption about Hispanic voters. Ernie believed that politicians and political parties that accepted Exon's assumptions did so at their own risk.

Ernie promptly began the search for a deputy sergeant at arms. After several interviews, he recommended to Senator Dole the individual he believed brought the best skills and motivation to the position: Trudi Morrison. She was an attorney and graduate of George Washington University Law School in DC. On June 13, 1985, the Senate approved her nomination. The Denver native was the first African American to serve as deputy sergeant at arms.

Ernie's advancement to sergeant at arms followed a group of individuals of Mexican heritage who had taken leadership roles in high visibility arenas in American culture. In sports, quarterback Jim Plunkett and Coach Tom Flores led the Oakland/Los Angeles Raiders to Super Bowl victories in 1981 and 1984. In 1980 Ben Fernandez entered the race for the Republican nomination for president. Fernandez shared a similar upbringing with Ernie's father, born in Kansas to a railroad family that also worked in the sugar beet fields. The Mexican or Spanish heritage of these individuals was neither kept secret nor highly promoted. But the public, particularly a young generation of Mexican Americans, saw through them that participation and leadership were within reach.

The *Garden City Telegram* and other newspapers and magazines within the state recognized Ernie's success. With the public recognition, he welcomed the opportunity to become a role model not only for young Mexican Americans, but also for all young people in southwest Kansas. Within days of becoming sergeant at arms, Ernie was inducted into the Garden City High School Hall of Fame. He was also invited to give the keynote address at the high school's commencement. Working with top government officials and receiving such recognition from home, Ernie was feeling a little heady. But there were some who, out of ignorance or contempt, put Ernie's feet back on the ground.

Tom Saffell, Ernie's high school principal and later the school's superintendent, introduced Ernie as the keynote speaker. In his opening comments, the superintendent made little attempt to recognize Ernie's successes and accomplishments, nor did he suggest to the graduating seniors that Ernie's efforts and work were models to follow. Instead, he took a personal jab at Ernie. Drawing attention to the weight Ernie had gained since high school, he commented to the students and guests that Ernie must be enjoying the cuisine at many of the good restaurants in Washington. Ernie did not understand the purpose of his comments. Surely, the superintendent knew the role of a keynote speaker. Perhaps he did not want to be bothered to find the words for a suitable introduction or maybe he remained irritated with Ernie's high school romance or academic performance. In any event, the superintendent's comments were so out of place that a Pentagon employee who had accompanied Ernie commented to him about the slight.

In response, Ernie addressed the Garden City High School class of 1985 and made every effort to inspire and encourage each student in the class. He wanted to take advantage of the opportunity to stand before them so they could see and hear someone who had once stood in their place and had since experienced a level of success.

As to Saffell's comments, Ernie relied on the counsel Evelyn Bowling had given him a decade prior: if someone had a problem with him, it was theirs to fix.

In his position as sergeant at arms, Ernie was responsible for more than 1,600 employees and an annual budget of more than $175 million. His primary responsibility was the safety and security of the senators. Other duties included providing security for the general public and high-profile individuals. More recent examples are Pope Francis and Prime Minister Benjamin Netanyahu of Israel, both of whom addressed Congress in 2015. As protocol officer, Ernie's ceremonial duties included escorting the president for the State of the Union address and greeting important dignitaries and high government officials such as the vice president, ambassadors, and foreign heads of state. Ernie met these individuals at the steps at the outside entrance to the Senate chamber. From there he would escort them to the appropriate senator's office, hearing room, or legislative chamber and accompany them when they departed.

The receptions and departures from the Senate were not always joyous events. Removal of high government officials begins with the House of Representatives sending articles of impeachment to the Senate for trial on the charges. Impeachment and Senate trials are extremely rare. Senate procedures provide that the sergeant at arms officially accept the articles and announce their arrival. On August 6, 1986, Ernie called from the Senate floor: "Hear ye! Hear ye! Hear ye! All persons are commanded to keep silent, on pain of imprisonment, while the House of Representatives is exhibiting to the Senate of the United States Articles of Impeachment against Harry E. Claiborne, US District Judge for the District of Nevada." It had been fifty years since the last pronouncement from the Senate floor by someone other than a US senator. Very few of Ernie's predecessors had the opportunity to do so. Judge Claiborne, despite a personal appearance during the Senate trial, was ultimately impeached. After the Senate ordered his removal, Ernie and federal marshals unceremoniously escorted Claiborne out of the Senate chamber and Capitol building.

One of the more difficult aspects of the duties of the sergeant at arms was accommodating the politics and personalities of the senators and the vice president of the United States. Officially, the vice president presides over the Senate. As the Senate president, the vice president traditionally goes to the Senate floor only if needed to cast a vote or to perform a ceremonial function. On those few occasions when the vice president is at the Senate, much of his time is spent in the office maintained for his use by the Senate. During Ernie's time as sergeant at arms, George H. W. Bush was vice president. As might be expected, during the waiting, Ernie and Vice President Bush spent considerable time talking in the vice president's Senate office. Ernie found Vice President Bush to be cordial and genuine, frequently asking about Ernie's family.

Bush was well aware when he became vice president that Ernie was one of Senator Dole's men. The senator and the vice president were political rivals, particularly after President Nixon's administration in 1972 installed Bush as chairman of the Republican Party, replacing Senator Dole. The change stung the senator, who had strongly supported Nixon during his difficulties in the White House. Rather than create more friction between the two men, the vice president told Ernie that he need not be seen in the Capitol building constantly doting on and pampering him. Ernie appreciated the vice president's concern and responded with a "Certainly, Mr. Vice President." Nonetheless, Ernie continued to carry out his duties and tend to the vice president's needs and comfort, albeit in a tempered fashion when in view of the public.

Not all of Ernie's visitors at the Capitol building were powerful government officials. His son, Felipe, now eleven years old, made his way from their nearby home to visit his father at work from time to time, just as Ernie had stopped to see his father at the jeweler's. Felipe was welcomed into the Capitol building by security guards with the mere showing of Ernie's business card. When Felipe was a small child, Ernie on occasion took him to Senator Dole's offices, where he played with the cache of toy trucks and tractors the senator kept in a closet. Over the years the senator had accumulated these tokens of appreciation from constituents and lobbyists.

At this time, Felipe was like many American children in that both of his parents worked to provide for their family and pursue their careers. In his middle school and high school years, Felipe went home after school and remained alone until Ernie or Ana Maria arrived. Felipe—called Phillip by his English-speaking classmates—had everything he needed at home except for the supervision and parental push to complete all of his homework on school nights. Felipe did enjoy some success in middle school and high school, serving as president of his sophomore class. But his overall academic performance suffered to some degree in the absence of supervision. At the same time, he did learn firsthand from his parents the value of hard work, long hours, and a determination to succeed.

When he was thirteen years old, Felipe served as a Senate page. The primary responsibility of the pages was delivering messages and materials to legislators and their staff. Their work may have been regarded as a convenience by some, but for the pages, it was an opportunity to see the people and places of government. The hope of the program was to inspire young minds as they observed the legislative process in Congress. The program allowed Felipe to walk among lawmakers who seemed to be gods or giants. But soon he saw the legislators as people, some with faults and quirks and a few adept at being rude and dismissive.

Although most Senate pages were in high school, Felipe, still in middle school, was able to perform his duties and find a place among his fellow pages. During his time as a page, he had complete access to the Capitol building. Later in life, Felipe had a better appreciation of his experiences in the Capitol, especially his father's role in the events taking place at the time. He has vivid memories of being with Ana Maria in the audience when Ernie escorted President Reagan to deliver his State of the Union address.

Ernie asked Senator Dole, members of Congress, and Capitol officials to sponsor many other Senate pages. He recommended students from across the state of Kansas, including students of Mexican heritage from Garden

City and Wichita. His recommendations included a student from California named Angela. She was Sharon Lee's daughter. Angela, at age fourteen, already had an interest in leadership at her school and had begun to imagine attending college and living away from home. She thought that the Senate page program would be a taste of independence. With a little hesitancy, Sharon Lee approved her participation.

When Angela stood on the Senate floor, she found it breathtaking and pictured herself working in that environment. The experience opened her mind to a world of possibilities for herself and started her on the journey to finding the career she would eventually choose. As a result of her time in Washington, Angela later enrolled at Trinity College, a Catholic women's college in DC, with the intention of earning a political science degree. She soon realized that she was too introverted for a political career, however, and in her sophomore year she studied English literature at Oxford in England as an exchange student. She found literature much more enjoyable and compatible with her interests. On her return to the United States, she graduated from UCLA and earned a master's in education from Claremont College. She chose to teach because she preferred a career that left her with a sense of giving rather than taking. Since 1993 she has taught English literature at a high school in California. There was some irony in the role the Cobb and Garcia families played in each other's pursuit of a college education and career.

All who serve as political appointees in DC understand that their future employment is at the mercy of elections. So it was with Ernie. The 1986 Senate elections gave the Democratic Party a majority and control of the Senate. The 100th Congress was sworn in on January 3, 1987. Two days later Ernie's term as sergeant at arms ended. Unable to find a suitable position in the Reagan administration after leaving the sergeant at arms position, he turned to the private sector and was hired as a vice president of Source One Management, Inc., which provided management and consulting services to government agencies and private clientele. Its home office was in Denver.

Ernie's role at Source One was consulting. His experience with Senator Dole and the Pentagon gave him firsthand knowledge of budgets and operating practices of federal agencies. As a liaison between private clientele and federal government administrators, Ernie frequently traveled to DC and other locations. His new employment did not include frequent interaction with high-ranking government officials, but that was not an issue for Ernie. His primary focus was the work and providing for Ana Maria and Felipe.

Ernie's new employer accommodated his pursuit of marine training and calls to active duty. Ernie spent his newly available spare time on maintaining physical readiness for his Marine Corps duties. He ran for longer and longer distances, including runs along the Rock Creek Parkway in DC and at Marine Corps Base Quantico in Virginia. In 1987 he ran the first of the seven marathons he would run competitively in the next ten years.

That year a reporter from the *Wichita Eagle* called Ernie. He indicated that he understood Ernie wanted to run for the House of Representatives seat currently held by Democrat Dan Glickman of Wichita. Ernie responded that he had given some consideration to the possibility but had not made a decision. Ernie had applied for a position as an aide for Glickman when Ernie was at KU, but he was rejected. Coincidentally, Glickman hired Ernie's cousin Patrick Garcia—whose father was Jesus, Rosa and Jose's second son—as a legislative aide in Wichita.

Ernie had, in fact, seriously considered the possibility of a run for Congress before becoming sergeant at arms. He spoke with Earl Brookover, Aunt Kay's employer, about the possibility. Ernie considered Brookover a friend and in some respects a mentor. Acknowledging Ernie's experience, character and military service, Brookover told him he had the potential to be a great candidate. But he also noted harsh realities. He identified two major problems with Ernie's potential candidacy: He believed that first, given western and central Kansas history, voters would not support a nonwhite candidate for national office; second, a great deal of money would be necessary to unseat Glickman. He emphasized that Ernie lacked a strong campaign fundraising organization. Ernie was disappointed that his prospects for a successful political run were poor, but he appreciated Brookover's blunt assessment of his likelihood of success. Brookover assured Ernie that if he ran for office, he would support Ernie politically and financially. A short time after Ernie became Senate sergeant at arms, Brookover passed away, and Ernie lost a confidant.

With a political career unlikely, Ernie continued at Source One for three years and remained largely out of government service in the DC arena. He spent a considerable amount of time in Denver and traveling to and from

Washington. During his time with Source One he was regularly called into active duty with the marines.

Ernie's absences from DC and the stress of pursuing careers had begun to take a toll on Ana Maria and Ernie's marriage. At the time Ana Maria was pursuing a successful career at the United States Department of Education, Bilingual Education Division, where she eventually became a senior federal employee. Unfortunately, their marriage did not survive the grueling environment of their career pursuits in Washington. In 1988 Ernie and Ana Maria agreed to separate. Though separated, they worked together to ensure that they continued to be loving and supporting parents for Felipe.

On August 2, 1990, Saddam Hussein, Iraq's dictator president, invaded Kuwait. The invasion was Hussein's ultimate rejection of US efforts to improve ties to Iraq. The following November Ernie's marine unit was called into active service for Operation Desert Shield, the US-led buildup of men and materials from various nations in preparation for a counterassault against the invading Iraqi forces in Kuwait and the Persian Gulf region. Armored vehicles, artillery pieces, and munitions were brought in by sea and air transport in support of the ground assault, codenamed Operation Desert Storm.

Ernie took a leave of absence from Source One to join his unit, the Fourth Civil Affairs Group out of Washington, DC. They trained at Camp Lejeune, North Carolina, before deploying to Saudi Arabia in January 1991. There they joined the First Marine Division as a part of Desert Storm. Their mission was to support the ground forces that would invade and liberate Kuwait. They were positioned near the southern Saudi-Kuwaiti border, approximately eighty miles south of the capital, Kuwait City, on the Persian Gulf coast.

An invading force waiting for the order to advance can easily become restless or bored. Ernie's challenge was to keep his unit at a high state of readiness. Not only did his unit constantly perform physical training, they continuously received instruction on the rules of engagement, the culture of the Saudis and Kuwaitis, and their standards of conduct. During the lull before the impending battle, Ernie moved about the encampment, particularly among lower-ranked marines, talking to as many as possible. As he did so, he became acutely aware that many under his command were young and inexperienced. Some were visibly nervous about what lay ahead. He turned his focus to the mental preparedness of these marines, reminding them that they were professional soldiers and that they were expected to carry out their mission as ordered. He resisted the temptation to become friends with his young marines, instead reinforcing the relationship of commanding officer and soldier. He fully understood that in the near future he might be required to order the men into battle.

On January 17, 1991, coalition forces began Operation Desert Storm with an air campaign against targets in Iraq and Kuwait. Ernie believed the coalition ground assault would begin soon after the air assault had weakened the Iraqi positions and targets. For five weeks, coalition air forces pounded Iraqi installations, infrastructure, and military assets. Finally, Ernie's unit received word on February 23 that they would be moving north into Kuwait the following morning. The day for the ground assault had arrived.

That night, Ernie and approximately two hundred other marines prepared to advance. As Ernie's unit was set to begin their advance, a gunshot was heard near their barracks. Ernie assumed the compound perimeter had been breached. He and several others rushed toward the sound of the gunshot. But when they arrived they found a group gathered around a marine lying on the ground. A young African American marine had put his rifle barrel into his mouth and pulled the trigger. Ernie knelt at his side. The marine was still breathing despite his horrific head wound. Ernie could only offer a prayer as the young man quickly died. Though the marine's death was tragic and gruesome, Ernie maintained his composure. His training guided his reaction and emotions.

Most marines strove to be committed to God, country, and courage, but some were unable to fit themselves into that mold. This young marine could not; he was overwhelmed by fear. Ernie later learned that the marine was twenty years old and did not want to die on the battlefield. He feared being gassed and believed he would suffer a terrible death, so he killed himself instead. Ernie was more troubled by the suicide long afterward than he was at the time it actually occurred. It became a lasting and haunting memory and remained the subject of occasional nightmares. Seeing young men suffer severe wounds and die during his several deployments accumulated over time and eventually tore at Ernie's soul.

The next morning coalition tanks and armored forces crossed into Iraq from their positions along the southern and western borders. The tanks overcame light resistance as they drove northward as far as one hundred miles. The tanks then made a right turn and headed east toward the Persian Gulf. Their objective was to reach Highway 8, the road connecting Kuwait City and Baghdad. If the tanks reached the highway while Hussein's army was still operating in Kuwait City, they would cut off the Iraqi army's escape route to Baghdad.

As the tanks maneuvered in the western desert, Ernie's First Marine Division began its drive northward toward Kuwait City. The goal of the infantry was to close the trap on Hussein's army between the coalition tanks to the north and their ground forces to the south. When Ernie's convoy vehicle began to move northward, he touched the Virgen de San Juan medallion that Luisa had given him. He said a prayer and asked for God's protection as he went into battle.

On February 26, Iraqi forces, including the elite Iraqi Republican Guard, began to withdraw from Kuwait City. The retreating forces included tanks, armored vehicles, trucks, and hundreds of cars. Iraqi soldiers stole many Kuwaiti-owned vehicles and filled them with loot from Kuwait City. In a convoy three miles long, the vehicles traveled north on the six-lane Highway 8 to the Iraqi city of Basra. The number of vehicles is disputed, but estimates are generally around 2,200, give or take three or four hundred vehicles.

By nightfall, the Iraqi convoy had passed through the city of Al Jahra, approximately twenty miles to the west of Kuwait City. Coalition tanks had not yet reached Highway 8 to cut off the retreat, so coalition air strikes were ordered. The Iraqi convoy was traveling with headlights on, thereby disclosing its position to the attacking planes.

The initial air strikes were aimed at the lead vehicles in the convoy. The strikes were accurate, completely destroying the lead vehicles. The burned-out vehicles blocked the highway, and those that tried to drive around the wreckage became stalled in the desert sand. Simultaneously, attacking aircraft destroyed the tail of the convoy, and those damaged vehicles further blocked the roadway.

The Iraqi Republican Guard and any civilians supporting them or the convoy were boxed in. Coalition forces had complete air superiority, as the Iraqis within the road block had no weapons to effectively counter the airstrikes. The Iraqi men on the ground were in panic and terror. Many of them abandoned their vehicles where they stopped and ran for safety in the desert. Those that remained with their vehicles attempted to find cover under or around them. The airstrikes continued throughout the night and for most of the next day.

To the south, Ernie's marine division was making its way to Kuwait City. On reaching the city, Ernie saw the destruction the Iraqis had left behind. Bodies were lying in the streets, buildings and homes were burning, businesses were looted, vehicles were vandalized and abandoned. The marines left Kuwait City and pursued the retreating Iraqi forces on Highway 8.

When Ernie and the marines came upon the convoy outside of Al Jahra, it was literally dead in its tracks. What Ernie saw was unimaginable. History had not seen the destruction of men and mechanized vehicles on such a scale. It appeared to Ernie that only the hand of God could have the power to scratch out three miles of roadway and fill it with massive of amounts of twisted metal and debris. He saw vehicles still burning and smoking. He and his unit also encountered injured Iraqi soldiers and captured others who had fled on foot into the desert. They were taken prisoner and treated for their injuries.

The air attack on the Republican Guard and its equipment and vehicles was so massive there is little agreement on the extent of the destruction. Reasonable estimates are that 500 to 1,000 Iraqis were killed, and 400 to 500 were taken prisoner. Almost all of the estimated 2,200 vehicles were destroyed. The stretch of road where the air attack on the convoy occurred became known as the Highway of Death. The next day President George H. W. Bush, Ernie's former charge in the Senate, declared a ceasefire, bringing the Gulf War to an end. Ernie's unit remained in Kuwait until the following May.

On Ernie's return to DC from the battlefield, he did not find employment that matched his experiences in government and the military. He started the new decade prepared to take every opportunity available and relocate if necessary. One of those opportunities included providing consulting services through Caribbean Basin Consulting Corporation. Caribbean Basin was headquartered in Miami and provided services for businesses contracting with federal and state governments. The CEO was Bob Medell, who had previously worked for the Central Intelligence Agency and the Drug Enforcement Agency. Ernie had met Medell when he was an aide with Senator Dole, when Medell had come to the senator's office to lobby as a representative of the Cuban Lawyers Association of Miami. Ernie was assigned to Medell in the belief that Ernie's ability to speak Spanish would facilitate their interaction. That belief proved accurate, and he and Medell developed a long-standing friendship.

Ernie's employment with Caribbean Basin did not require his presence in Miami and thereby enabled him to continue residing in DC. He was activated several times for duty with the Marine Corps Reserves for much of the 1990s while he worked with Caribbean Basin Consulting.

To add to his military credentials, Ernie pursued a scuba diving certificate in 1994. He and a small group of marines received diving instruction and training in DC. When the time came to qualify for his open-water dive, he and two others chose to travel to Zihuatanejo in the state of Guerrero, Mexico, on the Pacific Coast. (Fittingly, the name Guerrero means *warrior*.) They hired two local guides to take them offshore for the dive. The boat was small and without convenience or comfort. The guides took them to a location where the Mexican shore was barely visible, assuring the divers that the location was ideal for a qualifying dive with spectacular views of sea life.

The guides assisted Ernie in donning his wetsuit and air tank. Ernie took his turn and tumbled into the blue Pacific. The guides, themselves outfitted only in swim shorts, face masks, and air tanks—no wetsuits—took the marines to a depth of 110 feet, much deeper than planned. For Ernie, the experience was awesome. The underwater sea life was as the guides had described, spectacular in color and in form. Ernie saw fish of many colors, shapes, and sizes, and the rock formations and sea bed below. At one point a large gray fish, as big as Ernie, slowly approached him. Ernie's fight-or-flight response kicked in, and he instinctively stopped and remained motionless. He looked over to one of the guides. To his relief, the knowing guide gave Ernie a thumbs-up, indicating no threat, just an amazing work of nature.

When the dive ended, Ernie, at age fifty, had earned his certificate. However, he soon realized his Virgen de San Juan medallion was no longer around his neck. He searched his wetsuit but found nothing. Panic began to set in. He could not believe he had lost the medallion Luisa had given him years ago. Finally, he spotted the chain and medallion on the deck of the boat—it had fallen among the diving gear. He felt a great sense of relief and regarded his find as the result of good fortune. He immediately put it around his neck.

* * *

During the three years after his diving excursion, Ernie continued to be called to active duty for classified assignments. Many of them took him to several countries in South America, where he interacted with US government agencies and their foreign counterparts. On occasion he accompanied government and military officials as an observer of military exercises. Most of these missions were short in duration and conducted abroad with specific and limited objectives. The scope and details of these activities remain classified.

In the spring of 1998, Ernie's younger sister Alvina—nicknamed Vina—called and asked if he could provide a place for her while she and a friend, Amy, visited DC. Vina and Amy were coworkers at Saint Frances Hospital in Wichita and became close friends during the years Vina was nanny to Amy's boys, Jim and Kenton. Amy had planned a vacation to DC, and she had invited Vina to accompany her and her two sons. Ernie, as always, willingly agreed to Vina's request.

When Ernie met Amy, they had an immediate attraction for one another and easily carried on a conversation. She found him to be an interesting man and liked his eyes. Amy was petite and had auburn hair and green eyes. She was born Amy Gladden and was raised in the middle of America's heartland in Nickerson, Kansas, located two hours from the geodetic center of the United States. Ernie was impressed that she was a highly talented pianist, and well educated.

Ernie learned that Amy's family history was no less incredible than his. Amy's heritage was mostly Irish, Scottish, and English. She was a sixth-generation Kansan, whose ancestors had first arrived on the continent on the Mayflower in 1620. Several of her ancestors fought in the American Revolutionary War. The last of the immigrants in her family arrived in 1871 from Switzerland and Germany. Her family was Protestant and always moving westward. During the turmoil and Civil War over slavery, one of her ancestors, a Methodist minister in Tennessee, was scalped on the steps of his church. His daughter, Amy's great-great-grandmother, fled Tennessee for Missouri with a wagon full of kids. In Springfield, Missouri, in 1861, two of her great-uncles were executed by an angry crowd because they had voted for Abraham Lincoln. The surviving widows continued west in covered wagons to Kingman County in the south-central region of Kansas, just west of Wichita.

Amy's parents were teachers and farmed near Nickerson. She was raised Methodist, and her family was always active in the church and community.

She learned to play the piano and organ, eventually becoming a classical pianist. As a youngster, she began working early—in the local print shop, mowing lawns, and cooking for hired farmhands. She became a lifelong learner, earning a bachelor's degree in 1986 and a master's degree in nursing in 1994 from Wichita State University. Ultimately, she would go on to earn a doctorate in nursing practice from American Sentinel University and become chief nurse for Cerner Corporation, at one time the largest health information technology company in the world.

Within months of meeting Amy, Ernie left the DC area and returned to Wichita. Although he was unable to find employment in the city at first, he was close to Amy during his search. Fortunately, a contact in Ernie's network of friends and associates provided an opportunity that led to Ernie's hiring as the CEO of Research Development Laboratories (RDL), a Department of Defense contractor engaged in the development of space-based radar technology. In the past, Ernie had briefly served on RDL's board of directors. Unfortunately, the job site was the company headquarters in Culver City, California. Reluctantly, Ernie moved out to California, but after a year with many trips back to Kansas, he left RDL and returned to Wichita. In 1999 he and Amy were married at the botanical gardens in Wichita in July. He wore his white marine uniform and was attended by members of the Marine Corps.

Ernie was not the only member of his family to return to the Midwest during that time. After completing high school in Washington, Felipe had decided to attend college at the University of Northern Colorado in Greeley in 1994. His motivation stemmed in part from an unusually effective incentive: when Felipe was in high school, Ernie had arranged for him to work in Brookover's cattle feedlot back in Garden City. Felipe shoveled cow manure the entire summer. Each shovelful added to Felipe's appreciation of manual labor and his desire to get his degree. At college he majored in political science. During his senior year he served as the student trustee on the university's board of trustees. At the request of the dean of students, he gave a farewell address at graduation commencement ceremonies. After his graduation in May 1998, he spent a few months with Ana Maria visiting her family in Argentina before settling in Wichita.

Ernie was eventually hired as a senior assistant to the Wichita city manager in late 1999. His hiring occurred at a time when Wichita was particularly concerned with defense contracts and other federal funding that benefited the residents of the city. Ernie encountered some internal resistance to his hiring. Initially, he was told there were no openings. He suspected that the objections were political, but he had the strong support of Wichita's mayor, Robert G. Knight. The mayor, also a Republican, directed Ernie to contact the city manager. When Ernie did so, he was advised to report for an interview. He later discovered that the mayor had described Ernie as a "must-hire" and said that a place should be found for him. Ernie understood that the intensity of the resistance might increase given the process of his hiring, but he relied on his experience to avoid political pitfalls as he set about fulfilling his duties. He began working in the city manager's office in April 2000.

11

Return to War

2001–2004

By 2001 Luisa's health had begun to decline. She was eighty-two and becoming weaker and weaker with time. She became bedridden, and because her vocal cords no longer functioned properly, she could not speak. The dysfunction of the vocal cords also led to her choking on her food, requiring that she be fed with a tube. Initially, the doctor believed she was also exhibiting signs of dementia, but testing determined that the dementia symptoms were caused by her medication. In her better moments she was conscious and able to hear. Occasionally, she responded with her eyes or a grunt. Vina was her primary caregiver during this time, with Ernie's youngest sister, Ana, also helping.

Luisa and Ernie spoke in Spanish when last they were together. She told Ernie, "Mijo, mira como veni a llegar." Loosely translated, "Son, look where I have come to." She knew her health would not improve. It pained Ernie to see her become as dependent as a child. He understood when he left her side that they might never speak again.

On September 11, 2001, Felipe was working for Delta Airlines at Reagan National Airport in Washington, DC, and living with his fiancée, Christy Meek, in a condo in Falls Church, Virginia. From their unit on the twenty-sixth floor, they had a direct view of the airliner that terrorists crashed into the Pentagon. Ernie was on a golf course in Mexico when he learned of the attacks on the World Trade Center and the Pentagon. He was in disbelief and asked aloud, "How? How could this happen?" He realized immediately that he might be called to active duty. After contacting Felipe to check that he and Christy were safe, he and Amy promptly returned to Kansas.

It was always the case with Ernie that he wore two hats, public servant and military man. So two months after his hire with the City of Wichita in June 2000, he took on a relatively minor part-time administrative position with the US Selective Service System for the state of Kansas. The state headquarters was a resource for persons wanting to register and serve in the military. Its primary function was to maintain a state of readiness to meet the armed forces' responsibilities in peacetime and in the event of a national draft. Immediately after the September 11 attacks, many American men and women joined the military in the spirit of protecting and defending their country. Activity increased with a new urgency at Selective Service offices across the country, including the Kansas office.

Ernie felt the urgency as well, and a part of him wanted to answer the call to duty. He carefully followed the government's response to the attacks and found himself mentally preparing for active duty status, but the call to service did not arrive. By the end of the year, US and allied forces and the Afghan Northern Alliance had driven the Taliban out of the mountains of Tora Bora and into Pakistan. When the US-led forces installed a temporary government in Afghanistan, it appeared that the major conflict had ended without the need for Ernie to serve. In some ways, the end of hostilities was an emotional letdown for him, as he believed he was at his best when in uniform on active duty.

Luisa passed away at Vina's home in Wichita on March 12, 2002. Three of Luisa's children—Jim, Vina, and Ana—three grandchildren, and Aunt Kay were with her at the end. Ernie was in DC on assignment for the City of Wichita when he received the news. He grieved, but he also felt a sense of relief in that Luisa's long and difficult struggle in her last years of life had ended. Ernie regarded Luisa as a saint. She had nurtured her family when her husband died at an early age. She had been patient with Ernie when he was a child and did not squelch his sense of fun and adventure. She asked only that he be careful and not push matters to the limit.

Ernie's siblings as well knew the depth of Luisa's effort in providing them a secure life, one without want. Vina once asked Luisa after feeding her, "Do you know the real meaning of 'success,' not the definition in *Webster's*

Dictionary?" Luisa was only able to look at her with puzzlement. "I am going to tell you my meaning of the word 'success,'" said Vina. "The meaning of 'success' is Luisa Garcia. None of your boys are drug addicts or drunks. Your girls aren't streetwalkers. To me, that was success. Your children have done well. You did good, Mama." A tear ran down Luisa's cheek. Vina caressed her face and head and let her rest.

On March 19, 2003, the United States, leading a coalition of nations including the United Kingdom, launched the Iraq War with missile strikes on a palace owned by Saddam Hussein. Again, Ernie anticipated that he would be called to active duty. By the end of April, Iraq's capital city, Baghdad, had fallen to US forces. On May 1, rather than flying by helicopter to an anchored USS *Abraham Lincoln* off the coast of San Diego, President George W. Bush, wearing a flight suit, landed in a jet on its flight deck.

Upon his arrival on the carrier, President Bush gave a televised speech announcing that major combat operations in Iraq had been suspended. A banner clearly visible to viewers hung behind the president. The banner, against a red, white, and blue background, read, "MISSION ACCOMPLISHED." With the president's declaration, it again appeared that the conflict was resolved without the need for Ernie's service. But two months later, days shy of his fifty-seventh birthday, Ernie was activated in support of the global war on terror. Upon Ernie's activation, his position with the City of Wichita as assistant to the city manager ended. He did not know for some time to which theater of war he would be deployed.

In Iraq, US military commanders began planning the rotation to withdraw troops with the initial fall of Baghdad and Hussein's government. But those plans were never implemented. Within weeks of the president's declaration aboard the USS *Abraham Lincoln*, US and coalition occupying forces were targeted by religious, political, and tribal sects in Iraq. The government installed to replace Hussein's government also came under assault. Not only did the Iraqi factions attack coalition forces and authorities, they also attacked one another in a scramble for power and influence. The weapons of this insurgency included suicide bombs, car bombs, improvised explosive devices, grenade launchers, and small arms weapons. As a result of the rising insurgency, US troops were required to stay in Iraq until the country stabilized. The United States needed more troops in Iraq and in military installations across the globe to support the war effort in Iraq and Afghanistan.

Now a lieutenant colonel, Ernie thought he would be sent to Iraq or Afghanistan. He reported to Camp Lejeune, North Carolina, as ordered. To his surprise he was sent to Colombia. There he served as the principal instructor and trainer for Colombian marines fighting the war on drugs, specifically cocaine. He was required to develop the curriculum and multimedia material for the training program, which facilitated the collaboration between the marines and local civilian populations to identify and stop cocaine traffickers. His ability to speak Spanish again made him well suited for the assignment. He instructed one hundred Colombian marines over the course of a month in the Colombian Headquarters for Military Forces, Colombia's equivalent to the US Pentagon.

Apart from the program at the Colombian Headquarters, Ernie deployed several times to South America on special operations. During this time the United States maintained a relatively low profile in South America. Nonetheless, the United States and countries in South America were effectively collaborating not only on drug interdiction but also on military training relevant to each country's particular location. Despite the coordination, American military personnel remained hypervigilant for their safety, particularly in Colombia.

Colombia was unusually hostile for persons associated with the government or for those in an American military uniform. Antigovernment militias, including the Revolutionary Armed Forces of Colombia and the National Liberation Armies, promoted socialist ideologies and used violent tactics to advance their causes, such as attacks on military outposts and installations, assassinations, kidnapping and ransom, extortion, and cocaine trafficking.

As Ernie's missions in Colombia drew to a close, events in the Caribbean island nation of Haiti had become a storm of chaos. In November 2000, Jean-Bertrand Aristide was elected president of Haiti for a second time. He had previously been elected president in 1991, but after attempting to implement reforms, he was forced out of office by a military coup. With the support of the United Nations and the United States, Aristide returned in the fall of 1994 to complete his first term, which ended in 1996. When Aristide was elected again in 2000, Haiti still remained a nation in severe poverty and political disarray. Aristide had few means by which his government could begin to lead the country out of its poor condition. Given the country's history, the future held little promise for the people of Haiti. Aristide's political opponents began undermining the legitimacy of his presidency, and he was again threatened with rebellion.

By the end of February 2004, his rebel opponents were in striking distance of Port-au-Prince, the capital city. On the last day of February, Aristide left Haiti with the assistance of US security personnel. Within hours of Aristide's departure the United Nations Security Council voted to send troops to Haiti to keep the peace and stabilize the country. That day, the US Marines' Combined Joint Task Force–Haiti (CJTF-Haiti) began arriving to spearhead the peacekeeping effort. The CJTF-Haiti eventually included members of the armed forces of Canada, France, Chile, and Haiti, a combined total force of one thousand.

On March 25, 2004, Ernie reported at Camp Lejeune to Brigadier General Ron Coleman, the marine commanding officer of CJTF-Haiti. General Coleman told Ernie that he had been selected to serve as the civil affairs commander for the CJTF-Haiti. The general also advised him that Ernie would make the decisions to appropriately respond to both military and civil situations. Calling Ernie the "long pole in the tent," he further required Ernie to report directly to him.

Amy was disappointed to learn that Ernie would again be out of the country. She and Ernie had been looking forward to an extended period of time together at a slower pace. They hoped that Ernie could continue his part-time work with the Selective Service System, at least for a short time. Despite her disappointment, she remained supportive of his service.

Ernie traveled to Haiti in a C-130 transport plane. The transport touched down in Port-au-Prince on a rainy, hot, and humid evening. In the days to come, he found massive need and precious few resources. Ernie's team consisted of a multinational group of twenty civil affairs specialists and a hundred various specialists from UN member nations, including Chile, Canada, France, and the United Kingdom. Under his command, the team immediately began to reestablish the infrastructure. They distributed food, water, and medicine. When possible, they repaired water wells, schools, hospitals, communications, and airport facilities. Just as importantly, the team kept order and stopped or prevented looting.

Ernie had seen poverty in his travels, but the poverty in Haiti was unlike anything he had ever encountered. The gross lack of clean water, food, shelter, sanitation, health services, and security was shocking. Children were thin with hunger in their eyes, barefoot, and wore little clothing. Some, without parents, were left alone in the streets, begging. He did not hesitate to call upon the navy to provide Medical Civic Action Programs, medical doctors, and specialists equipped with supplies to establish a temporary field clinic for the local population, especially inoculations for the children.

Ernie saw the opposite end of the wealth spectrum in Haiti as well. As the civil affairs commander, he met with high government officials, military officers, and business leaders. Often these meetings were held at the Hotel Montana, a resort hotel that provided luxurious comforts and conveniences. It was located on a hill in Pétion-Ville, a suburb of Port-au-Prince. Although Ernie appreciated the conveniences, the contrast with the people in need below troubled him. He knew the difference was extreme and unjust. Haiti's problems were incredibly immense, perhaps ultimately insurmountable in the short term and, with ineffective governmental institutions and corruption, extremely challenging in the long term.

After three months, Ernie's team had substantially begun to address the most pressing needs of the Haitian population and contribute to some basic stability for the people. For his leadership, Ernie was awarded the President's Meritorious Service Medal, the Secretary of Defense Meritorious Service Medal, and a letter of gratitude from the UN coordinator. The citation that accompanied the Defense Meritorious Service Medal noted that Lieutenant Colonel Garcia had "contributed to the success of untold humanitarian assistance projects, including schools, food distribution centers, medical care, and other projects to improve Haitian quality of life."

Ernie was scheduled to end his service in Haiti on June 10, 2004. Shortly before his departure date, he received notice that he was to be deployed to Iraq. He was assigned to the Twenty-Fourth Marine Expeditionary Unit (MEU). The MEU provides an immediate reaction capability for crisis response and is capable of limited combat operations. Ernie was granted thirty days' leave before he was to report to Camp Lejeune to await transport to join the MEU, which had already deployed to Iraq.

After anticipating deployment immediately after 9/11 and the Iraq War, Ernie was mildly surprised that he was ordered to Iraq now. After missions to Colombia and Haiti, he concluded that the marines preferred his services in Central and South America. His assignment to the Twenty-Fourth MEU was new in every respect. He had no prior service with this unit, nor did he know any of the MEU's officers or other personnel. He would have to rely on his performance and ability to connect with people to become part of the unit.

Once again, Amy was not happy with Ernie's new orders. The military news from Iraq suggested a slow spiral of death and destruction for US military and civilian personnel. She was already thinking that his admirable thirty-year career should be brought to an end. But as Amy had done many times before, she put aside her disappointment and did not let Ernie see her frustrations with his impending absence. When Ernie returned to Wichita on leave, they spent their time enjoying one another's company and, to the extent possible, talked about his deployment in positive terms. Amy expressed her belief that his time away would pass quickly and not drag on. She assured him that she would continue to send him care packages with conveniences and goodies unavailable in the field. And most importantly, she reminded him that they would exchange daily emails.

Before his deployment to Iraq, Ernie trained at March Air Reserve Base in California. There, along with other marines, he trained in a mock Iraqi village in preparation for house-to-house operations. When the training was completed, Ernie was sent to Camp Lejeune to await transport to Iraq. During this period of predeployment training and processing, Ernie and his Second Marine Expeditionary Force Operations officemate, Lieutenant Colonel Rich Wersel, waited for the order to deploy. Rich was a by-the-book marine who took no shortcuts in executing his duties. He and his wife Vivianne, who is of Mexican heritage, are from California.

When deployment orders were issued, Rich was to report to the Green Zone in Baghdad, a highly fortified area for primarily American personnel. His time in Baghdad would be his second tour of duty in Iraq. Ernie was to report to Camp Kalsu, approximately thirty miles south of Baghdad. In late July, Ernie, along with soldiers from different branches of the military, departed for Iraq in a chartered DC-10. They left from the Marine Corps air base in Cherry Point, North Carolina, and upon landing in Kuwait, stepped out into 135-degree temperatures. From there, Ernie reported to Camp Kalsu, while Rich reported to the Green Zone in Baghdad. As they went their separate ways, they agreed to keep in touch by email.

Ernie's next stop was Al-Taqaddum Air Base, forty-five miles west of Baghdad. From there, a CH-46 marine helicopter flew him to Camp Kalsu near the city of Iskandariya, Iraq. The base was named after Bob Kalsu, a former pro football player for the Buffalo Bills who was killed in the Vietnam War. Iskandariya was named after Alexander the Great, whose armies had reached the Middle East two thousand years before. Camp Kalsu was a forward operating base used by the marines to support military forces in the area. It was on the southern edge of Iraq's Triangle of Death, an area that experienced heavy insurgent combat activity including mortar attacks, rocket fire, roadside improvised explosive devices, and suicide attacks on both civilians and military personnel. Most combat situations in the triangle were those of urban warfare with few open-field battles.

Upon arriving at Camp Kalsu, Ernie reported to Marine Colonel Ron Johnson, the commanding officer. Johnson was not a desk commander. He was always out in the field on patrol and making assessments on the ground. Ernie came to respect and admire his ability as a commanding officer. Johnson reiterated to Ernie that he was to command and lead the Military Civil Affairs Unit. He made a special effort to emphasize to Ernie to keep his head down and always wear his protective gear, including a Kevlar bulletproof vest. The protective gear, though heavy, actually worked to cool the body in the stifling July heat. Ernie had not experienced such extreme heat in his previous deployment in the Gulf War in 1991.

When Ernie arrived at Camp Kalsu, insurgents were firing ten to fifteen rockets a day on the camp, usually from the beds of Toyota pickups. The insurgents drove the pickups to a stop within a mile or two of the Camp, fired the rockets, and sped away. To avoid detection and counterfire, the insurgents did not take the time to carefully take aim. Consequently, only by chance did their rockets and mortar fire hit a worthy target. Unfortunately, in the minds of the insurgents the most highly valued targets were US Marines.

On Ernie's first night, as he was being shown to his tent, he heard the sizzle of rockets flying overhead. The sound made him keenly aware that in this place, his life was constantly at risk. With his training and prior experiences, he beat down any initial moments of fear or apprehension. He shifted into a state of hypervigilance, a mandatory survival strategy in the triangle. He tried to lighten the gravity of the risk by joking aloud to himself, "I'm not in Kansas anymore."

A few days later, Ernie joined a group of young marines on a night patrol of nearby Iraqi villages. They rode out in a column of four Humvees armed with small arms weapons and a mounted .50-caliber machine gun. Looking for insurgents, the marines came upon a house that appeared to be abandoned. Some of the walls of the house had been knocked down; others were riddled with bullet holes. Ernie and Chief Warrant Officer Michael James—Jimmy—carefully approached the house while the others remained near the road. Ernie was confused by what he saw within the house. He thought he saw the shadowy figure of a horse. Whatever the actual figure was, it was out of the ordinary. He felt an adrenaline rush. He and Jimmy then heard a noise within the house and dropped to the ground to take cover. The other marines opened fire on the house. When the shooting stopped, they inspected the house and found nothing but a horse. It was not injured and had not fled during the shooting. The marines laughed—all that shooting and the horse was left standing. The result strongly suggested to Ernie that the young marines needed to spend more time at the shooting range.

Every mission served to bond its warriors. Together they set out and experienced the adrenaline of danger and standing at death's edge. They hoped to return unharmed and be able to laugh at their escape from the grim reaper's grasp. Warriors who went into battle together and walked out together are bonded forever. So when a fellow marine falls or is harmed in battle, the survivors deal with grief, anger, and later, the guilt of surviving.

Shortly after arriving at Camp Kalsu, Ernie became close friends with the MEU's executive officer, Lieutenant Colonel Tim Maxwell. They had met briefly when Ernie left Haiti and first reported to Camp Lejeune. Tim was the second-in-command of the Twenty-Fourth MEU at that time, and it was readily apparent to Ernie that he was especially dedicated to the safety of the men and women under his command. He wasted no time in telling Ernie that the safety of the troops should be his number one priority as well. At Camp Kalsu they found themselves working long hours together in the command center, eating at the camp's chow hall, and maintaining their physical fitness training. They were in each other's presence twenty hours a day.

One afternoon after lunch they returned to their respective tents to relax and get some sleep. Camp Kalsu was a sprawling encampment, with Ernie's quarters on one end and Tim's a short distance away. As Ernie awakened from a short nap, he heard incoming mortar rounds and three small explosions. Looking out from his tent, he saw a plume of smoke. Immediately, he realized the smoke was rising from Tim's quarters. He and other marines ran toward the smoke.

When Ernie arrived, he saw Tim lying on the ground. Shrapnel had struck the side of his head. He was unconscious and bleeding profusely. Ernie saw that Tim was missing part of his skull; he could only watch as navy corpsmen fought to save his life. He thought Tim would not survive.

Tim was evacuated on a Black Hawk helicopter to Baghdad, where he was stabilized. Then he was sent to an air force medical unit in Balad, Iraq, and eventually flown to the Landstuhl Regional Medical Center in Germany, where seriously wounded marines from Iraq and Afghanistan were treated for their injuries. Ernie later learned that Tim survived his traumatic injuries but needed a cane to walk and spoke with an impediment.

Men in combat must guard against being overwhelmed by the great harm their comrades suffer. Ernie knew that unless he pushed aside his anguish for Tim, he might lose a degree of vigilance. So he tried to focus on the day before him. He tried to move on and bury his sorrow within himself.

Ernie's days at Camp Kalsu were long—twenty-four-hour days were not uncommon. With his rank of lieutenant colonel, Ernie had the option to stay in the camp, "inside the wire." But he preferred to be out in the field with his marines. His approach was that a static marine ends up a dead marine. At the start and end of each day, he participated in briefings and updates with unit commanders. He reported to the MEU command staff on the status of civil affairs operations.

Ernie's unit worked to develop a cooperative partnership with Iraqi tribal and village leaders. Once trust was established, US military forces and nongovernment agencies were able to interact with the villages regularly. US embassy staff members, United States Agency for International Development staff, United Nations agencies, the Red Crescent, and others also provided humanitarian services to help the Iraqis rebuild their homes and villages. Together they built and repaired schools, hospitals, bridges, and roads that had been destroyed by the insurgents.

After members of Ernie's civil affairs team made initial contact with Iraqis in the villages, Ernie followed up with other members of his team. Most of his contacts with Iraqi civilians took place during daytime hours. On occasion a helicopter took him to meet contacts in hot spots in Anbar Province, such as Fallujah and Ramadi. His ground excursions usually involved three or four Humvees. Not only did the vehicles run the gauntlet of roadside IEDs, they also encountered snipers, small arms fire, and mortar fire. Though Ernie's unit developed a cooperative arrangement with Iraqis, the work remained dangerous. One particular Iraqi civil engineer who worked with Ernie and the marines was later shot in the stomach by insurgents in retaliation for cooperating with the marines. He survived the small caliber bullet, and when he recovered, he courageously continued his cooperation.

As part of the civil affairs mission in the Triangle of Death, Ernie processed and investigated claims by Iraqis that US Marines or other military personnel had abused or killed Iraqi civilians. In one case, an Iraqi claimed he was held at gunpoint with a rifle to his chest. Ernie denied the claim after talking to other members in the village and learning that the claimant was an informant for insurgents. Another claimant wanted $1 million for the death of a nephew at the hands of the US military. Ernie asked the claimant to complete forms and supply the facts of the death along with the names and addresses of all concerned. The claimant never returned with completed forms, nor did any other person seek compensation claiming to be related to the nephew. Ernie concluded that the claim was fraudulent. Ernie's investigations did not reveal any misconduct by the marines, but other investigators did find instances where Iraqi civilians had been harmed by marine and other military personnel misconduct. Legitimate claims for harm or injury resulted in significant compensation to Iraqi families.

In mid-September, Ernie was notified that he would be returning to Camp Lejeune in a few weeks. He was thrilled and told Amy the good news. He emailed his Camp Lejeune friend, Rich, who was still in Baghdad, and informed him of the same. Rich replied that he was right behind Ernie and that he too would return shortly.

On September 24, 2004, the temperatures at Camp Kalsu were still very high. When Ernie sat down for lunch in the chow hall he removed his protective armor. As he ate, the camp was hit by mortar fire with rounds landing near the chow hall. Ernie and a large number of other marines in the chow hall ran for one of the narrow doorways to the chow hall, resulting in a crush of bodies. They pushed and shoved to get out to the safety of the bunkers.

Ernie finally made his way out and ran toward a bunker. As he did so, the concussion of a mortar blast knocked him down. He was not hurt. He gathered himself and continued his escape. A second blast knocked him against a concrete rail, a road divider similar to those used during road construction. This time he felt sharp pains in his neck, arm, shoulder, and groin, but he was again able to get to his feet and keep moving toward the bunker.

Ernie finally reached the bunker, but just as he was entering, another mortar shell hit the bunker. The blast knocked him into the air and slammed him hard against the wall. He was dazed for a few moments. As he gathered himself, he again felt severe pain in his neck, shoulder, and groin. He heard the screams of the wounded and the yelling of navy corpsmen running to them to provide medical care. After a few moments, Ernie realized that he had not been hit directly by shrapnel and that he was not bleeding. When the shelling stopped, despite his pain, he and other marines aided the wounded. Two marines and several Iraqi civilian contractors later died from their injuries.

Two days after the mortar attack, Ernie's pain and discomfort intensified. The vertebrae in his neck had been bruised and sprained, and he had suffered two abdominal hernias. After he was medically assessed, he was medevaced by helicopter to a hospital in Baghdad that once served as Saddam Hussein's private hospital. He remained in great pain but was grateful to be mobile despite the injuries. After he was examined, he waited for an empty bed.

While he waited, more seriously wounded marines and soldiers were carried in. The medical personnel immediately tended to those in critical condition and left the stable for later care. The face and arms of one of the stable patients were covered in dried blood, dirt, and mud. Ernie saw that the medical staff had stopped tending to the marine. Ernie got off his cot and found a clean towel. He poured water onto the towel and carefully cleaned the wounded marine's face, arms, and hands. The young man said to Ernie, "Who are you? Sir, why are you doing this?" He was clearly surprised that a lieutenant colonel was tending to him. Ernie's response was simple and straightforward. "Marines take care of each other, no matter the rank." During Ernie's stay at Saddam Hussein's hospital, he tried to provide whatever comfort he could to his fellow marines and soldiers.

Ernie called Amy and told her about his injuries. She was thankful they were not life-threatening. He remained at the hospital for a week before he was flown to Landstuhl Medical Center. Upon learning that he was to be moved to Germany, Amy immediately made plans to join him.

On the medevac flight to Germany, Ernie sat next to a marine whose arm was badly injured and heavily bandaged. The wounded marine struggled to position his arm to relieve the pain. When he saw the marine unable to move his arm, Ernie unbuckled his seat belt, approached him, and carefully placed his arm in a more comfortable position. When he returned to his seat, he noticed an air force general sitting across from him. The general looked at the two of them, never saying a word. A tear slipped from the general's eye and rolled down his face. Moments later he walked over to Ernie and the injured marine. The general presented them with his personal challenge coin and said, "Job well done." These coins usually bear the insignia or emblem of a military group or organization. High-ranking officers within the group award the coins to honor and recognize special efforts and achievements of group members and to help raise morale.

When Ernie arrived in Germany, he felt relief that he was out of danger. He was grateful for the medical attention and morale boost he received there. An army general was present to welcome the wounded. A nurse was assigned to each of the approximately twenty-five marines and soldiers. Ernie was placed in essentially a small apartment with pillows, sheets, and his own bathroom with toilet paper. These were conveniences not always available in Iraq. With the relief and comfort, he slept a great deal.

Shortly after Ernie's arrival, at a debriefing at the medical center, he began to feel his emotions rising to the surface. He could no longer hold them in. So he excused himself to an adjoining room. There, he quietly wept and began to release the tensions and emotions of his combat experience. After a few minutes, he rejoined the debriefing.

Amy arrived in Landstuhl in time to be at Ernie's side during surgery for his injuries. She provided care and comfort in support of his recovery and healing. During her time in Landstuhl, she stayed at the Fisher House, a no-cost temporary home for military families within walking distance of the medical center. Families in the Fisher House support not only their wounded but one another's families as well with small acts of kindness—food, drink, conversation, words of comfort and encouragement. The families endured their own stresses as their loved ones recovered from their wounds.

After Ernie's surgery, he was notified that he would be sent back to Iraq to rejoin the Twenty-Fourth MEU. Amy was livid. She was certain he would be sent back to Camp Lejeune for further care and rehabilitation. Ernie, however, was not surprised by his new orders, since he was quite familiar with the mission of military medical care: Fix them up and send them back to the front lines, not home. He returned to Camp Kalsu in late November. Three weeks later he received orders to return to Camp Lejeune in North Carolina on December 15, 2004. He was filled with mixed emotions. On the one hand he was relieved to be going home, but on the other he regretted leaving his marines behind to continue the fight.

Ernie would not see combat on foreign soil again. His combat duties ended when he, now fifty-eight years old, boarded the freedom bird at the small dirt helicopter pad at Camp Kalsu. But he did serve in the Marine Corps Reserves for another eighteen months.

During his time in Iraq, Ernie had remained entirely focused on his military mission. There was never a moment during or after his deployment when the controversy surrounding the Iraq War led him to question his country's call to war. In both of his deployments to Iraq, he had observed some evidence of nonnuclear weapons of mass destruction. He saw no lack of justification for military action.

Ernie returned to Camp Lejeune for postdeployment processing, including a full medical exam. The exam confirmed the fracture in his neck and the hernia, but it also revealed tears in both rotator cuffs and an additional hernia. However, the most pressing diagnosis was the emotional stress and fatigue he was suffering. Even before Ernie left Landstuhl, he had begun to experience sleepless nights, nightmares, and hypervigilance.

Amy met him at Camp Lejeune and was thrilled to have him home. But her focus quickly turned to his health. Her nurse's training enabled her to understand his condition, and her skills helped Ernie deal with the challenges he faced in recovering his health. With counseling, medication, and Amy's unwavering assurances of improvement, Ernie began to improve. He also resumed running in an effort to lower his stress levels. After several weeks in the military backlog of requests for medical care, Ernie's request was processed and granted. Finally, his prayers for time to heal were answered.

With his improvement Ernie was able to meet with his friend Tim Maxwell, who had been hit by shrapnel at Camp Kalsu. Tim's condition had improved, but he was still in rehabilitation at Camp Lejeune. Ernie volunteered to drive Tim to various medical appointments on and off base in nearby Jacksonville. It was difficult for Ernie to see Tim, his wife, and their children suffering. Tim had been a marine's marine. He was an avid runner and a muscle builder. The weight and pain of survivor's guilt were heavy in

Ernie's mind and heart. Over time the guilt would subside, but it left its lasting mark.

Ernie was also reunited with his friend and fellow officer Rich Wersel at Camp Lejeune. They were again assigned to the Second Marine Expeditionary Force Operations Office. Ernie often joined Rich and Vivianne for dinner at their home on Emerald Isle near Camp Lejeune. After dinner they sat on the beach drinking a beer as the sun slowly set beyond the horizon.

One afternoon Ernie drove to the base finance operations office to complete postdeployment processing paperwork. There he met Rich, who was standing by his vehicle in the parking lot. Rich asked, "Hey, Ernie, before you leave, help me out here. I think I have a loose fan belt and I need to tighten it." Ernie was more than willing to help. "Sure, okay." They lifted the hood and worked the problem, with Ernie applying pressure on the alternator and Rich tightening the bolts.

Rich wanted to continue talking, but Ernie had an appointment in the office. He told Rich, "Look, I gotta git."

"Yeah. Okay. Thanks," said an appreciative Rich.

Ernie entered the finance office, and Rich headed for the gym. While returning to the Second Marine Expeditionary Force Operations Office, Ernie received a call from the office. The clerk told him, "Rich has been rushed to the base hospital!" Ernie immediately drove to the hospital. As he hurried he kept asking himself in disbelief, "What could have happened?" He finally reached the nurses' station in the emergency room and asked to see Rich. The receptionist called over to a woman wearing a nurse's cap. The nurse said to Ernie, "I am sorry, sir. You will have to speak to his family if you want more information."

Her words hit Ernie hard. He was shocked and in denial. He thought, *He cannot be dead. This cannot be true! I was just talking to him! How does a man survive Baghdad, only to come home and die?* He wanted to scream, "This is not right! This cannot be!"

Ernie arrived at the hospital before Vivianne, but it was not long before she too arrived. Ernie reached deep into his heart and turned his thoughts to supporting Vivianne. When she returned after meeting with hospital staff, Ernie embraced her and consoled her.

Rich died of a massive heart attack he had suffered during his workout. As a child, Ernie saw his father suffer for years, then pass away. He had seen death and carnage on the battlefield. But Tim's injury and Rich's death impacted him profoundly. He was close to both men. Ernie thought that he was the one who should not be alive. His life's experiences included events where his death could or should have resulted. Ernie felt his death must be near, like a cat on its eighth life.

Vivianne asked Ernie to be the principal escort at the funeral and burial at Arlington Cemetery, Virginia. He remained in contact with Vivianne and Rich's son and daughter. Ernie's mind and body suffered a great deal of wear and tear in Iraq. He dreaded the remaining surgeries needed to relieve the pain from his neck, shoulder, and hernia injuries. But still Ernie was durable and persistent. He was able to focus on the next day and move on, banged up as he was.

12

The Road Home

2005–2014

Ernie began to consider employment possibilities even before he returned to inactive status. After his service in Iraq, he preferred a position connected to the military, ideally the Marine Corps. He was eligible to return to his position with the City of Wichita, but he was hesitant to return given that many of his colleagues in the city manager's office were Democrats and regarded him as an outsider. Adding to the chilly work setting in Wichita was the Republican mayor's description of Ernie when he first applied as a "must-hire." Ernie's colleagues interpreted the mayor's comment as a directive to grant Ernie undeserved special treatment.

President George W. Bush was reelected in November of 2004 and had nominated William A. Chatfield to serve as the director of Selective Service. Chatfield's nomination was confirmed by the Senate, and he assumed the directorship in late November. Ernie knew Chatfield from his earliest days in DC. Chatfield had been the doorkeeper of the House of Representatives when Ernie was a staffer for Senator Dole. They had both worked in the Pentagon during the Reagan administration. Like Ernie, Chatfield had a long career in the Marine Corps. Ernie regarded him as a good friend with a reputation of helping others advance their careers.

During his tour of duty in Iraq, Ernie had technically remained the part-time director of the Selective Service System for Kansas. He thought that perhaps with his ties to the Republican Party, his career in the Marine Corps, his part-time status with Selective Service, and their prior interaction in the Capitol building, Chatfield might look favorably on his application. Ernie had his sights set on the position of deputy director of the Selective

Service System, but Chatfield had already filled the position. Instead, he offered Ernie a position as his chief of staff. He accepted the offer and soon thereafter, with the president's approval, Ernie assumed the duties of chief of staff. He was pleased to be back in Washington with an agency connected to the military.

In his new position, Ernie would be actively involved in the management of the agency. Internally, his duties included oversight of the administrative functions of the agency, including budget, planning, and personnel. Externally, he maintained contact with regional offices and provided guidance for implementation of the policies of the director and deputy director. He was actively engaged every day with the upper levels of the organization, reviewing and establishing policy and procedures to efficiently register men and women for military service. The hands-on work with the nuts-and-bolts operations of Selective Service appealed to him.

Finding a home was the first order of business when Amy and her son, Kenton, joined Ernie in DC. They encountered sticker shock as they viewed prospective homes in the area. In the spirit of experiencing something new and exciting, not to mention the seller's real estate market, they decided to buy a boat to live on. Despite none of them having lived previously on the water, they quickly adjusted to the constant motion.

Over a three-year period, they maintained a slip in a marina along the Maryland side of the Potomac River in Fort Washington and later moved the boat to a marina on the Chesapeake Bay near Annapolis, Maryland. They found evenings on the deck of the boat a welcome relief from the activity and stress of a DC workday. Whenever possible, for the pleasure of the ride itself, they took the boat down the Potomac to the Chesapeake Bay. These were good days for the family.

Ernie's work with Selective Service continued a level of stability for him and Amy and kept him close to the military arena. They enjoyed a period of relative calm for the next three years, particularly because he was no longer under the risk of a call to military service. Contributing to that sense of calm was the heavily bureaucratic and bland nature of his work with Selective Service. He was not traveling to locations abroad in the middle of stressful and dynamic events requiring hypervigilance.

Amy, meanwhile, had begun working with the National Association of School Nurses in 2006. The association conducts advocacy for children's health and produces journals and books for both nurses and agencies in support of improved student health. One of Amy's major responsibilities was advocacy through the media. She was a special guest on national television networks and the subject of major national newspaper interviews addressing such topics as vaccinations, outbreaks of various illnesses, and preventative health care. When she was called upon to collaboratively pursue funding and grants with members of Congress, their staff, governmental departments and agencies, Ernie was able to offer suggestions on the appropriate contacts in the Senate and various agencies.

On July 10, 2006, two days before his sixtieth birthday, Ernie retired from the Marine Corps. After forty years and two months, he would no longer put on his cammie uniform, a patterned clothing used to disguise military personnel on the battlefield. For four decades he had answered his country's call to serve. Initially, the call had disrupted his life and pursuit of a college degree. But in the end, he had success in both education and the military.

In uniform Ernie did what was asked of him and more. Beginning with his days as a recruit, he developed the confidence to meet the challenges put before him. This approach allowed him to embrace the core values of the Marine Corps: honor, courage, and commitment. Marines with a love of God and country and who led by example were men to be emulated. He enjoyed the company of men with a sense of camaraderie and adventure.

The corps's values were easy to recite, but for many they were a far more difficult challenge to uphold, particularly in combat. The fear of death can easily overtake the mind. Ernie relied on his life experiences and marine training to meet those challenges. He had been in the presence of dying men. He had seen the carnage of war on the Highway of Death. The carnage was revolting, but he did not become sick or weakened. Ernie knew how to manage his emotions at the sight of flesh and blood—he knew the meaning of slaughter. As a boy, he had seen his grandfather empty the blood and organs of animals. As a marine officer, he was trained to avoid dwelling on the gore of combat and the death of men in battle. Officers did not have the luxury to stop and reflect. The emotional impact of what Ernie saw had to be suppressed. He understood that any hesitation placed him and the men under his command at risk of injury or death. The men had to move on and proceed with their mission.

Before missions and battle, Ernie prayed for the courage to execute his orders as he was trained. Nonetheless, what he saw and experienced ultimately had its impact. At times, when he considered his actions on the battlefield, he was uncomfortable with himself. He thought, *What kind of man prays for the strength to put aside the suffering of wounded and dying comrades during the heat of combat? Was I so callous, or was it my duty to protect the living and myself?* As it was for most soldiers, the resolution and answers would require time, and care, and patience.

With all the hardships and internal conflicts, Ernie still regarded his time in the Marine Corps his best career experience. He had risen from a reluctant draftee to a lieutenant colonel. While he took pride in his combat experience, he was most proud of the lives he had improved by providing security, disaster relief, and basic services for civilians.

Ernie's military retirement ceremony took place in the ornate Mansfield Room on the Senate side of the Capitol building, one of the larger meeting rooms near the Senate chamber. Many family members, friends, and dignitaries joined Ernie and Amy at the ceremony, including Felipe and Christy; Amy's parents, Jim and June Gladden; Ernie's brother and sister-in-law, Frank and Joyce; and his brother Jim and two of his daughters. Dignitaries included Senator Dole, Bill Chatfield, and Major General Cornell Wilson, a three-star marine general.

Part of the retirement ceremony included honoring the retiree with a folded US flag. Before the ceremony Ernie had asked that two flags be made available. After receiving his flag, Ernie asked Frank to rise and be recognized for his service to the country as a United States Marine. Those in attendance stood and applauded. Ernie asked Frank to step forward and presented the second flag to Frank. An emotional embrace between the brothers followed. Another tradition of the retirement ceremony is the presentation of flowers to the parents of the retiree. Amy's parents, Jim and June, received them in place of Felipe and Luisa.

After his retirement, Ernie had a shadow box made with his military rank insignia from private to lieutenant colonel. The shadow box also contained thirty-two medals and two combat action ribbons. The shopkeeper who prepared the shadow box told Ernie, "I have never seen anything like this before."

Indeed, Ernie's military career was quite unique.

In January 2008 Ernie's performance over the previous three years as Chatfield's chief of staff paid dividends when he was promoted to deputy director. But yet again presidential elections and new administrations altered the lives of federal employees in DC. Even if an election results in the same political party holding the presidency, careers are changed and families are relocated. And so it was for Ernie in 2008. On November 4, in a historic election, the Democratic candidate, Barack Obama, was elected president. The Republican bureaucracy serving under President Bush began to prepare for the transition to the newly elected Democratic administration.

During this transition period, Ernie resigned his political appointment. His resignation allowed him to become a senior executive service employee in the federal government's civil service system. This meant he could continue working with the Selective Service System as a career employee rather than a political appointee. With that status, he kept the option to remain in his position until his retirement if he did not find a position outside of Selective Service and related to the military.

President Obama's nomination for a new director of Selective Service and Senate confirmation of the nominee were delayed. Finally, in May 2009, Director Chatfield could wait no longer and submitted his resignation as director. In Chatfield's absence, Ernie was appointed acting director of Selective Service. With his appointment, Ernie became the head of the very federal agency that had pulled him from college and sent him into the military. Forty-two years earlier when Ernie had received his draft notice, he had believed the Selective Service System's decision was unfairly and arbitrarily made. Now here he stood, leading the entire agency. As acting director Ernie did not merely babysit the agency. He proceeded with measures to improve the operation of the agency, given its personnel and budget issues. He continued to interact with the Congress and congressional staffers, military services, and members of the executive branch.

The Obama administration eventually settled on Lawrence Romo of Texas as its nominee for director of Selective Service. Ernie was prepared to work cooperatively with the transition to the new administration. He believed his knowledge would facilitate a seamless and efficient transition. He spoke with Romo on the phone before his Senate confirmation. In that conversation, Romo made it clear that he had no need for Ernie's advice and counsel. Ernie was effectively excluded from any conversation and negotiation that normally occurred in an administration transition. He found it regrettable that his assistance was disregarded.

Romo's appointment was finally confirmed in December 2009. For the first five months of 2010, Ernie was relegated to a small office in the Selective Service System building. His small office reinforced the leadership's view of his place within the system. He was given no responsibility for matters of any significance.

During this time, Ernie spoke with US Senator Sam Brownback of Kansas at several social functions in DC. At those meetings, the senator informed Ernie that his governor's campaign was doing well. In turn, Ernie expressed his interest in returning to Kansas to work in Brownback's administration should he be elected.

In June Ernie was admitted to the Veterans Administration hospital in Martinsburg, West Virginia, for injuries he had sustained in Iraq and for ongoing stress. He spent nearly five months in the hospital, but regarded his stay and recovery as part of the sacrifice made for his country. He believed that during his hospital stay, Romo and his political staff conducted an investigation to confirm that he was actually in the VA hospital. It was clear to Ernie that he was a persona non grata under Romo's leadership. He believed the new administration was looking for reasons to further alienate and discipline him.

When Ernie left Martinsburg, one of his goals was to increase his interaction with family, which had been limited by the time he devoted to service in government and the military. His hope was strengthened after learning of the experience of his second cousin, Mary Ann Frey, in making contact with members of the Garcia family previously unknown to her.

Mary Ann's grandfather, Benjamin Garcia, was the youngest brother of Jose Garcia. Her father, Alberto, was first cousin to Ernie's father, Felipe. In December of 2009, Mary Ann, her husband, Floyd Frey, and their young adult daughter, Ann Marie, drove from Illinois to El Paso in search of living relatives of Pedro Garcia. It was Ann Marie's childhood question, "Where did we come from?" that put them on this journey to the border to seek out generations from the past—a past untold to Mary Ann by her father, Alberto. Living in Kentucky across the river from Cincinnati, Ohio, in the 1930s and 1940s, Alberto came to understand that his white neighbors believed that he and his children, born of a white mother, were not white. But neither did his neighbors believe they were black. Perhaps Alberto chose to withhold information about his family's heritage lest they be subjected to the same prejudices suffered by the black community.

After researching the family history, Mary Ann believed that a granddaughter of Pedro, Manuela Rodriguez, if still living, might be the last member of his family to have known him. To find Manuela, Mary Ann directed Floyd, who was driving their pickup truck, to a modest red brick home on Grenoble Drive in El Paso's southeast side. Mary Ann and Ann Marie got out of the pickup, with Mary Ann leading the way. Mary Ann wore a white turtleneck with a flowered sweater vest. She was in her mid-fifties and stood five feet tall at most. Ann Marie, who stood head and shoulders above her mother, was in a black turtleneck and wore an elegant, thin, gold necklace. Both were wearing glasses, and both women had light skin with rosy undertones and brown hair. Mary Ann carried a three-ring binder and a picture in a frame, while Ann Marie followed her mother holding a file folder.

Anxious and hopeful but not hesitant, Mary Ann knocked lightly on the screen door. Her knock was quickly answered by a woman of her own height, with light brown skin, perhaps in her mid-thirties or early forties, and with shoulder-length black hair. Mary Ann asked the woman, "Are you Maria Contreras?" Without waiting for an answer, she explained, "My name is Mary Ann Frey, and I may be a distant relative of Maria's."

The woman hesitated, but answered, "I am Maria Contreras."

Mary Ann was delighted and pleased that Maria Contreras spoke English. Maria Contreras could not recall ever having met Mary Ann, nor did she recognize Mary Ann's name. She was quite sure that the woman at her doorstep was no relative of hers. Mary Ann explained that the family connection was through Manuela Rodriguez and that she had been trying to locate Manuela in El Paso. Maria Contreras was shocked at hearing the name Manuela Rodriguez. She softly responded to Mary Ann in disbelief that she might be looking for her grandmother, Manuela. Maria Contreras explained that Manuela did not live with her, but that Manuela's home on Montesito Road was about ten minutes away. She gave directions and indicated to Mary Ann that she would join them there shortly.

Floyd drove the pickup to a small white house on Montesito Road. It was set back from the street and surrounded by a chain-link fence enclosing a yard of sand and desert rock. Mary Ann, with picture frame and binder in hand, hoped that today at long last, Ann Marie would get an answer to her question.

A petite older light-skinned woman with short salt-and-pepper hair answered Mary Ann's knock and slowly opened the door, peering from behind the screen. With a Spanish accent the woman asked with an uncertain but polite, "Can I help you?"

Mary Ann forged ahead. "I'm looking for Manuela Rodriguez. Does she live here?" The older woman remained unsure. "For who?"

"Manuela Rodriguez. I would like to speak to her, if I may."

The woman turned and spoke in Spanish to someone further inside the home who was not visible to Mary Ann. "Mama, I think this woman is looking for you and wants to speak to you."

"What do they want?" said Manuela.

"I don't know. She just said that she wants to speak to Manuela Rodriguez."

Manuela stepped closer to the door and surveyed her visitors. She responded with certainty, "I don't know any gringas. Tell her I don't know them."

The woman who had answered the door turned to Mary Ann and shook her head, "No, no, sorry."

Mary Ann noted that the woman's response was not a direct denial that the elderly Manuela lived at the residence. She pressed on. "I am trying to find Manuela Rodriguez. I may be related to her. I would like to speak to her." It was clear from the woman's expression that she did not understand Mary Ann. Mary Ann repeated that she was trying to find Manuela Rodriguez, whom she believed might be the granddaughter of Pedro Garcia.

By this time Maria Contreras had arrived and joined them at the doorway. She kindly invited them in the house, "Come in. Please come in."

As Mary Ann and Ann Marie entered, Maria Contreras explained, "My grandmother's last name at birth was Cegarra, but her stepfather's name was Rodriguez. We'll talk to her, but she's ninety-five years old. Some days she has a hard time remembering things." Maria Contreras stood next to Manuela, who was tiny and thin, not five feet tall. Her hair was still salt and pepper in color. The lines in her face were slight, leaving her with a soft expression. Her brown eyes were bright and aware. On this day there was no suggestion of a failing memory.

Maria Contreras introduced Manuela to Mary Ann and Ann Marie. But without any explanation, she advised Mary Ann that Manuela was called Nellie. Rather than invite more confusion, Mary Ann thought better of asking why that was so. Maria Contreras then introduced the older woman who answered the door as her mother, Juanita. With Maria Contreras providing the interpreting, Mary Ann responded by introducing herself and her daughter, Ann Marie.

The five women then seated themselves on a small couch and chairs in the crowded living room of the house. Mary Ann said to Maria Contreras, "Please tell Manuela that we might be related." Mary Ann watched Manuela as her words were interpreted. She then continued, "I believe my grandfather, Benjamin, was your mother's younger brother."

When Maria Contreras finished interpreting, Manuela looked at Mary Ann and responded in Spanish, "That cannot be; my mother's brother did not know any gringos." Mary Ann continued, "I think my great-grandfather was your grandfather. His name was Pedro Garcia." Manuela hesitated and did not offer a response. She was clearly puzzled by the information she had just heard.

Mary Ann reached for the framed 8½" × 11" photo that she had carried into the house. She slowly turned it around for Manuela to see an old man with a dark hat seated on a chair in front of a screen door, a dog at his side.

On sight, Manuela clasped her hands at her chin. "Othello! Othello!" she exclaimed.

Mary Ann looked at Ann Marie and whispered in surprise, "I think we might have the wrong family!" Maria Contreras continued interpreting Manuela's words for Mary Ann. "I loved Othello. I haven't seen him in so long!" Manuela said as she thrust her hands open toward the photo.

"Or maybe the wrong picture," said Mary Ann, now more confused.

"Maybe she can't remember," Ann Marie replied.

Manuela looked at Mary Ann and Ann Marie, and said in a voice of frustration tinged with anger, "They shot him! They shot him!" On hearing Maria Contreras's interpretation, Ann Marie asked Manuela in disbelief, "They shot him? They shot him? Who did?"

"The border guards," Manuela answered.

"Why?" Ann Marie asked, still in disbelief.

"Because he kept going back and forth across el rio," Manuela answered. Ann Marie was outraged. "The guards shot my great-great-grandfather just because he kept crossing the river?" Manuela was puzzled by Ann Marie's response, then said to her, "No, no." She shook her head. "They shot Othello, the dog, not Pedro."

"Oh. Oh!" Ann Marie said in relief.

Though slightly embarrassed, the women laughed at the misunderstanding.

Now with more interest, Manuela asked, "Who did you say you are?" Mary Ann looked at Manuela with certainty and said, "My grandfather Benjamin was the younger brother of your mother. Benjamin's older sisters were your mother, Maria, Juana, and Guadalupe. One of Benjamin's older brothers was Jose. They were sons and daughters of Pedro."

"My uncle Benjamin was your grandfather?"

"Yes. Exactly."

Manuela, Juanita, and Maria Contreras sat in stunned silence. Each in her own mind tried to determine how these gringas could be related to them.

Finally, seeking more proof of their claim, Manuela asked, "Where did you get that picture? I have not seen it for a long time. The Garcias from Kansas took it and never returned it." Mary Ann explained that her family in the Midwest had been in contact with the Kansas Garcias since the 1970s. She had obtained a copy of the picture from them. The Kansas Garcias were the sons of Jose and Rosa.

Mary Ann continued, "When I got a copy of this picture I studied it closely. I could see in the background, on the other side of the screen door, a woman holding a baby in her arms. Is that you, Manuela?" With her finger Mary Ann outlined for Manuela the figure of a woman with a headscarf holding a baby behind the screen door.

After a few moments inspecting the photo, Manuela could not say. Juanita then related that she recalled an aunt telling her that Manuela's mother liked to wear a headscarf as she completed her house chores. They considered the times when Pedro lived in El Paso and the likely age of the infant in the photograph. They concluded that yes, it was Manuela being held in the photograph.

The women spent the rest of their time telling their family stories and taking photographs to fill the empty space in their history created when one of Pedro's older sons, Jose, moved to Kansas, and Benjamin, the youngest son, moved to Detroit and later Cincinnati.

On her return to Illinois, Mary Ann sent, as promised, three copies of Pedro's photo to the women in El Paso. Manuela was again able to keep in her mind her grandfather Pedro's image and that of her beloved childhood pet, Othello, until she passed away in 2010.

Ernie found Mary Ann's tale intriguing and the confusion over Othello's demise amusing. He appreciated the time and effort she had spent in search of unknown family, and he began to think that he might want the same experience. He knew much of the Garcia history but little of the Ayala family in Mexico. But he had no time to research or travel in pursuit of the Ayala history and would have to put aside and delay that effort for the moment.

Senator Brownback was elected governor of Kansas in November 2010. The governor-elect subsequently offered Ernie a state cabinet position as superintendent of the Kansas Highway Patrol (KHP). It did not take long for Ernie to reach a decision. He took some pleasure in submitting to Romo his notice of resignation from the Selective Service System.

Ernie and Amy soon began the transition to Kansas. They sold their boat and started to look for a home in Kansas, eventually purchasing a beautiful two-story home in a quiet, shade-filled neighborhood in Overland Park, on the Kansas side of Kansas City. At that time Amy was working with the American Nursing Association, headquartered in Maryland. She would be unable to join Ernie in Overland Park until 2012.

After Ernie's appointment was unanimously confirmed by the Kansas Senate, he reported for duty as superintendent of the KHP in January 2011.

Ernie's appointment as superintendent, unfortunately, was not warmly welcomed by the leadership of the Kansas State Troopers Association, an organization that operates similarly to a union. The association's leadership promoted the argument that because Ernie had not been a trooper, he did not possess the knowledge or the skills to properly lead the KHP. The leadership argued, in essence, that Ernie was not one of them. He did not share their image and likeness and therefore should be disregarded as someone able to effectively lead the KHP. The association leadership downplayed the finding by KU researchers that the driving forces behind low morale at KHP were the troopers' low pay and a shortage of troopers on the road.

Ernie's response was the same as it always was—to work hard to fulfill the responsibilities before him and to do more than what was asked. Leaving the objections to those making them, Ernie established KHP's administrative priorities: the safety of the public, securing adequate funding for compensation for the troopers, equipping and training the troopers and supporting staff, and instilling a sense of public service.

Ernie secured the KHP's participation in and assigned several KHP troopers to the FBI-sponsored Joint Terrorism Task Force. The task force combined state and local law enforcement agencies with federal law enforcement agencies in the investigation of internal and external threats.

The KHP was a part of the federal investigation and arrest of Terry Lee Loewen, who was charged in December 2013 for attempting a car bombing at the Wichita airport. One of the principal undercover agents in the investigation was a KHP trooper. During the investigation Ernie received regular briefings on the surveillance and developments in the case. He was also present when US Attorney Barry Grissom held a press conference to announce Loewen's arrest and the nature of the charges. Loewen eventually received a twenty-year sentence for attempting to perpetrate a terrorist attack.

Ernie's administration secured the authority and recommended funding for the construction of a new KHP regional headquarters in Wichita. The new headquarters addressed the KHP's severe need for additional operating and administrative space. Groundbreaking for the new building took place in August 2014. Plans for the new headquarters building included housing the Kansas Bureau of Investigation as well. The construction of the building was surprising in that it took place during a time of extreme funding cutbacks by the state. No taxpayer funds were available for construction costs, as Governor Brownback's tax-cutting policies did not result in increased tax revenues as promised, and so the $3.5 million cost was funded with the KHP's share of asset forfeiture funds.

Ernie's administration also recommended continued funding for the operation of the air unit of the KHP. During Ernie's leadership, two small Cessna aircraft were purchased with asset forfeiture funds. These planes and the KHP helicopter are especially useful in search-and-rescue missions and in transporting patients and blood supplies across the state during medical emergencies.

Ernie insisted on a proactive KHP in the belief that residents of Kansas were better served. He contacted other state and federal law enforcement agencies to encourage and increase the flow of information and communications. As in every state, Kansas has diversity in language and culture in its population. Ernie and KHP staff met with organizations and leaders of the different communities and opened lines of communication between the two.

With the rise of school shootings and active shooters in public settings, Ernie directed his senior staff to develop an informational and instructional program for school administrators and the general public. Their information and presentations were well received by local law enforcement officials and the community at large.

During Governor Brownback's term, the leadership of the troopers association continued its criticism of Ernie. They contended that some KHP staff believed the upper-level command, consisting of Ernie, his assistant superintendent, and four division commanders, had engaged in excessive discipline and illegal labor policies. Ernie met with the association leadership to encourage more cooperation. Several times after their initial meeting he invited the association leadership to meet further. But they did not act on his invitations and showed little interest in working together. Ernie believed the association's continuing management-labor issues undermined the cooperative effort needed to benefit the troopers and, most importantly, the security of the people of Kansas. State funding levels for law enforcement had limited the number of troopers in the field. A unified management and labor front might convince the legislature to fund not only more boots on the ground but also an increase in pay for those currently serving the public, who had not seen a raise for some time.

As the November elections approached in the fall of 2014, Ernie assessed his position with the KHP. He was grateful for the opportunity that Governor Brownback had provided him, but the reality of the state's budget shortfall tied his hands and limited the KHP's effectiveness. He had long been a strong proponent of keeping law enforcement, a core function of government, at funding levels determined by the needs of public safety, rather than the needs of politicians and political parties. Even when serving as sergeant at arms, he strove to ensure that law enforcement was properly funded and without personal and party politics. But the state's funding policies were set in stone and left him frustrated.

Meanwhile, Ernie was now sixty-seven and still in need of abdominal, neck, and shoulder surgeries. After retiring from the marines, he had attempted to maintain a level of physical fitness, running or jogging when possible. But even before leaving DC for Overland Park, he had begun to experience an excessively rapid heart rate. The episodes were occurring more frequently when running. After a short rest period, his pulse slowed to a normal rate. His doctor in Kansas City told him that he suffered from an arrhythmia that was life-threatening if not treated or corrected. Ernie suspected that the time for the corrective surgery, called an ablation, had arrived.

Accepting the totality of his circumstances, Ernie conceded that he needed to stop working and begin taking care of himself. His career had been a great ride, including the obstacles and challenges, but it was over. The governor faced a difficult reelection campaign in the fall of 2014 and needed every possible vote. Ernie felt that an announcement of his retirement shortly before the election might secure a few votes for the governor. At the least, his retirement might keep the association's complaints against the governor's handling of the KHP out of the news cycle. Governor Brownback survived the scare and was reelected in November. Ernie retired in the first week of January 2015.

13

Reflections

2015

Although his last day at KHP was imminent, Ernie and Amy spent their 2015 New Year holiday on a cruise ship exploring the Mediterranean. The difference between the rolling prairies of Kansas and the rocky terrain rising up out of the Mediterranean Sea allowed Ernie to easily put aside the frustrations of the KHP and politics. The ship's slow pace on the sea gave him an opportunity to decompress and reflect on his life and career. In looking back, he thought, *Did it really happen? Was it a dream?* He was grateful that his life had been filled with so many experiences. It seemed to him that by the grace of God and the support of his family and friends he led an amazing life. He retired knowing that many times during his career, his efforts improved the well-being of others, especially the less fortunate.

Ernie had no regrets about his life's path, with one exception: the time he spent away from his family and loved ones. From nightly homework to sporting events and school plays, he frequently was not present in support of Felipe. He hoped that his regret might diminish to some degree knowing that he and Ana Maria, by their examples, had instilled a strong work ethic in Felipe. He contemplated whether Felipe saw in him and Ana Maria the same straightforward approach to life's challenges that Ernie saw in his father and Luisa—overcome challenges with hard work, resourcefulness, and resilience.

Ernie took comfort in the success that Felipe had enjoyed, albeit from a distance. In the aftermath of September 11, Felipe and Christy left DC and returned to Kansas. They were married in July 2002. Two months later, Felipe was the second person hired in Kansas by the Transportation Security

Administration. His primary responsibility was to assist in establishing the TSA's presence in Wichita's Mid-Continent Airport. At the same time, he began pursuit of a master's degree in public administration, which he completed in 2005.

Felipe became a loving and caring husband and father. With the birth in 2011 of Felipe and Christy's first son, Christian, Ernie became a grandfather. By the time a second son, Jordan, was born in 2013, Felipe had advanced to the position of assistant federal security director for screening at Mid-Continent Airport and Christy had completed her KU doctorate in pharmacy. Rather than Felipe accepting a TSA promotion in Michigan, the couple decided to pursue Christy's career opportunities in Kansas, where they had more stability and family support. Eventually, Felipe left TSA in 2013 and started a successful property management business in Wichita, while Christy began working for a pharmaceutical company.

Ernie retired believing that too few Hispanics participated in the decisions of government, particularly those who were younger. He saw the need for Hispanics and other people of color to take their rightful place at the decision-making table. It was obvious that nonparticipants were at the mercy of others. He wanted all Hispanics to understand that one cannot wait for power to come one's way. If Hispanics desire power, they must act within the political system to seize it. A favorite maxim of Ernie's was, "Those who sit at the table eat; those who don't watch." In his view, it was of no consequence whether a participant walked through a Republican or Democratic doorway. Far more important, by any measure, was becoming adept at bringing about changes in government policies from within the system.

When Ernie began his pursuit of his master's degree in public administration, he had no specific plans or hopes to work for Republicans or in Republican administrations. But after a Democrat had rejected his application for employment, a Republican senator gave him the opportunity to pursue his career. He acknowledged that his work with Senator Dole and Secretary Weinberger at the Department of Defense inevitably shaped his political views. But when he initially arrived in DC, he was already receptive to GOP policies because of his upbringing, which included a strong Catholic faith, a strong work ethic, and the honoring of military service. As a boy, he knew the president's name was Eisenhower and that he was a general and a Republican from Kansas. And he knew military service can require sacrifice, as his father's fatal illness proved.

Despite Ernie's allegiance to the Republican Party, he did not agree with every position advanced by Senator Dole or the GOP. He was not a blind loyalist who believed that his party acted without error. At times he sat at the GOP decision-making table and called attention to public policy issues that he believed benefited the public. On some occasions his colleagues responded positively to his proposals; other times they did not.

For the most part, the Republican Party's conservative to moderate policy views were acceptable to Ernie, particularly its support of economic strength, a strong military, smaller government, and support of religious freedom. As a civil military affairs officer, he understood that a fundamental role of government in all countries, including the United States, was to help their people meet their needs. The preamble to the US Constitution specifically acknowledged that promotion of the "general welfare" was a legitimate purpose of government.

Ernie strongly embraced as part of the general welfare a policy of lawful immigration with a fair process to citizenship and a watchful eye for immigrants who pose a security risk. He did not oppose government assistance to those in need. His family had been in need and was a recipient of government benefits after his father's illness and death. Again, he cautioned against awarding benefits to those who were ineligible and to those wanting to defraud the government. He regarded any policies that did not fund essential community services, such as law enforcement, safety, and education, as a failure to promote the general welfare.

When he left government service, he was concerned that younger Hispanics were unaware of the struggles their parents and grandparents had suffered for opportunities now available. Without that knowledge, he believed they were unprepared to overcome the obstacles that lay in wait.

After his return from his Mediterranean cruise, Ernie began the pursuit of information about his Ayala family in Mexico. His desire to get the search underway had been growing since Mary Ann Frey had planted the idea four years earlier. At the end of January, he and Felipe traveled to Penjamo, Chalio's hometown. It was a blind search, as Ernie and Felipe had no reliable information to help them locate family members. A short distance from Penjamo, they located a small village named El Refugio de Ayala. They spoke with villagers there and in surrounding villages who were potentially related. But they needed more information to confirm the blood ties.

On Ernie's return to Kansas, he and Amy met with Aunt Kay, then ninety-five years old, to ask about her knowledge of the Ayala family in Penjamo. Despite being in a weakened state, Aunt Kay's mind was sound, and she proved to be a treasure trove of information. She confirmed that Chalio had a family in Mexico and revealed that she and Luisa had a half-brother, Carmen, and a half-sister, Tomasa. Aunt Kay told them that she and family members in Penjamo had exchanged letters decades before. In 1947 Aunt Kay had visited the men in the family home in the nearby village of Abosolo. She showed them the letters and photographs taken when she traveled to meet them. Ernie and Amy studied the letters for clues to identify Ayala family members and planned another trip to Penjamo for August when Jim, Vina, Frank, and his wife Joyce could join them.

In August when the six of them left for Penjamo, they took with them photographs that Aunt Kay had provided. They were able to find three first cousins, Tranquilino, Leon, and Carlos Vargas de Ayala. These men were children of Tomasa Ayala, Luisa and Aunt Kay's half-sister. Ernie and his siblings also spent several days with an elder, Don Manuel Arroyo Balver. Balver's grandfather was Catarino Ayala, who may also have been Ernie's great-grandfather.

During her visit in 1947, Aunt Kay photographed the sister of Don Balver. When Ernie showed the picture to Don Balver's sister, she was surprised to see herself as a young girl, sixty-eight years before. Apparently, family photos from the 1940s were precious few in Penjamo and Abosolo. The photo was the beginning of the confirmation that bloodlines existed between them. Cheers erupted, and hugs were many for the newfound relatives.

For Ernie the time in Penjamo and Abosolo was a time of family discovery. He felt a stronger connection to the Ayala family in Mexico beyond his mother, Aunt Kay, and Chalio. He did not know that after the 1910 Mexican Revolution, the Mexican government attempted to implement socialist policies that were particularly harsh on Catholics. In response, Chalio and many other Mexicans came to the United States, not only for work and a better life, but also to escape religious persecution.

As Ernie became familiar with the Garcia and Ayala family members who had lived long before him and their histories of overcoming hardships and poverty, he began to understand that he was part of a lineage of strong, determined survivors and daring adventurers. As a child and youth in Garden City, the character of that lineage had been out of view. The successful people he saw, especially in the areas of education and businesses, were not familiar to him. They spoke a different language, ate different foods, lived in bigger houses in a different part of town, rode in newer cars, and danced to different music. Ernie saw few trappings of that type of success in the Santa Fe barrio.

When the young see and are familiar with their ancestors, they view themselves differently—capable and worthy. Very often they are more confident and inspired and will attempt to duplicate their ancestors' success. But despite often being in unfamiliar settings, Ernie's immediate families passed on to him a sufficient number of the qualities to form the platform from which he leaped to success. Ernie hoped for successes and worked for them, but there was always uncertainty. When they occurred, he was always surprised.

A few weeks after returning to Kansas, Ernie learned that Don Balver had passed away. His death tempered the joy of Ernie's trip to Penjamo, but he was thankful that he and Don Balver had the good fortune to have met one another. He began planning yet another trip to Penjamo for later in the year. Sadly, Aunt Kay did not live long enough to know the results of Ernie's second trip. She died on May 9. She was the last of Chalio's children to pass away. Luisa, Aunt Kay, Carmen, and Tomasa all lived into their eighties and passed away in the United States.

With Aunt Kay's death, Ernie again felt the pain and anguish of losing those close to him—his parents, his friends in the military, and the marines who died in the line of duty. Ernie and all of his siblings and their families gathered for Aunt Kay's funeral services. Though she never married, she cared for and nurtured her nieces and nephews as though they were her children, and she worked alongside Luisa to see that they thrived. Because Ernie had spent so much time away from his siblings, he was unsure of his place with them as they dealt with Aunt Kay's death and funeral. He preferred to keep a little distance from them to avoid saying or doing something hurtful or inconsiderate. In some ways it was easier for Ernie to be alone at that time.

At times, he felt a distance from his extended family as well. Ernie had always opened his home to his siblings, nieces, and nephews and to many of his forty or so Garcia first cousins as they traveled to DC. He was unable to recall a time when his family or friends treated him poorly or distanced themselves because of his career and political leanings. Still, his contact with them was infrequent and lacked the closeness of regular interaction. During his career he had been unable to attend many of the Garcia reunions that had been held every three years since the mid-1970s. Conflicts with his work and military duties always interfered. In his absence from the reunions, it was difficult for him to recognize that his extended family held a great amount of love and respect for him.

After his retirement, he began to use social media to help strengthen his ties to the extended family. He also planned to attend as many family events and reunions as possible, including the reunion scheduled for Garden City in 2017.

Throughout the years, Ernie remained in contact with many of his high school and college classmates and friends from Garden City, including Ann Regan, Randy Bowling, Sharon Lee Cobb, Enrique Avila, and Paulasue Patterson. Some of his classmates, at his twentieth and later reunions, congratulated him on his successes given the difficulties of an upbringing on the other side of the tracks. Ernie understood how his success might be seen in that light by his classmates. But he saw it differently. He accepted that his father's death ended any further father-son experiences, but he did not feel deprived by it. He felt fortunate because in his father's stead were his mother, grandfather, aunts, and uncles. By their examples, they instilled in him the values that led him to the success he experienced.

Before his return to Penjamo in August, Ernie met with his cardiologist at the Veterans Administration Medical Center in Kansas City. The doctor suggested that the time had come for Ernie to undergo the procedure to address his heart ailment. He explained that the cardiac ablation procedure could be completed within two hours while Ernie was under anesthesia. They agreed to set the date for surgery for October 14, 2015.

On the morning of the surgery, Amy accompanied Ernie in support. After three hours she received word that the surgeon had found more damage than had been anticipated. Amy's nursing experience took over her thinking. Focusing on the medical procedures that were required to successfully complete the surgery, she did not panic nor become filled with fear or worry.

The surgery dragged into a fourth hour with still no end. In the fifth hour, the surgeon emerged with the news that the surgery was successfully completed. Ernie was stable and doing well in recovery. After two days in the hospital, he went home. He had survived and was on his way to recovery.

After his heart surgery, Ernie acted with less urgency. He toned down the hypervigilance and quick-response mechanisms that were instilled in the corps. More than ever, he appreciated the peace and quiet of his neighborhood. He understood that he needed to regain his strength to undergo another round of surgery for his neck and remaining hernia.

Ernie spent some of his retirement time providing care for his grandsons while Felipe and Christy pursued their careers. As Chalio had, he insisted that his grandsons help him in the yard, raking leaves, gathering branches, and weeding the garden and flower bed. He was not too concerned with their actual work product—his real purpose was to instill the ideas of work and helping others. But it was not all yard work for the boys. They spent hours digging for worms and learning to shoot and dribble the basketball under Ernie's guidance. It was a time of contentment with his grandsons. Christian and Jordan lovingly refered to Ernie and Amy as Paka and Nana.

Ernie did not retire his sense of wanderlust and adventure, which Amy fully shared. In early November 2016, he traveled to England and spent time in the villages along the eastern coastline. Later that month, he and Amy went on a cruise in the Caribbean. He traveled to 135 countries; she traveled to 77. But when the trips conclude, they always looked forward to returning to their lives and beautiful home in Overland Park.

When Ernie and Amy were youngsters, they never thought for a moment they might live in such a home with a manicured lawn, beautiful trees, and a backyard that sloped down into a small stream. Their upbringings were challenging and filled with hardships. But the challenges and hardships they overcame do not stand alone. They have a history. Pedro, Jose, Rosa, Chalio, Alvina, Felipe, and Luisa labored mightily to ensure that their children and grandchildren would be secure in their homes and live without want.

Ernie's and Amy's lives are the living dreams of their ancestors. They brought the values and character of their diverse immigrant history into their home. Those values and that character enabled Ernie's and Amy's successes, and they will enable their children and grandchildren as well. That blend of values and character is America's future. It is America's destiny manifested.

Epilogue

East Los Angeles, April 2016

An old dark blue sedan turned slowly into the cemetery located at the corner of Whittier and Downey. The driver was alone. The sedan took the lane to the left, passing in front of the cemetery offices and mausoleums. The lane ran parallel to the cemetery's western boundary, Downey Boulevard. It was a cool midmorning with a sky left unusually blue by wind and rain the night before. The cemetery grounds were a blend of sunlit grass and emerald green shade.

In no hurry, the sedan passed a dark green open funeral tent standing off the roadway. The tent was surrounded by grieving family and friends dressed in black. Many wore dark glasses. The sedan continued on and climbed a small rise before stopping next to the curb. The number painted on the curb where the sedan stopped was 220.

A brown middle-aged man got out of the driver's seat. He was of average height, barrel-chested, and a little long in the torso. He wore black jeans and a gray sweatshirt with a hood. He also wore a blue Dodgers baseball cap with white LA lettering and white button on top. He walked across the lane carrying a small brown paper bag in one hand and a white paper cup with a brown sleeve in the other. He walked to the second row of grave markers from the curb, where he looked at a few headstones before stopping and looking down at one for a few moments.

The headstone lay flat in the grass. Its left side depicted in black the image of the Santo Niño de Atocha. The right side, inscribed in white lettering, read: JOSE C. GARCIA, FEB 27 1880–ENERO 17 1938, RECUERDO DE SU ESPOSA E HIJOS. The brown man began to speak, still holding the paper bag and cup.

"Buenos dias, abuelo. Como manecio?" He paused for an answer. "Grandfather, I brought us some tamales from La Indiana Café down the street."

He slightly lifted the brown bag so it could be seen. "And some coffee from a fancy coffee shop. They serve good coffee, but they charge a little too much." He walked to the side of the grave so he could easily see the gravestone. He then sat down, cross-legged, and put down the brown bag and cup. He rested his forearms on his knees.

"I've been meaning to come by and visit you, but you know how it is. You get busy with everything, and the day is gone before you know it."

"I don't have to work this morning, and I remembered to come see you. So here I am with breakfast. I got two tamales, one for me and one for you." The grandson reached in the bag and pulled out a tamale and a small package of salt. He began to peel away the corn husk and tapped a little salt on the tamale.

"Abuelo, my mom always told me that you were now a spirit and you could go anywhere, like an angel does." He paused to take a bite of the spicy shredded pork embedded in the steamy warm masa. "I'm not sure I believe what she said." He took another bite and a sip of coffee. "So just in case, I came here to tell you some things I've been thinking about."

"Grampo, I'm betting that when you were alive you had some dreams for your sons. Am I right?" He paused, looking at the headstone. "But it was God's will that you died before you even knew if they got married and had children of their own." He took another bite.

"Here's what happened. A couple of years after you died, the United States fought in another war, like World War I. Actually, we have been in a lot of wars since you died. Some of your sons and grandsons fought in those wars. Anyway, because of the war, your sons stopped working in the fields. They got jobs in town and got married. They married good women." He took another sip of coffee. "I got a big surprise for you, Grampo, a big surprise. Altogether, your sons fathered forty-four children! Can you believe that? You have forty-four grandchildren!" He took the last bite of his tamale.

"I got more news for you, Abuelo. Your sons and grandchildren have done great things. They have accomplished a lot. One of your grandsons talked to the pope, went to China, and taught the president of the United States to say a few words in Spanish. That grandson has been in the newspapers and on TV—" he interrupted himself. "You don't know what TV is, do you? It is like a camera taking pictures. Only the pictures are sent to a box in your house, like radio. The box has a glass screen, and you can see the pictures right away as they are taken. There is no waiting for the pictures to be developed. Pretty amazing, don't you think?"

"Grampo, you are not eating your tamale, so if you don't mind I will help you." With that, the grandson grabbed the second tamale, peeled the husk, tapped a little salt onto it, and took a bite. "Anyways, you know the grandson I was telling you about? His success was very public. Lots of people saw it. But what I want you to know is that all of your sons and grandchildren have had great success that is not seen by the public. They have taken care of their families and got them educated." He took another bite of the tamale and followed it with a sip of coffee.

"They are teachers and nurses. They are businessmen. They are administrators in schools, colleges, and universities. Some have been elected to public office. They work in law enforcement. Some work for newspapers and magazines. A couple of them are lawyers. The men have served in the military, and fought in our country's wars. You have a great-grandson who flies planes for the air force!"

The grandson took another bite of the tamale and another sip of coffee.

"I wanted you to know, yours and Gramma Rosa's hard work—when it got cold and was snowy, when it got hot and was dusty, when the work did not end and you got exhausted—all your work paid off. The little house you bought on Fourth Street, it stayed in the family until 2009. That's eighty-one years. Your granddaughter sold it to a man from Mexico. He is a plumber and fixes houses, and he works hard. I thought you might like that."

"Congratulations, Grampo, your dreams have come true. You just didn't get to see it happen before you died." He took the last bite of the tamale and tipped the paper cup for the last drop of coffee. "Grampo, today we use a word to describe where a man has been . . . *footprint*. You left a very, very big footprint. Bien hecho. Well done."

The brown man gathered the husks and paper cup into the bag. He stood up and looked at the headstone.

"I will be back to see you soon, I promise. Till then, I will leave you in the care of the Santo Niño de Atocha. I gotta get to work, Grampo."

He turned away from the gravestone carrying the brown bag, walked across the lane to the sedan, and drove away.

Index

www.ingramcontent.com/pod-product-compliance
Lightning Source LLC
LaVergne TN
LVHW011318070926
847404LV00052BA/318

* 9 7 8 0 7 0 0 6 4 3 7 0 7 *